Daily Life through American History in Primary Documents

Daily Life through American History in Primary Documents
Randall M. Miller, General Editor

Volume 1: The Colonial Period through the American Revolution
Randall M. Miller

Volume 2: The American Revolution to the Civil War
Theodore J. Zeman

Volume 3: The Civil War to World War I
Francis J. Sicius

Volume 4: World War I to the Present
Jolyon P. Girard

Daily Life through American History in Primary Documents

Randall M. Miller
GENERAL EDITOR

Theodore J. Zeman
VOLUME EDITOR

AN IMPRINT OF ABC-CLIO, LLC
Santa Barbara, California • Denver, Colorado • Oxford, England

Library of Congress Cataloging-in-Publication Data

Daily life through American history in primary documents / Randall M. Miller, general editor.
p. cm.
Includes bibliographical references and index.
ISBN 978-1-61069-032-4 (hard back : alk. paper) ISBN 978-1-61069-033-1 (ebook)
1. United States—Social life and customs—Sources. I. Miller, Randall M. II. Zeman, Theodore J., 1965– III. Sicius, Francis J. IV. Girard, Jolyon P., 1942–
E161.D35 2012
973—dc23 2011040023

ISBN: 978-1-61069-032-4
EISBN: 978-1-61069-033-1

16 15 14 13 12 1 2 3 4 5

This book is also available on the World Wide Web as an eBook.
Visit www.abc-clio.com for details.

Greenwood
An Imprint of ABC-CLIO, LLC

ABC-CLIO, LLC
130 Cremona Drive, P.O. Box 1911
Santa Barbara, California 93116-1911

This book is printed on acid-free paper ♾

Manufactured in the United States of America

CONTENTS

SET INTRODUCTION

Historians and anthropologists, among others, have long insisted that discovering the character of any civilization requires finding and understanding the "small things," as anthropologist and historian James Deetz termed them. In essence, they argue, it is not only the big things such as theology, statecraft, and diplomacy, but also, and even more so, the daily habits and doings of people, that reveal any and every people's true values, interests, and identity. Thus much historical and anthropological inquiry has looked to locating the "small things" and placing them in their proper context. Such is the purpose of these four volumes, *Daily Life through American History in Primary Documents*, which present and set in historical context many of the "small things" that made up Americans' daily life from the first English settlements to today.

The "small things" are myriad and many. They have changed over time and according to circumstance. They have varied according to place, position, and personality of individuals and communities. They have sometimes grown into big things, such as the individual efforts at improvement that over time became the collective American interest, as evidenced in massive investments in public and private education and whole industries devoted to improving one's prospects for getting work, getting married, and even getting happiness. Yet the small things have also remained small, as in the persistent belief that improving the self is the essential step toward any societal improvement. Thus Americans, like no other people, write and read all manner of self-help books and advice columns that supposedly teach, and have taught, them how to raise their vegetables and their children, how to fatten their portfolios and trim their waistlines, how to get along with the in-laws or without them. These and other "small things" are highly personal, even as they are also very public in the selling and showing off of promised improvements or the consequences of people wanting and trying to do them. They are daily concerns. And to those people thinking about and doing them, they are not small at all.

What has mattered, and still matters, to people in their daily lives is best found in their own words. Thus, *Daily Life through American History in Primary Documents* gathers representative and revealing examples of the "small things" and also many big things that marked the daily rhythms, rituals, and requirements Americans have followed over the past five hundred years. As a very reflective people, almost from the first landing of Englishmen in Virginia, "Americans" have thought about how to make their way in the world, even to make a "new world," and why they should care about doing so. They have sought new lands and opportunities. Americans have prided themselves on inventing new ways of getting about and getting ahead, and even getting inside with all manner of medical diagnostic technology, surgical instruments, psychiatric examination, and meditative spirituality. In all this, they have been observers because they expected to be users of what they saw, whether it be nature's bounty or human imagination. And so they have recorded their observations as perhaps no other people have done. They have left musings on the world(s) they have tried to know and master and jottings on the problems and prospects of each day. Such is the "stuff" of history that gives the people voice in it. And such is the "stuff" of these volumes.

It is almost presumptuous to suppose that anyone can catch the whole of American daily life over the centuries in a mere four volumes. A people so vibrant and varied, dynamic and diverse, almost defies any single definition that holds for the many, much less the all. The assertion in *e pluribus unum*—one out of many—expresses a hope as much as a fact. Yet America is not and has not been without form and focus. The very diversity and dynamism that have marked its history point to a salient fact that undergirds all—namely, that Americans are and have been a people always in the process of becoming. They are unfinished and almost wish to be so, because of a common faith, or conceit, that their future is brighter than any other people's. Indeed, as the mightiest and meekest have proclaimed since the first English settlements in the New World a half millennium ago, America would be, and must be, different in history. Thomas Jefferson once called it "the last, best hope of mankind," and Lincoln and others after him would echo the sentiment. Such belief has informed not only public policy but also private lives. The striving for improvement as much as anything else has defined private lives. So it is in the documents in these volumes.

Features and Uses

Daily Life through American History in Primary Documents is an integrated set of four volumes that provides documents from the people themselves describing and relating the interests, ideas, identities, and institutions that defined their daily lives. It brings together samplings of the people's own public and private voices—from diaries, letters, memoirs, speeches, advertisements, public notices, travel accounts, court documents, newspaper and magazine articles, poetry, novels, and more—to suggest the many and varied ways people ordered, or sought to order, their public and private worlds.

The volumes are organized chronologically, but they are not separated by fixed dates. Social history has more fluid time demarcations than, say, a political calendar with set times for elections, inaugurations, legislation, court cases, and such. It is more attuned to a person's, or a people's, life cycles and more part of larger cultural, intellectual, and economic currents shaping and directing a society. In its time frames, *Daily Life through American History in Primary Documents* uses wars as the principal markers. Wars that engage the whole people have been, and are, times of self-reflection and collective action. They also are times of upheaval and great social change. Witness the disruptions of the American Revolutionary War, which shifted authority more downward to "the people," challenged slavery, and forced the migration and expulsion of many erstwhile "Americans." Or the Civil War, in which more than 600,000 men died as soldiers, countless people were uprooted by armies tramping about, roughly four million slaves became free by their own actions and then by constitutional amendment, and one section of the country was left economically prostrate and the other encouraged by its strength in saving the great experiment in democratic government. Or World War I, in which many women entered work previously closed to them, many blacks began the "great migration" out of the Jim Crow South and poverty to the "Promised Land" of jobs and "freedom" in the North, many immigrants were subjected to rigorous Americanization programs, and many Progressives were able to give their ideas on social planning and a regulated economy a full test. Such an organizational principle necessarily led to some "spillover" from one volume to the next, which process should remind readers, again, that any people's history is not only a neat staking off of dates.

The volumes are as follows:

Volume 1, *The Colonial Period through the American Revolution*, contains 137 documents covering the time of settling British North America and transplanting Old World plants, animals, and people in a new land; interacting with native peoples; laying out holy experiments in living; exploiting indentured and enslaved labor to create new wealth; growing dramatically through immigration and natural increase; establishing English law and governments; and challenging arbitrary power, whether at home or from abroad, to the point of declaring independence.

Volume 2, *The American Revolution to the Civil War*, contains roughly one hundred documents covering the time of winning independence; creating a new nation; getting saved by God in Protestant revivals and worrying about Catholic immigrants crowding into cities; becoming "American" in literature and popular culture; entering a market economy; reaching across a continent; and coming apart over social, economic, and political concerns, most especially slavery.

Volume 3, *The Civil War to World War I*, contains 103 documents covering the time of fighting the Civil War and dealing with its effects, especially the nature and extent of "freedom"; "winning the West" and occupying it; extending an industrial revolution; organizing labor; drawing massive immigration; moving to and remaking cities and adopting a more "modern" urban culture; marveling at technological wonders that light up the night and span great rivers; discovering nature; and experimenting with social and political reforms and a regulated marketplace as Progressives.

Volume 4, *World War I to the Present*, contains seventy-eight documents covering the time of mobilizing to win the "war to end all wars"; becoming modern in the age of automobiles, radio, jazz, and Republican prosperity; losing jobs and hope during the Great Depression and building a New Deal with the promise of recovery, relief, and reform to America; winning World War II; standing up for "freedom" during the Cold War; moving to the suburbs and into a middle-class society; bringing up baby from the "Boomers" to the X Generation and after; marching for civil rights and against Vietnam; tuning in, up, or out with all manner of technological devices; and wondering what a postindustrial and information-driven economy means for the American Dream.

Each volume opens with a historical introduction that offers a panoramic view of the time period, followed by individual chapters that give close-in views of the nature and dynamics of daily life in each of seven intersecting categories: "Domestic Life," "Economic Life," "Intellectual Life," "Material Life," "Political Life," "Recreational Life," and "Religious Life." Such a common organizational pattern allows, even invites, considerations of the ways particular aspects of Americans' daily life have changed or remained constant over time, as it also encourages investigation into the ways those particular aspects reflected a specific time. Thus, for example, one might follow the character and meaning of the home or household as it moved from being a place of reproduction and production during the colonial period, when families not only lived within the household but also made their livings from the products they spun, sewed, processed, manufactured, or otherwise made there, to the separation of work from the household with the coming of the Industrial Revolution and the market revolution, which pulled men from their homes into factories and offices while leaving women as the homemakers, to the reemergence of the household as the place for raising a family and making money, with an Internet connection and FAX machine in a bedroom converted to an office used by both parents or partners, as the case may be. At the same time, as the introductions make clear, the larger context in which people lived has affected the smallest aspects of people's lives. Thus natural disasters (e.g., floods, tornados, hurricanes, droughts), epidemic diseases, population movements, and governmental policies, to name several, have profound impacts on where, how, and even why people live as they do, or whether they survive at all.

Within each of the categories, each volume considers common concerns of daily life, which include such topics as work; housing; marriage and family formation; growing up and growing old; education; customs; and accumulating, using, and making sense of the bric-a-brac of daily life. The coverage of and emphasis on such topics varies according to the time period and availability of documents, but all have their place in each volume. Again, by comparing particular topics, such as education, from volume to volume, it becomes possible to chart the place and development of particular subjects over time and at any time. And readers might move backward as well as forward, or even sideways, to discover the genesis, gestation, and growth of a habit, custom, practice, and more, or to see its vitality and variety at a given time, or even its decline and dismissal as old ways give way to new ones.

The substance of each volume derives from the documents in it. Each individual document has a headnote that introduces the author and subject of the document and locates them within a larger historical context. Thus, for example, a document on a train trip might note the person keeping the account of the outing and the significance of such travel, which might be a comment on the ways improved transportation opened nature to urban visitation or an observation on the marketing of railroads to a public eager to see a wider world. The source note identifies the document, both for reference and in case any reader wants to look further into the document and subject. The note points the reader to the bibliographical particulars necessary to locate the document.

Each volume also contains a chronology that provides useful context about important events and developments during the period represented in that volume. Not all of the events noted in the chronology, or time line, are represented with documents in the volume. Rather, they represent the larger architecture of the society, polity, and economy during the time period.

Each volume also includes a bibliography of suggested readings. The bibliography is not a mere listing of sources cited in the volumes. It is rather a listing of important secondary works that provide useful context and significant analysis of the period or the particular subjects affecting daily life within that period. The bibliography, like the selection of documents, thus is both information and an invitation to explore the issues more fully.

That invitation extends to moving beyond the volumes to connect with other related resources on the daily lives of Americans. These volumes continue the American story in documents anticipated in the three-volume set *Daily Life through World History in Primary Documents*, published in 2009. Indeed, in terms of categories and basic organizational structure, these American volumes borrow from the world one. More important, they offer a wider and deeper comparative investigation of the "modern era" by setting them alongside the *Daily Life through World History in Primary Documents*, so that it becomes possible to observe common themes and interests across cultures and to map the convergences and divergences of people, plants, products, pathogens, and more over the past five centuries. *Daily Life through American History in Primary Documents* also can trace its conceptual lineage to the *Greenwood Encyclopedia of Daily Life in America*, published in 2009, which covers the period from the American Revolution to 2008. All the authors/editors of the *Daily Life through American History in Primary Documents* were involved in the encyclopedia project and have used it as a touchstone for both particular subjects and larger patterns of daily life in America. The volumes also connect with the *Greenwood Daily Life Online* database, which promises a continued expansion of materials and an easily searchable resource. In a word, these volumes, like the American people themselves, are of many parts but directed to a common purpose.

These volumes make no claim to being comprehensive in subject or coverage. The daily lives of some people are underrepresented or not represented at all. This is not out of any strategy of exclusion. Rather, it is a result of circumstances, because some people have left little or no accounts or accounting of their daily lives. Thus, enslaved Africans during the seventeenth century "appear" because others in their day observed them and wrote about them, not because the enslaved left any personal accounts that have survived. They did not in that century. Likewise, finding the daily lives of native peoples before "contact" with Europeans remains principally the province of archaeology and anthropology rather than in any recorded accounts left by the native peoples themselves. Then, too, the daily lives of the working class and the poor at any time remain more elusive than those with the wealth and time to set down their own daily doings and strivings and to leave other expressions of their identity and interest in the form of material culture (e.g., portraits, samplers, home furnishings) that society has collected, preserved, and prized. Because of "investigations" into the lives of working-class and poor people at various times, data exist on their living conditions and other aspects of daily life, but again, such information is principally from the perspective of others, often social reformers or critics, looking in, rather than from the people doing so themselves in diaries, letters, memoirs, or other traditional means of recording life histories. To be sure, oral history helps to give voice to many people otherwise left outside the normal course of historical investigation, and personal narratives and other recorded oral history inform these volumes. But the "many" of American history remain less visible than the few in having the power to make their own case in history. Realizing that imbalance, the editors/authors of these volumes hope readers will use the documents represented herein to seek out more and varied ways to discover and recover the daily lives of the many. In that regard, these volumes are not complete and never will be. They represent a process more than a product.

In fact, a principal benefit of these volumes to readers and users lies in the invitation to consider ways of expanding their reach rather than simply closing the book on the subject. Getting to know the daily lives of Americans, which the documents in these volumes help so much to do, is the way to get to know America. It is to try to answer the unanswerable but necessary and persistent question, asked during the American Revolution and echoed thereafter—namely, in the words of Hector St. Jean de Crèvecoeur, "What then is this new man, this American?"

A Note on Origin and Method

Daily Life through American History in Primary Documents grew out of discussions with editors at ABC-CLIO about how best to open ABC-CLIO's bank of documents for use by teachers, students, and researchers in a responsible way and how to provide a fuller documentary foundation for books on "daily life" that the press has been publishing. And as noted above, the editors sought to build from and on the Daily Life encyclopedias and documentary collections. From such discussions, the press enlisted the editors/authors of these volumes to draw on the documents bank as necessary and appropriate and to expand the sampling of documents from other sources as necessary and appropriate. At ABC-CLIO Michael Millman took the lead in moving the project from conception to production, encouraging and prodding, as necessary, to keep the editors/authors on task, on target, and on time. He also has gone beyond the normal definition of editor by providing templates for the bibliographies and working up the chronologies. *Daily Life through American History in Primary Documents* is, in important ways, his product as much as that of the editors/authors.

Each editor/author assumed the primary, almost complete, responsibility for his individual volume. Early on, the general editor and Michael Millman agreed on the scope of each volume and the principal strategy(ies) for accessing, assessing, and using the ABC-CLIO documents file and acquiring additional documents as needed. The general editor coordinated these and subsequent discussions, met and corresponded with the individual editors/authors to discuss matters pertinent to their work, read the individual volumes in their various stages of development for content and coverage and their fit with the overall design of the four volumes, and made suggestions for content, coverage, and revisions, where necessary and appropriate. It is important to note that each individual editor/author assumed principal responsibility for the content and correctness of his volume, which included setting the documents in a meaningful historical context, getting permissions to use any material(s) still in copyright, fact-checking, and proofing and revising text. The individual volumes are the work of the individual editors/authors, and they are properly so named and recognized on the title page of each volume. It also is important to note that the editors/authors did more than gather up and compile documentary collections. They were authors as well as editors, writing the volume introductions, chapter introductions, and headnotes that give historical perspective and substance to each work.

The documents in the volumes are presented as written in the original source from which they came. The editors/authors intruded little into the texts, except to excerpt them when necessary. The presence of ellipses usually means the editors have excerpted material not pertinent to the subject. Where necessary for meaning, the editors/authors inserted a definition or the modern term for a word; in such instances, the inserted material is set in brackets to distinguish it from the original document. Spelling, punctuation, and grammar are printed as found in the document source being used. Doing so literally lets the writer of the document have his or her own voice. Capturing the authenticity of the voice is an important editorial principle to which all the editors/authors subscribed. It also speaks to the purpose of this work—to let the American people tell about themselves, about their daily lives, on their terms. Thereby we might discover who they really were and wanted to be.

Randall M. Miller

ACKNOWLEDGMENTS

While working on this volume, I had the opportunity to read many accounts by people who lived during a very important time in American history, and I have gained a greater appreciation for the lives people led during this time. It is always exciting for me to read the words of those writing about their everyday lives. I would like to thank my colleague, Randall Miller, at Saint Joseph's University, for once again asking me to work with him on this project, and for all the patience he showed as the project progressed. As an editor, he has no peer. I would also like to thank my friend Anthony Marino, who helped with the research process, picking up things that I may have overlooked. I would also like to express my thanks to Michael Millman at ABC-CLIO for his infinite patience and his help in guiding me along to the project's culmination. I finally would like to thank my mother, Lucy Zeman, and my uncle, Theodore Drobnicki, for all their patience and encouragement as I worked my way through the volume.

CHRONOLOGY OF SELECTED EVENTS, 1791–1865

1791 Congress approves the Bank of the United States Act (1791) to establish a national bank, on February 25.

The Bill of Rights, the first ten amendments to the U.S. Constitution, goes into effect with ratification by Virginia on December 15.

1792 The presidential election fuels the development of two political parties: the Federalist Party, led by Alexander Hamilton and John Adams, and the Democratic-Republican Party, led by James Madison and later Thomas Jefferson.

1793 Eli Whitney invents the cotton gin, a machine that greatly improves cotton production levels in the United States and allows cotton to become a dominant crop in the South.

The Fugitive Slave Act (1793), passed on February 12, provides a mechanism for the enforcement of a slave owner's right to recover runaway slaves as mandated in the Constitution.

1794 Mounting discontent over a 1791 tax on whiskey boils over in Pennsylvania in July. The Whiskey Rebellion is put down peacefully after President George Washington orders troops into the area in August.

1798 Between June 18 and July 11, Congress passes four Alien and Sedition Acts, which allow for greater control of foreign nationals and immigrants and limit freedom of speech.

1800 The United States conducts its second census. There are over five million people in the states, nearly 900,000 of whom are slaves.

1803 The United States purchases the Louisiana Territory from France for $15 million on May 2. The Louisiana Purchase doubles the size of the country.

Beginning a three-year voyage of exploration in the Louisiana Territory and other parts of the West, Meriwether Lewis and William Clark's expedition sets out down the Ohio River on August 31.

1809 On July 2, Shawnee leader Tecumseh and his brother Tenskwatawa establish a confederacy of American Indians to resist further land cessions to the United States.

1812 On June 1, President James Madison sends a message to Congress asking for a declaration of war against Britain in response to British harassment of American ships, impressment of American sailors, and encouragement of Indian hostilities. The declaration is approved, and the War of 1812 begins on June 18.

1814 The British defeat the U.S. forces at the Battle of Bladensburg outside Washington, D.C., on August 24. The U.S. government flees, and British troops burn many of the city's prominent buildings.

On December 24, Britain and the United States sign the Treaty of Ghent, which ends the War of 1812.

1820 The Senate passes the Missouri Compromise, which allows Missouri to become a slave state with the stipulation that all lands west of the Mississippi and north of 36°30′ latitude within the territory of the Louisiana Purchase be free states.

1823 President James Monroe issues the Monroe Doctrine on December 2. Though the U.S. military is too weak to enforce that doctrine, Monroe claims hegemony over the entire Western Hemisphere and warns European governments not to interfere.

1825 The completed Erie Canal opens in Buffalo, New York, on October 26 and provides the connections necessary to create a water route from New York City to the Great Lakes.

1830 Joseph Smith founds the Church of Jesus Christ of Latter-day Saints (Mormon Church) in Fayette, New York.

President Andrew Jackson signs the Indian Removal Act, requiring all Native Americans to relocate west of the Mississippi River.

1831 Nat Turner organizes a slave insurrection in Southampton County, Virginia.

1836 To prevent Texas independence, Mexican general Antonio López de Santa Anna's siege on the Alamo begins on February 23 and lasts until March 6, when all the Texas volunteers are killed. Anglo settlers in Texas declare independence from Mexico on March 2.

On April 21, Sam Houston defeats Mexican general Antonio López de Santa Anna at the Battle of San Jacinto and forces the Mexican Army back across the Rio Grande.

1837 The Panic of 1837 begins on May 10, as New York banks can no longer make payments in specie (gold or silver coins) and fail. Before the year is over, 618 other U.S. banks will fail.

1838 U.S. government forces march the Cherokee from Georgia to the Indian Territory beginning in October and through the fall and winter. At least 25 percent of the Cherokees die on what becomes known as the Trail of Tears.

1840 President Martin Van Buren creates a ten-hour workday for federal employees on March 31.

1841 The first covered wagon train, consisting of forty-eight wagons, arrives in Sacramento (in the Mexican state of Alta California) by way of the Oregon Trail, the Sierra Nevada Mountains, and the Humboldt River.

1845 Beginning in 1845, the potato famine in Ireland pushes 1.5 million Irish immigrants to come to the United States over six years.

1846 On April 25, the Mexican Army takes U.S. soldiers prisoner in the disputed Texas territory, and on May 13, the United States officially declares war. The Mexican-American War has begun.

1848 The state of New York grants women the right to own property with legal status equal to that of men.

On February 2, the Treaty of Guadalupe Hidalgo ends the Mexican-American War. Mexico cedes Texas north of the Rio Grande, California, and New Mexico in exchange for $15 million.

1849 Bringing gold hunters from the East, the ship *California* arrives in San Francisco on February 28. An estimated 80,000 "forty-niners" travel to California by land and sea during the first year of the California gold rush.

1850 The Compromise of 1850 is signed by President Millard Fillmore on September 9. It includes the Texas and New Mexico Act, creating the New Mexico Territory and fixing its border with Texas; the Utah Act, creating the Utah Territory; and a bill admitting California to the Union as the thirty-first state.

1852 In April, Harriet Beecher Stowe publishes *Uncle Tom's Cabin*, which emphasizes the cruelty of Southern slavery. The book is both hugely popular and controversial; it sells more than one million copies and heightens abolitionist sentiments.

1854 The Kansas-Nebraska Act is approved on May 30. It creates the territories of Kansas and Nebraska and repeals the Missouri Compromise of 1820, which had prohibited slavery north of the 36°30′ parallel line.

1856 Republican senator Charles Sumner of Massachusetts gives a speech in the Senate on May 19 regarding what he calls the "crime against Kansas," the installation of a proslavery legislature there. Three days later, in reaction to that speech, Congressman Preston Brooks of South Carolina severely beats Sumner with his cane. Brooks is fined $500.

1857 On March 6, the U.S. Supreme Court announces, in *Dred Scott v. Sandford*, that because Dred Scott is black, he is not a citizen and cannot sue for his freedom in federal court. The Missouri Compromise of 1820 is also ruled to be unconstitutional.

1858 In Illinois, Republican Abraham Lincoln and Democrat Stephen A. Douglas compete for a seat in the U.S. Senate. They meet in seven highly publicized debates, in which Lincoln speaks out against slavery and Douglas speaks in favor of states' rights.

1859 In an attempt to free slaves and establish an abolitionist republic, John Brown leads eighteen others in the Harpers Ferry raid in Virginia and seizes the federal arsenal on October 16. Many are killed, and Brown is captured two days later by Col. Robert E. Lee.

1860 On November 6, Abraham Lincoln wins the presidential election.

In reaction to Lincoln's election, South Carolina becomes the first state to secede from the Union, on December 20. Ten more states will secede in 1861.

1861 The Union Army garrison at Fort Sumter, South Carolina, is bombarded by Confederate artillery on April 12. The Civil War has begun.

In the first major confrontation of the war, on July 21 Southern forces rout Northern troops in the First Battle of Bull Run.

1862 The year is characterized by heavy fighting and high casualties on both sides as the war rages in the South, throughout Mississippi, Tennessee, and just outside Washington, D.C.

1863 The Emancipation Proclamation goes into force on January 1. Since its provisions apply only to regions where the Union Army is not in control, its effect is primarily psychological.

Union victory at the Battle of Gettysburg. Confederate general Robert E. Lee's army incurs losses of nearly 30,000.

1864 On November 16, Gen. William T. Sherman departs a virtually destroyed Atlanta and commences his famous March to the Sea. Sherman strikes major Southern cities and military centers throughout eastern Georgia, South Carolina, North Carolina, and southern Virginia.

1865 The Freedmen's Bureau is established by Congress on March 3 to provide former slaves with economic, medical, and educational assistance in their transition from slavery to freedom.

Lee abandons Petersburg to end the siege begun by Gen. Ulysses S. Grant the previous June. On April 9, Lee agrees to Grant's terms, presented at Appomattox Court House, Virginia, and surrenders the Army of Northern Virginia.

On April 14, President Abraham Lincoln is assassinated by John Wilkes Booth during a performance at Ford's Theater in Washington, D.C. Lincoln dies of his head wound the next morning, and later that day, Vice President Andrew Johnson takes the oath of office to become the seventeenth president.

On December 18, after long debate, the Thirteenth Amendment, prohibiting slavery in the United States, goes into force.

Part I
HISTORICAL OVERVIEW

Revolution and a New Nation

The American Revolution forever changed the course of American history. Over the course of the next eighty-five years, the effects of the Revolution significantly altered the everyday lives of Americans. They would see profound changes in government, the economy, and society. With the exploration of the regions west of the Mississippi River and the settlers who followed in their wake, the new nation grew into a continental empire. Technological developments such as the steamboat, the steam locomotive, and the telegraph added to the expansion of the factory system, transforming the nation from an agrarian-based economy to one founded on industry. At the same time, America continued to experience the effects of the Second Great Awakening, including a renewed sense of Christian purpose that led to increased interest in social reforms such as temperance, aid to orphans, and antislavery. Although their accepted role continued to be defined in terms of family care, women began to take a greater role in shaping American society. And even as white Americans experienced the freedom of a new nation, slaves continued to struggle for that freedom. Slavery came under increasing attack during this period. Antislavery societies grew in number and influence, although participation was largely limited to native Northerners. Southerners, yeomen as well as planters, continued to defend and promote the South's "peculiar institution," which had economic and political as well as social ramifications. The slavery controversy continued to fester throughout this period; defying political solutions, it took a bloody and destructive war to provide a resolution.

The year 1775 was a critical moment in the American Revolution as the colonies dramatically asserted their rights as British subjects. In April the opening shots in what became a war for independence were fired at Lexington and Concord as British regulars and American militiamen exchanged fire and both suffered casualties. The clashes in Massachusetts left ninety-five Americans and seventy-three British dead. They revealed that a negotiated settlement of long-festering American grievances was no longer possible, and that full-scale military confrontation was imminent. When the Second Continental Congress met in Philadelphia in May 1775 to decide the colonies' next step, delegates' opinion was divided about whether the colonies should continue to seek redress for their grievances against Parliament and King George III or to declare independence. The opinions of ordinary Americans were similarly mixed. Many wanted to remain loyal to Britain, while others believed a complete break was a necessity. As the debate continued, so did military operations. On June 16, 1775, British troops in Boston launched an assault on the American positions on Bunker and Breed's Hills. The British gained a tactical victory by driving the poorly trained and equipped but determined Americans from their entrenchments. In the process, however, the attackers suffered more than 1,000 casualties while inflicting 450 on the Americans—a strategic setback. The disparity convinced many American civilians that their army could resist the British and, through courage and perseverance, win in the end. Increasingly Americans began to believe that their virtue was their armor; the typical yeoman farmer was more than a match for a mercenary employed by a corrupt Old World government. Thus emboldened, the delegates in Congress determined to press on; they decided that a full-fledged army should be recruited and organized to resist British coercion. Command of the so-called Continental Army was assigned to a forty-two-year-old planter and militia officer from Virginia, George Washington. Upon his shoulders rested the hopes of American resistance.

While Washington slowly formed and trained an army of volunteers, the debate in Congress over the path that America should take heated up. Those who supported reconciliation traded barbs with colleagues committed to American independence. The failure of the Olive Branch Petition, which had been sent to the king upon the insistence of John Dickinson, a conservative delegate from Pennsylvania, prompted those who favored independence, headed by the eloquent and passionate John Adams of Massachusetts, to call for an open break with the mother country. Adams's cause was aided by the pamphleteer, Thomas Paine, whose *Common Sense* (1776) helped persuade uncertain and wavering Americans that the king was a tyrant undeserving of their continued allegiance. In June 1776 the introduction by the Virginia delegation of a formal resolution calling for independence resulted in the drafting of a document designed to provide the philosophical foundation of the independence movement. Thomas Jefferson of Virginia drew the task of writing the Declaration of Independence. The document clearly enumerated the colonies' grievances against the British crown and called for America to separate from its parent country. On July 4, 1776, the wording of the Declaration of Independence was approved and the text was read aloud before a crowd gathered in front of Independence Hall in Philadelphia.

The Declaration of Independence drew mixed reviews from ordinary Americans. Many doubted that separation from Great Britain was either wise or possible. Throughout the conflict that followed, thousands of so-called Tories supported attachment to Britain; many openly waged war against their "patriot" neighbors.

Numerous patriots and Tories alike assumed that the war would be short and would not create widespread suffering. Yet the war lasted eight years and produced an estimated 50,000 American and some 20,000 British casualties. A large percentage of these were felled by disease rather than bullets. The total number of civilian casualties, most of which were caused by small-scale but deadly partisan clashes and Indian raids, has not been firmly established, but it was large enough to leave an indelible mark on American society for decades to come.

For the patriot cause, the war was a fluctuating mix of victories and defeats. The Continental Army achieved early success when British troops were forced to evacuate Boston in March 1776, but the loss of strategic New York and New Jersey later that year seriously hurt American morale and took Washington's forces to the brink of disintegration. On Christmas evening 1776, however, the American commander led a surprise raid on the Hessian outpost at Trenton, New Jersey, capturing the garrison, and then followed up with a victory over British regulars at Princeton nine days later. These successes restored American confidence and kept the Continental Army intact.

During the first year of the war it became clear that it would take a great and sustained effort to drive the British from American soil. Americans soon realized they had to make sacrifices to attain their independence. The politicization of the military effort became more pronounced as the war progressed. Efforts to keep the revolutionary fires burning took many forms, including musical propaganda. One example was the song "Yankee Doodle," originally a tune that expressed British derision of the typical American volunteer that evolved into an expression of patriot pride. Another symbol of the war effort that was turned into political propaganda was the Continental Army's winter encampment at Valley Forge, Pennsylvania. The suffering borne in this venue of squalor by the soldiers in the name of independence became an enduring image of American spirit and tenacity.

The course of the war took a critical turn in 1778 when the French empire intervened militarily in America's behalf. Three years later French soldiers and sailors helped Washington gain a decisive victory at Yorktown, Virginia. The war continued for another two years, however, during which America survived the threat of a military coup that would have destroyed all that had been fought for since Lexington and Concord. The leadership and influence of Washington, who repeatedly reminded his soldiers that they fought for liberty, not their own gain, defeated those behind the cabal. Washington's public deference to civilian authority saved America from collapsing into civil strife and military dictatorship, the fate of many revolutions elsewhere in the world.

The Treaty of Paris brought the war to an official conclusion on September 3, 1783. The veterans who had endured so much over the previous eight years returned to their homes to resume their everyday lives. Independence had been won, but Americans now had to determine how to build upon their triumph. That process led to experiments in government at the state and local level and eventually to the creation of a strong central government to secure the rights of the people and serve as a beacon of freedom to the world.

At war's end, hundreds of Tories left America to settle elsewhere, uprooting their lives and families and in many cases losing everything of value they had accumulated. For many of those who supported the patriot cause, the war likewise meant dislocation and disruption, although the majority of those who had actively or tacitly supported independence could bask—at least for a time—in the glow of victory and freedom.

A New Government and an Expanding Nation

In the wake of the Treaty of Paris, most Americans settled down to their everyday lives and looked forward to a peace that they had not known for eight years. But as time passed, there were signs that the new nation was having difficulty governing itself. The federal government that had been established under the Articles of Confederation in 1781 was weak, principally because the power of the states was superior to any central authority. Many people began to fear that this weakness was retarding economic growth and undermining the stability of social institutions. Conflicts arose between states over the payment of debt; clashes between debtors and lenders led to arguments that culminated in Shays' Rebellion in Massachusetts, which began in August 1786 and was not put down until February 1787. Shays' Rebellion marked a critical point in the development of a strong central government. It suggested that the newly established state governments were unable to enforce laws to promote domestic tranquility.

As a result, calls were made for developing a more powerful central government that would address the problems that were confronting the nation. In May 1787, delegates from the twelve states (Rhode Island did not send a delegation) met in Philadelphia to amend the Articles of Confederation. The meetings, held between May and September, did more than that. The delegates completely scrapped the document and drafted a constitution that produced a strong central government, one that would ensure the future success of the nation. Public reaction to the work of the Constitutional Convention was mixed. Many citizens applauded the Constitution, believing the only way the United States could survive was through a strong government that would settle disputes between states and secure the confidence of other countries in American political and economic stability. Opponents viewed a powerful federal structure as a threat to the republican freedoms that had been won in battle against the British. The debate that ensued between the Federalists and Anti-Federalists played out as the state ratification conventions deliberated whether to accept or reject the Constitution. The public also debated the question via the press, informational pamphlets, and public gatherings. Eventually the Federalists prevailed, although their opponents gained a concession: a Bill of Rights was later written into the document that guaranteed certain basic rights under the Constitution.

A glaring limitation in the Constitution left the issue of chattel slavery in the hands of the states, thus protecting southern economic interests. The debate over the Constitution had produced threats by the southern states that they would bolt the convention if the federal government was given the power to eliminate slavery or limit its practice. In a saving compromise, the delegates agreed that slaves were to be counted as three-fifths of a free person for purposes of representation, which helped increase southern influence in the Congress. Furthermore, the importation of slaves could not be terminated until at least 1808, and fugitive slaves were recoverable anywhere in the nation. The inability or unwillingness of the Founding Fathers to solve the slavery problem sowed the seeds that would lead to civil war in 1861.

With the formation of the new government and the election of George Washington as its first president, America embarked on a period of growth; by 1860 the country had expanded to the Pacific Ocean and transformed in numerous ways. For the most part, people were able to go about their lives without interference from their national leaders. Local governments touched people more directly. Rather than rule with a heavy hand, the government concentrated on economic development. Thanks to its support, the country benefited from investment in the development of new technologies that spurred economic growth and protected property interests.

As the economy expanded, questions arose about the nature and extent of government's role in its development. Many citizens believed that America should remain true to its agrarian roots; others contended that if the nation were to reach its economic potential, it must invest heavily in mercantile and industrial enterprises. The result of this contest during the first decade of the new government was the emergence of political parties. Those who supported the traditional agrarian orientation of the economy, such as Thomas Jefferson and James Madison, coalesced into the Democratic-Republicans. Those who supported a strong mercantile-industrial economy, such as Alexander Hamilton, formed the Federalist Party. The parties became the base upon which the political shape of the nation would form, and partisan politics would shape the nation for centuries to come.

Even before the Revolution ended, Americans began to move beyond the boundaries of the colonies westward toward the Ohio River. With the close of the war, settlers headed farther west to put down roots and establish communities. Westward expansion brought settlers into contact with Indian tribes, who were wary of the numbers of whites entering their lands. Resistance led to major conflicts between white men and Native Americans. The new federal government sought to negotiate with the Indians with the intent of creating safe areas for the preservation of the tribes, but it was not very successful. Eventually the conflicts led to tragedy, as government officials adopted a policy of forced resettlement on reservation lands and many tribes resisted being compelled to relocate in regions unsuitable for the kinds of agriculture and hunting and fishing they had practiced for years.

As America entered the nineteenth century, its people looked forward to a period of peace and growth. But optimism soon wavered in the face of signs that the nation's political, economic, and social growth would not occur evenly or smoothly. The portents were troubling. During the presidential election of 1800 Thomas Jefferson defeated the incumbent John Adams, successor to Washington. The significance of this election was that it reflected the emergence of political parties on a national level. Both the Federalists, who supported Adams, and the Democratic-Republicans, who championed Jefferson, had gained considerable strength during Washington's administration. For decades to come the parties would struggle mightily for control of the government, each using the ever-growing power of the press to place their views before the public. The parties did not always prize consistency or orthodoxy. Jefferson, for instance, warned against concentrating too much power in the federal government, but he was almost single-handedly responsible for expanding that power through his purchase of the Louisiana Territory and enforcement of the embargo during the Napoleonic Wars.

The greatest achievement of America's government at the turn of the century was the Louisiana Purchase of 1803. Taking advantage of Napoleon's need for money, the government purchased the Louisiana Territory for $14 million. Its acquisition moved the nation's western border beyond the Mississippi River as far as the present states of Washington and Oregon. To gain a detailed picture of the lay of this land and those who inhabited it, Jefferson sent Captains Meriwether Lewis and William Clark to explore the new territory. Embarking on this mammoth undertaking in August 1803, the forty-man expedition, known as the Corps of Discovery, spent two and a half years mapping out the territory and recording its plant, mineral, and animal life. The Corps returned to its starting point, St. Louis, on September 23, 1806, having amassed an abundance of information that would prompt many thousands of settlers to move to the new territory.

Other explorations also spurred westward settlement. In July 1806 Lieutenant Zebulon Pike was ordered to explore that portion of the territory that bordered the region long claimed by Spain. His expedition penetrated the Rocky Mountains to as far as present-day Colorado. For decades a direct water route to the Pacific had been considered a myth, but by the 1830s the first overland migrations were heading via river to the Pacific Northwest. People read accounts of these explorations with great avidity. The observations, maps, and specimens that resulted from the expeditions of Lewis and Clark, Pike, and others proved invaluable to scientists and naturalists as well as to potential settlers.

As more people moved west, the nation's economy began to change, from Jefferson's cherished agrarian system to one more heavily dependent on industrialization. By the turn of the century more and more of those goods that had been produced by and purchased from Europe, primarily England, were being manufactured in America. Much like the Industrial Revolution of late eighteenth-century England, America's manufacturing "take-off" began with the dramatic growth of the textile industry. Over the succeeding decades hundreds of factories were built to fill the demand for goods ranging from cloth to soap. The era of the single artisan was passing away and by 1860 would be all but gone in several important industries. This economic transformation demanded skilled or semiskilled workers to operate the looms, presses, and furnaces that constituted the most visible manifestations of an industrialized society.

Technological innovations hastened the American worker's transformation from using simple tools to using heavy machinery. Improvements in harvesting and processing crops, machine tools, and interchangeable parts greatly increased output and made better use of a laborer's time and energy. An early example of a machine that revolutionized an industry was the cotton gin, patented by Eli Whitney in 1794. The cleverly designed device expedited the production of short-staple cotton, a product long rendered unprofitable by the need to remove cotton seeds slowly and carefully by hand. As a result, the production of cotton became more profitable—and slavery more productive. The demand for cotton and the ability to process it quickly spurred the expansion of slavery westward and southward. The belief that slavery would die out as a consequence of making importation of slaves illegal after 1808 was proven wrong: for decades afterward, slavery would expand through natural increase. Soon planters and politicians were looking to make slavery legal in the lands beyond the Mississippi.

Another invention that had a major impact on the economy during the early and mid-nineteenth century was the development of the steamboat by Robert Fulton. Others had attempted to apply steam power to river travel, but had been unsuccessful. In 1807 Fulton's *Clermont* successfully steamed up the Hudson River from New York City to Albany in two days—half the time it took a sailing ship to cover the same distance. Modifications to Fulton's invention over the following years allowed for the transportation of goods to ports around the country at a much faster—and therefore more profitable—rate than ever before. With the emergence of shallow-draft vessels able to navigate upstream, the steamboat conquered the western rivers. River traffic increased dramatically on trans-Appalachian waterways as well as on the mighty Mississippi.

Other developments in what became a transportation revolution included improved roads and canals. The federal government proposed a national road system, begun in 1811; although it eventually stretched from Maryland to Illinois, it was not completed until 1852. More important as a spur to commerce was the Erie Canal, which upon completion in 1825 connected New York City with the vast hinterlands of the Great Lakes region. Its dramatic success encouraged other states to fund canals. The "canal boom" flourished, creating America's first great transportation network, which facilitated the movement of goods and people through the nation's east-west corridor.

As the United States expanded geographically, its government began to develop a foreign policy. The Washington administration had managed to keep America out of the war between England and France in the 1790s, but President Adams had been unable to prevent attacks on American merchant ships by both belligerents. The situation led to a quasi-war with France in 1798, in which the small U.S. Navy defeated the mighty French Navy in several engagements. Adams was able to negotiate a peace treaty with the French government, but the raids against American shipping continued during his successor's administration. Much of the damage was inflicted by Barbary pirates in the Mediterranean. Although Jefferson did not believe in a large military, these widely publicized depredations compelled him to send ships into the Mediterranean to enforce shipping rights. For a time the attacks ceased, but as Jefferson's administration entered its second term, Great Britain began to impress American seamen into its navy. To combat the illegal practice and the renewed British interdiction of American ships headed to Europe, Jefferson announced an embargo that would prevent goods from being traded to, or imported from, Britain. The edict proved disastrous to the American economy, and Jefferson left office having failed to establish American rights on the high seas. The continued impressments of American sailors and depredations of American maritime commerce would prove a factor in the War of 1812, "America's Second War of Independence."

The War of 1812 to the Age of Jackson

The continued aggression of the British Navy, which stopped American ships and impressed their sailors, added to British support for Indians threatening the American frontier and other military and economic policies, led President James Madison to ask Congress to declare war on June 19, 1812. Once again America faced the greatest military power in Europe. Although the English were preoccupied with fighting Napoleonic France, the war did not go well for the United States. The lack of a professional army and the small size of its navy meant that America could not prevent the British from blockading U.S. ports and raiding American territorial possessions. The defeat of an American army at Detroit in August 1812 demonstrated the need to build a standing, highly professionalized army, which the United States sought to do after the war by establishing a military academy and training a cadre of officers. The U.S. Navy achieved limited success in engagements against British ships, notably the victories of the U.S.S. *Constitution* over several British warships, but the tiny force was soon bottled up by the British. Makeshift naval forces led by Commodore Oliver Hazard Perry defeated a British naval force on Lake Erie in September 1813, helping keep the British at bay. A victory by forces under General William Henry Harrison at the Battle of the Thames stopped a combined British and Indian force from further incursions into the northwest frontier and killed the great Indian leader Tecumseh.

These successes notwithstanding, the Americans faced a crisis once Napoleon was defeated in April 1814. The British were now free to concentrate their vast resources against America. They extended their blockade until they were able to choke off all trade and shipping with the United States. The war's downturn prompted Federalist politicians in New England to call for an abrupt end to the fighting during the Hartford Convention in December 1814; the alternative was to risk the secession of that region from the union. This demand came on the heels of the burning of Washington, D.C., by British forces in August, including the destruction of the Executive Mansion (White House). In September, however, the British failed to take Baltimore thanks to the stout resistance of Fort McHenry, whose commander refused to surrender even in the face of an intense naval bombardment. Such tenacity inspired Francis Scott Key to compose "The Star Spangled Banner," which more than a century later became the national anthem of the United States. By this point, negotiations between the antagonists were underway in Ghent, Belgium; they were concluded successfully on December 24, 1814. The treaty was ratified by both nations in February 1815. By then the Hartford Convention had adjourned, its antiwar protest having been voided, first by the dramatic victory of Andrew Jackson's forces at the Battle of New Orleans (January 8) and then by word of the peace settlement. The threats of secession emanating from New England effectively destroyed the Federalist Party.

Having survived the war, America considered not only its independence but also its economic prosperity assured. The nation would continue to grow as an industrial and commercial power well into the twentieth century. America would further assert its rights as a nation in 1823 through the Monroe Doctrine, which warned that interference in the Western Hemisphere by the states of Europe would not be tolerated. Although the Doctrine was probably unenforceable when it was announced, it would guide American foreign policy for centuries to come.

The War of 1812 reaffirmed the sovereignty America had won during the Revolution. With most of the Old Northwest delivered from Indian incursions, westward migration redoubled. The molestation of American merchant shipping having ended, commerce and manufacturing expanded at a rate unknown in the Old World. Although the life of the average citizen was not radically changed, over time it became clear that life was being transformed in a multitude of ways.

Postwar America embarked on a program of internal improvements that facilitated the transportation of goods to and from markets—from interior points to ports up and down the Atlantic and Gulf of Mexico coasts. The various states led the way in developing and funding internal improvement projects, with profitable results. The money invested by New York in the Erie Canal would be paid back many times over. While work progressed on the canal, Henry Shreve's steamboat *Washington* inaugurated service between Louisville and New Orleans, an early indication of the western reach of the new means of river traffic.

The nation also began to get its finances in order. The Second Bank of the United States was established in 1816 to facilitate credit and, by its ability to issue bank notes that operated as currency, to regulate the nation's finances. The bank's charter had been allowed to expire in 1811 by the Democratic-Republicans then in power, who regarded the institution as a threat to public sovereignty. The charter was reinstated, however, in the spirit of progress and buoyant nationalism that followed victory over Britain. The bank owed its revival to the growing belief that government should take a more active role in public works projects and stimulate the economy in general.

From 1790 to 1819 nine states entered the Union. Their admission came about smoothly, but a controversy erupted in 1819 over the pending statehood of Missouri, which straddled the heretofore easily defined line between North and South. Congressional debate centered around whether slavery would be permitted in the new state, the first to be carved from the Louisiana Purchase. Northern politicians—many of whom wished to make the country more open to white labor, with a zealous minority desiring to eradicate slavery altogether by limiting its expansion—strove to curb slavery's growth in the newly acquired territories. They banded together to block Missouri's admission unless slavery was made illegal there. Southern congressmen, who considered slavery's expansion critical to their region's economy, fought back. A compromise was finally reached under which Missouri was admitted as a slave state; slavery was outlawed in the Louisiana Purchase north of latitude 36°30′, and Maine was admitted to the Union as a free state, thus maintaining an uneasy balance between slave and free states in the Senate. A possible crisis had been defused, but the political wrangling revealed that the issue of slavery had threatened to tear apart the political and social fabric of the nation.

With the Missouri Compromise in place, America continued to expand, while involving more and more of its people in the political process. By 1825 only three states (Virginia, Rhode Island, and Louisiana) retained property restrictions on the right to vote, which meant that almost the entire adult white male population could cast a ballot. This was the result of white men's growing interest and participation in the political process. Many gained insight into that process through the rapidly proliferating press, which enabled them to make informed decisions about the issues and the candidates for office. The period also saw an increase in the number of public meetings in which issues of concern to the electorate were disseminated, discussed, and debated. Public awareness of the governmental process was facilitated by the growing availability of public education, which helped raise not only political consciousness but also the literacy rate.

The presidential election of 1824 polarized the American political system even as it strengthened the nation's faith in the efficacy of popular government. At the outset several candidates vied for the presidency, but ultimately the contest came down to John Quincy Adams, son of John Adams, and the military hero Andrew Jackson. Because neither man gained enough electoral votes to win the election, the decision was passed to the House of Representatives. After a long and contentious debate and numerous votes, Adams was declared the winner. Many political observers believed this had come about because the influential Speaker of the House, Henry Clay of Kentucky, was offered the post of secretary of state in an Adams administration. Jackson's supporters charged that a "corrupt bargain" had stolen the election from their man, thus subverting the foundations of popular government. Although the accusation was later proven untrue, it would stick to Adams and lead to his defeat four years later.

In 1828, following one of the most contentious elections in the nation's history, Jackson gained his revenge by defeating Adams. Jackson's inauguration in March 1829 ushered in a period marked by increased popular participation in elections, the rise of national party systems, and the widespread distribution of patronage. The political credo that characterized the so-called Age of Jackson can best be described as "to the victor belongs the spoils."

The political party system was in part an outgrowth of differing visions on the role that the federal government should play in fostering the economy. There were those who believed that the states and private business should be responsible for the funding of projects such as the building of canals and roads, as well as the financing of another form of transportation that would play a key role in the economic development of the nation, the railroad. The development of a steam locomotive in the United States in 1830 led many to believe that rail transportation was the future for the transport of goods and people. As a result, charters were issued by states for the building of hundreds of railroads throughout the country. Supporters of government finance believed that government participation would enhance the country's finances, but opposition came from those who believed that government involvement would eventually strangle the ability of individuals to prosper in a free economy. Jackson and his supporters stuck to this view. This difference in ideology led to a split in the Democratic-Republicans, to the formation of the Democratic Party led by Jackson, and then to the creation of the Whig Party, led by Henry Clay, established in 1834. The two parties would develop not only differing ideologies but also the party organizations that are the model for political parties in America to this day.

The presidency of Andrew Jackson was marked by two controversies that had long-lasting effects on the nation: the Nullification Controversy of 1832 and the fight over a new charter for the Second Bank of the United States in 1832. The nullification issue arose when the state of South Carolina, supported by then vice president John C. Calhoun, refused to accept a federal law that raised tariffs on imports into the United States. This had been passed in 1828, and many southerners viewed it as an attack on their freedom to do business, as well as an extension of northern interests that could ultimately threaten slavery. Calhoun had written in 1828 that a state had a right to negate a federal law that violated the compact that existed between the states in the formation of the national union. A further tariff was passed in 1832, which led to South Carolina nullifying the law. Although Jackson was not a believer in big government, he believed that nullification was wrong, and in January 1833 he had Congress enact the Force Act, which allowed Jackson to mobilize the army and navy to enforce federal authority. The lack of support from other states led to South Carolina backing down; Calhoun resigned as vice president and was elected senator from South Carolina, where he continued to make a call for the idea of nullification. The seeds planted during the Nullification Crisis would sprout in 1860, with disastrous consequences to the nation.

The second controversy also arose in 1832, when Jackson opposed rechartering of the Second Bank of the United States. Jackson believed that big government stifled the rights of the people and that private investment and state governments should drive economic growth and development. As a result, he threatened to void the bank's charter, which was not due to expire until 1836. Whigs believed the bank was necessary not only to help the American economy, but to prevent state and private banks from loaning too much money and extending too much credit to those who could not pay. In the end Jackson won. He withdrew government funds from the Bank in 1834 and allowed the charter to expire in 1836. A year later, during the first term of President Martin Van Buren, a severe depression struck the United States, and many people blamed it on the speculative venture of state and private banks and the inability of the government to intervene to prevent it.

During the 1830s Americans continued to stream westward. One region that many began to settle was Texas. At this time the territory belonged to Mexico, and the influx of Americans into the territory increased tensions there, especially as the Americans insisted on their "right" to bring slaves into the territory and follow their own rules, irrespective of Mexican law. Americans living in Texas wanted to create an independent republic or be annexed by the United States. With tacit support from the federal government, a Texas independence movement gathered strength; it led to a war between the Americans in Texas and Mexico in 1836. In March Mexican president and general Antonio López de Santa Anna captured a fortified church in San Antonio known as the Alamo, killing every defender there. In April, however, General Sam Houston's Texas forces defeated Santa Anna at San Jacinto and forced him to recognize the Republic of Texas. Within ten years, conflict would again arise with Mexico over Texas and start a war that would expand America's borders to California.

The increasing pressure of westward expansion began the policy of relocation of Indians in Alabama, Mississippi, Georgia, and Florida beyond the Mississippi River. Jackson believed this was the best policy to protect the Indians from further contact with whites. Eventually the Cherokees were forced to march overland in what became known as the "Trail of Tears," in which over 14, 000 Indians were marched 1,200 miles and 3,000 elderly and young Indians perished. This forced removal and the continued actions of the federal government in relocating Indians throughout the rest of the century engendered more conflicts and suffering for America's natives.

During the 1830s the number of immigrants coming to America increased dramatically, principally Irish, English, Germans, and others seeking political and economic opportunities in the United States denied them in their native countries. During the 1840s and 1850s immigration increased further as economic and political conditions in Europe forced many to leave for the United States. The Irish fled famine and political oppression in their land, as did Germans who fled after the failed Revolution of 1848. Chinese immigrants flocked to California to seek work and escape the poverty of their native lands. The influx of such large numbers of foreigners into the country excited a strong nativist movement in the country that sought to limit the impact the new arrivals had on America. The Democratic Party by and large supported open immigration and won the loyalty of immigrants in cities especially, where it aggressively recruited them and provided support in the form of jobs and help in personal crises. The beginnings of so-called city machine politics were at work. Whigs, in contrast, generally looked to limit the power of the immigrants by calling for restrictive immigration laws and laws that increased the number of years immigrants had to live in the country in order to vote, and they argued for "moral reforms" that would enforce temperance and other Protestant values on Catholic immigrants. In the 1850s nativism took an overtly political form with the emergence of the Know-Nothing Party, which pledged to limit the number of foreigners entering the country before the Civil War, but was not successful. The Know-Nothing Party did not survive the coming apart of the party system over slavery in the 1850s, but nativism continued as a factor in American public life after the Civil War.

The issues that confronted the nation during the 1830s heightened the political participation of its citizens. With the expansion of the franchise to all adult white males came a call for further political involvement for women. Women were already involved, albeit indirectly, in the political life of the nation by encouraging men to act on particular issues such as temperance or other reforms. But the normal role for women was to support their husbands by managing household affairs. Even that, however, had political meaning, for they were also expected to raise their children in the proper ideals of republican government. Reformers such as Catharine Beecher made that obligation explicit in the growing literature on household management and child raising. Other women wanted a more direct role for women as both a matter of right and to improve the moral character of politics. They argued for the right to vote.

Another factor in the increased involvement of women in the political arena was the scores of religious revivals known as the Second Great Awakening. The renewed sense of Christian purpose led to increased interest in social reforms. The work that women performed in the temperance, antislavery, and childcare reform movements brought them into the political arena, albeit in an indirect way. Although it was considered unseemly for women to speak in public, many did so. Others lobbied politicians to make changes in laws affecting women, such as control over property and access to divorce, and to change conditions for those who had no voice. The work of Dorothea Dix to reform the way society and governments dealt with people suffering from mental disabilities was but one example of women's increasing role in the public sphere during this period, which would continue beyond the nineteenth century. Significantly, many women reformers argued for creating institutions, or asylums, that could remove a troubled person from the hurly-burly of everyday life in order to get treatment and a sense of order. They emphasized nurture over nature in shaping human behavior, a belief that potentially extended women's roles, for womanly nurture promised a cure for crime, drunkenness, domestic abuse, and a host of social ills—provided the proper care was available—and education, with women as teachers, promising to inculcate values and habits that would prevent those very social problems. In other words, as some reformers insisted, women needed to extend their private sphere from the home into the public. Many did so.

Despite the rise of nativism, the ongoing controversy over slavery, and the economic course of the nation, visitors to the United States noted the great future that country was moving toward. Books published during this period by many foreign travelers noted the differences between Europe and the United States. They left a detailed description of everyday life in America during this period. One of the most widely read and influential observers was the Frenchman Alexis de Tocqueville, who had been sent to observe the prison system, but expanded the scope of his mission to an assessment of American democracy. Tocqueville noted how democracy in America balanced the interests of the individual with those of the community. He also noted that it was possible in America for one to achieve higher social standing through hard work. The Christian values of the nation constituted another of his themes. He observed that unlike Europe, where religion and freedom ran in diametrically opposite directions, in the United States the two were intertwined, and that this spirit guided the work of the people to make things better. The fact that so many religious groups existed in America was proof of this. The spirit of freedom, combined with Christian values, guided many Americans during this period of reform.

Education was a potent force in helping Americans improve their lives and increase their opportunities for success. During the 1780s Thomas Jefferson wrote about the need for American schools to become superior to European schools in order to maintain the health of the American republic. The public education system in the United States by the 1830s and 1840s, though largely confined to northern states, was seen by many foreign observers as being superior to the educational systems of Europe. It was widely believed that a proper education would imbue the children of the republic with proper ideas about industry, honesty, and virtue, thereby ensuring the health and wealth of the nation. For adult men this meant being "independent" by working one's own land or making goods and by voting; for women it meant maintaining proper households and raising children who would extend the values of the republic. The result was a more literate public that was aware of the responsibilities of republican government.

The Road to Civil War

Throughout the 1840s the nation continued to divide over the issue of slavery. Both the North and the South became more suspicious of each other as conflicting issues and interests pushed them toward an inevitable confrontation. In 1836 Congress had passed a gag order that prohibited the submission of petitions to abolish slavery in the District of Columbia and in those territories where Congress had the authority to act. Despite the efforts by former president John Quincy Adams, now a congressman from Massachusetts, who continued to fight for that right until his death in 1848, the gag order operated for several sessions of Congress. In 1845 the publication in the North of *Narrative of the Life of Frederick Douglass, an American Slave*, and the subsequent publication of books by other former slaves illustrating the horrors and wrong of slavery, added to the continuing sectional tensions. An uncompromising abolition movement had emerged in the North, led by William Lloyd Garrison through his newspaper *The Liberator*. That movement argued that slavery was morally wrong and corrupted everything it touched—family, religion, work, democracy. Douglass addressed such themes in his work. Southerners, in turn, preached a proslavery gospel that insisted that slavery was a divinely sanctioned institution and that slavery in the South provided the foundation for American prosperity. They also reiterated the obligation of the nation to protect slavery's interest, as confirmed in the Constitution. Most white northerners hardly subscribed to abolitionism, but a growing number were sympathetic to arguments about the need to stop slavery's spread westward, where it would compete with free labor, and to stop a supposed "slave power" from trampling on whites' civil rights and civil liberties with gag rules in Congress, attacks on the press, interdicting the mail, and forcing northerners to do southerners' bidding in chasing down fugitive slaves. For each side, slavery was an issue that was becoming nonnegotiable. That was a principal reason why the major political parties sought to keep "silent" on the issue, lest discussion of it cause the political system, and the nation, to unravel. That changed when Texas and the prospect of slavery's expansion forced the nation's hand in the 1840s.

The most vexing diplomatic issue facing the nation in the 1840s was the annexation of Texas and the war with Mexico from 1846 to 1848. It had serious implications for the internal politics of the Union. There had been calls in 1836 for Texas to join the Union, but because it would be admitted as a slave state, and because of its size, Jackson had deferred a decision rather than risk an antislavery protest, and Texas became a republic. By 1845, many in Texas were petitioning to join the Union; others called for the country to expand throughout the continent, into Mexico and Canada. The campaign of "Manifest Destiny" was the product of the press, and it became louder as the decade progressed. Many warned that this expansion would open up the issue of slavery and would lead to sectional conflict. Southern politicians used the border dispute with Britain over Oregon to gain the support of northerners for the admission of Texas to the Union. Texas was admitted as a state as the new president, Democrat James K. Polk, took office. He settled the boundary dispute over Oregon and then concentrated on the deteriorating situation along the Mexican border. Polk sought to purchase from Mexico the territories of California and New Mexico and entered into formal negotiations to that end. At the same time he sent an army under General Zachary Taylor to the Nueces River in Texas to await further orders. When negotiations broke down, Taylor was ordered to the Rio Grande, which the United States claimed as the border with Mexico; the Mexicans claimed the border was the Nueces. When the Mexicans attacked Taylor's army, Polk used the incident as an excuse to ask Congress to declare war on Mexico in 1846.

The war lasted two years, although fighting virtually ended with the capture of Mexico City in September 1847. The Whigs claimed the war had been started under suspicious circumstances and corrupted by political motives. Many of these critics, particularly those who hailed from the Northeast and Midwest, saw the conflict as a calculated attempt to expand slavery through conquest. The U.S. Army and Navy captured California and New Mexico; then, as the forces of Taylor bogged down after the capture of Monterey, President Polk called on General Winfield Scott to lead an expedition to take Mexico City. Part of the reason for this was political, as Taylor's early success marked him as a potential presidential rival in the 1848 presidential election. Scott led a force of 14,000 men on a march from Vera Cruz to Mexico City, defeating the Mexicans there. Under the 1848 Treaty of Guadalupe-Hidalgo, Mexico sanctioned the boundary with the United States at the Rio Grande and ceded California and New Mexico to the United States as well. The United States agreed to pay Mexico $15 million and to cover any claims the citizens in the new territory had against the United States. But as Henry Clay predicted, the war had reopened the slavery issue, with grave consequences for the United States.

During the war, when Congress deliberated on the appropriations bill for the army, a Pennsylvania representative, David Wilmot, had attached a proviso prohibiting slavery in any territory gained from Mexico. Southerners decried the Wilmot Proviso as an attempt by northern and western politicians to destroy slavery, whereas northerners and westerners wanted to keep territories free of slavery, both to encourage "free soil" settlers and to limit slavery's power from growing. The proviso passed the House but was defeated in the Senate. Still, the war had once more brought the slavery issue to the political forefront in the 1848 presidential election. The Whigs won the White House when Zachary Taylor defeated Democrat Lewis Cass, but the election also produced a third national party, the Free Soil Party, with former president Van Buren as its standard bearer. This party, most of whose adherents were more interested in securing opportunities for white laborers than in freeing slaves, garnered almost 300,000 votes by calling for slavery's exclusion from the territories. The discovery of gold in California in 1849 exacerbated the problem, as many flocked to California to make a quick fortune, although the majority would come away empty-handed. The influx of Americans and immigrant Chinese led to growth in population in California and pressure for it to be admitted to the Union.

Many who traveled to California were recent immigrants who hoped to "strike it rich" and lead better lives than the ones they had left behind in their native lands. Determined, risk-taking Americans made the dangerous journey across mountains and deserts to reach a land that promised a better future. Many were guided by the explorations of men like John C. Frémont, who explored the route to California in the early 1840s. Others were helped by guidebooks, which prepared the travelers for their journey and had become very popular among travelers. The experiences of many of these travelers would become the source of popular novels and books throughout the remainder of the century, and they are part of American popular culture to this day.

President Zachary Taylor believed that California should be admitted to the Union as a means of settling the issue of slavery in the territories. Since it would enter as a free state, and because Oregon, New Mexico, and Utah likely could be admitted as free states, southerners feared that western and northern interests would dominate the government and began to talk of secession from the Union. In an attempt to avoid secession, Henry Clay proposed a compromise that would admit California as a free state, establish territorial governments in the land gained from Mexico with no restriction on slavery, abolish the slave trade (though not slavery) in the District of Columbia, and enhance the power of the federal government to recover fugitive slaves. A great deal of controversy arose when Clay introduced this proposal. Taylor threatened to veto the bill, but he died after falling ill during a Fourth of July picnic in 1850. His successor, Millard Fillmore, sought to push the bill through Congress.

Democratic senator Stephen A. Douglas of Illinois maneuvered a compromise bill through Congress. In September 1850 President Fillmore signed the compromise into law. The legislation did not resolve the slavery question, as Congress and the White House had hoped; in fact, it intensified the debate. The Compromise of 1850 began the disintegration of the Whig Party, as many left to join the Free Soil Party. The presidential election of 1852 saw northern Democrat Franklin Pierce defeat the Whig candidate, Mexican War hero Winfield Scott. Pierce's administration was marred by the continuing deterioration of the relationship between the sections. The newly strengthened Fugitive Slave Law was roundly ignored or subverted by northerners, who resented the extraordinary powers it gave to federal officers charged with recovering runaway chattels. Outraged by stories of the "kidnapping" of fugitives and conscience stricken by their own complicity in allowing slavery to grow, many northerners opposed the last southern demands outright. Harriet Beecher Stowe captured this feeling in her best-selling novel *Uncle Tom's Cabin* in 1852. The success of that novel in turn enraged southerners, who thought northerners were becoming "abolitionized" and could not be trusted.

In time the slavery issue became entangled in efforts to build a transcontinental railroad. Railroads by this time had become important, especially in the east-west flow, and very profitable. This, coupled with the invention of the telegraph in 1844, had led to the development of new towns and cities along the emerging rail lines, much as had occurred with the land boom earlier and along waterways traversed by steamboats. Now the time had come for the building of a railroad across the nation. The location of the eastern terminus for the railroad became a bone of contention between the North and the South. Northerners favored Chicago, while southerners favored St. Louis, New Orleans, or Memphis. The southern route had originally been blocked by Mexican territory, but James Gadsden was sent by Secretary of War Jefferson Davis to work out a deal that would get the land, which lies between New Mexico and Arizona today, for $10 million. In an effort to get the terminus to be in Chicago and therefore benefit his constituency, Stephen Douglas proposed in 1854 that the Nebraska Territory be opened to settlement. Southerners opposed the bill, because Nebraska was above the Missouri Compromise line and its admission as a free state would upset the balance between slave and free states. So Douglas proposed to create two new territories, Kansas and Nebraska, and let the people in them decide their character under the principle of "popular sovereignty."

As Douglas saw it, popular sovereignty would determine whether the territories would be slave or free. This compromise became known as the Kansas-Nebraska Act. The bill destroyed what was left of the Whig Party; it also led many northern Democrats to leave their party in protest over the repeal of the Missouri Compromise. Those who left the two parties joined a new party that had formed in opposition to the Kansas-Nebraska Act, the Republican Party, a sectional party committed to no further extension of slavery into the territories. Enough Republicans were sent to Congress in the midterm elections that when they worked with the nativist Know-Nothings, they controlled the House of Representatives.

The basic elements of popular sovereignty had much appeal to Americans, as the concept highlighted their involvement in the political process. The political movement in America reached down to the local levels of government, and the high rate of literacy in America meant that most adult white males who were eligible to vote followed local and national politics closely. The proliferation of newspapers in the United States meant that coverage of political debates and news reached nearly everyone. Most newspapers were the mouthpieces of political parties, so readers read the papers that suited their political leanings. The 1840s also witnessed growth in the number of political magazines that appealed to readers of different political stripes. *The American Whig Review* and *The United States Democratic Review* are two examples. *The American Whig Review* introduced the poem "The Raven" by an obscure writer named Edgar Allan Poe to American audiences.

Newspapers, magazines, tracts, and books printed in America proliferated during this period, as improved transportation, new technology in papermaking and print, and a wider market drove down the cost of print and circulation. The "penny press" arose in cities—daily newspapers that reported the latest events, often with lurid details on crimes and scandals to attract a wide readership. The American Bible Society and the American Tract Society turned out tens of thousands of Bibles and religious and reform tracts, with the intention of getting one in every household in America. Magazines of all types catered to those interested in science, household management, fashion, the arts, politics, and a host of other subjects. *Scientific American*, for example, discussed the new inventions that were becoming available for industry and farming. *Harper's New Monthly Magazine*, which began publication in 1850, brought works already published in Europe to American readers, but soon began publishing the works of American artists and writers. *Godey's Lady's Book* kept women up-to-date on the latest trends in fashions and furnishings for the home. The growing availability of reading material helped in developing an "American" culture during this period and throughout the remainder of the nineteenth century. One aspect of this development was ironic, for the growing "American" literary culture derived in part from reliance on local lore and regional stories, thereby enhancing local and regional identities while building an American identity free of European forms.

Although some journals avoided political issues, as they sought a national readership, the sectional issue began to play out in most newspapers and magazines during the 1850s and further polarized the nation.

It soon became evident that the Kansas-Nebraska Act had inflamed the already raw issue of slavery in the American South. The controversy began to manifest itself in violence; fighting that broke out in Kansas in the mid-1850s constituted a preview of the greater bloodshed to come. In 1855 settlers began to move into Kansas and held elections to choose a state legislature. Armed proslavery forces from Missouri provided the muscle necessary to have a proslavery legislature. The legal inhabitants then held an election in Topeka and elected a legislature that wrote a constitution and elected a governor in Lawrence. They then applied for statehood, but were rejected by the Pierce administration, which recognized the proslavery government as the legal government of Kansas. This encouraged proslavery forces to attack the "illegitimate" free soil government, which they did by sacking the "free soil" capital town of Lawrence and burning the "free soil" governor's house there. In retaliation, antislavery forces led by John Brown attacked the town of Pottawatomie and hacked five proslavery men to death with machetes.

In May 1856 the fight reached Congress when a South Carolina congressman, Preston Brooks—who had been incensed by a speech in which Massachusetts senator Charles Sumner, while condemning the violence in Kansas, slandered Brooks's kinsman, South Carolina senator Andrew Butler, and his state—attacked Sumner on the Senate floor with a cane. The badly beaten Sumner became a martyr in the North, and Brooks a hero to southerners. The presidential election boded ill for the nation's unity. James Buchanan of Pennsylvania was nominated by the Democrats for president, while John C. Frémont, the well-known explorer of California and the West, was nominated by the new Republican Party. The Know-Nothings and Whigs, following a platform of anti-immigration, nominated former president Millard Fillmore. Buchanan won a narrow victory, mainly, it would seem, because he had been out of the country as ambassador to Great Britain during the Kansas-Nebraska crisis and thus was untainted by the bill and its consequences. Yet president Buchanan could or would do nothing to stem the tide of sectional conflict, proving to be a weak and vacillating pro-southern president.

Three events between 1857 and 1859 crystallized the national debate and led directly to civil war. The first was the *Dred Scott* decision handed down by the U.S. Supreme Court in March 1857. Dred Scott was a slave from Missouri who was owned by an army surgeon, who had taken him to Illinois and Wisconsin during his army duty. After the master died, Scott sued his widow for his freedom on the basis that his stay in a free state and a free territory had liberated him. A circuit court in Missouri had upheld his case in 1850, but the surgeon's widow appealed to the Missouri Supreme Court, which reversed the decision. Scott then appealed to the U.S. Supreme Court to overturn the Missouri Supreme Court's ruling. In the case *Dred Scott v. Sandford*, the Supreme Court ruled that Scott's petition to the court was illegal because Scott was a slave, and the Fifth Amendment prohibited Congress from taking property without "due process of law." Essentially, the ruling declared the Missouri Compromise unconstitutional. In so doing it undermined popular sovereignty, since no territorial legislature created by Congress had the authority to prevent slavery. Southerners hailed the decision as a vindication of their stance that the federal government had no right to interfere with slavery, whereas northerners saw it as another instance of southern "slave power" subverting the will of the people.

The situation was only made worse by Buchanan, who both supported the Court's decision but sought to end the fighting in Kansas. He supported a proslavery constitution in Kansas that had been rejected by the majority of the voters in the state. The Lecompton Constitution clearly violated the concept of popular sovereignty, and it was only defeated when Stephen Douglas managed to allow the bill to die in Congress. He put forth a plan that called for a new vote on the question of slavery in Kansas, and in 1861 citizens in Kansas voted against slavery. Kansas was admitted as a free state, but the Civil War had already begun.

The second event that polarized the nation at this time was the series of senatorial debates in Illinois conducted by Stephen Douglas and a one-term U.S. congressman who headed the Republican Party in Illinois, Abraham Lincoln. Lincoln believed that under the Constitution the government could not interfere with slavery where it already existed, but he also believed that slavery was wrong, because it violated the right of freedom spelled out in the Declaration of Independence. Lincoln took the Republican position that slavery should not be allowed to extend into the territories. The debates between Douglas and Lincoln were closely followed across the nation, and although Douglas retained his seat, Lincoln's strong performance in the debates catapulted him onto the national stage. He would become a force within the national Republican Party and won the party's presidential nomination in 1860.

The third event that pushed the nation toward civil war was the October 1859 raid by abolitionist John Brown on the federal arsenal and armory at Harpers Ferry, Virginia. At the head of sixteen followers, Brown seized the arsenal in the hope that local slaves would flee their masters and flock to his side. He planned to arm them so they might spread the revolt throughout the South. It was a forlorn hope. Brown and his followers were surrounded by a detachment of Marines commanded by Lieutenant Colonel Robert E. Lee, who stormed the armory, killed ten of Brown's followers, and captured their leader. Brown was put on trial for treason in Virginia. Convicted, he was sentenced to death. In December 1859, shortly before he was hanged at Charles Town, Brown declared in a handwritten note that the sin of slavery in the country could only be purged through the shedding of blood, a prediction that would come true less than two years later. The Brown raid and the sympathy many northerners expressed for his courage—Ralph Waldo Emerson likened him to a Christ figure—outraged millions of southerners, who viewed the positive response of the North as final proof that slavery's continuance could be achieved only at gunpoint.

In the wake of these tumultuous events, the country entered perhaps the most critical presidential election in its history. The Democratic Party disintegrated when northerners attempted to nominate Douglas for president at their convention in Charleston, South Carolina, and southern Democrats walked out. The remains of the party nominated Douglas at a convention in Baltimore, while the southerners held a convention in Richmond that nominated former vice president John C. Breckinridge. With the split in the Democratic Party, the last national institution claiming loyalties in both North and South was torn asunder. Several churches had already split over slavery. The nation was literally coming apart. A Constitution Party, committed to the Constitution and avoiding discussion of slavery, nominated John Bell. Meanwhile the Republican convention in Chicago, after several votes, nominated Lincoln as their standard bearer. In the election that followed, the fractured state of the nation was evident as the South voted for Breckinridge, while northern Democrats went for Douglas. The party rift permitted the Republicans, who gained a majority of northern votes, to elect Lincoln. His victory prompted southern leaders to call openly for secession. Buchanan, a lame duck president, stood by as the southern states began to secede. South Carolina led the way in December 1860, followed by six more states over the next two months. By April 1861, one month after Lincoln's inauguration, the weapons of war were poised to open fire.

Part II
DOMESTIC LIFE

The physical environment in which people live shapes their everyday lives and often determines their outlook on life. The "home," perhaps more than any other place, plays such a formative role. Thus a look at domestic life promises to reveal important aspects of the interests and identities of everyday people. When viewing domestic life, one encounters a variety of activities and relationships within individual households, including the preparation of food, eating, sleeping, clothing, caring for oneself and others, and the daily routine that makes up everyday life. In its essence, however, domestic life is about relationships within the household. Those relationships changed as the nature of the household changed from the time of the American Revolution to the Civil War. The most striking change was the transformation of the household from a place of reproduction and production to one of reproduction alone for urban middle-class families. The household as the center, or an important part, of economic production continued on farms and plantations, but by the mid-nineteenth century even working-class people were moving their work away from their households, though women might still take in boarders, laundry, and sewing to supplement family income and maintain the household. Thus the particular circumstances of each household, or "home," are an important consideration in examining domestic life.

One focus of this section is on women and women's roles in domestic life. Men are not included in this section, not because they are unimportant in domestic life, but because the roles women played in domestic life during the growth of the republic symbolized the work that women performed in the growth of the nation. Also, maintenance of the household was principally the woman's charge. By the time of the Civil War, the "ideal" of true womanhood emphasized separate spheres, with men working outside the home and women assuming more authority in it.

Another aspect of life covered in this section is childhood. The raising of children by mothers and their education were, and are, an important element in domestic life. Depending on class, condition, and circumstance, childrearing and education remained the province of women; were partially shared or even delegated to others, such as teachers; or were almost impossible for the mother to control and determine, for example among slaves, whose families were always vulnerable to breakup by sale and separation. In considering childrearing, it is instructive to assume the perspective of the child as well as those of the parents and others involved. To that end, this section doesn't deal with the experiences mothers had in raising their children per se; rather, the documents give a glimpse of the lives children lived and look at the lives of a free white child, a boy slave, and a girl slave, and their different experiences within American life.

Old age is the final topic covered. During the period after the American Revolution life expectancy was much shorter than it is today. But again, class, condition, and circumstance could, and did, lead to various outcomes. Not surprisingly, working-class immigrants and slaves had shorter life spans, on average, than persons engaged in less strenuous and dangerous work on a daily basis and with better diet and hygiene. At the same time, aging was recognized as a "normal" process. American culture prized youth but still respected age. Older people had value, out of necessity at least, to take care of themselves. But in an age when the rudiments of life demanded constant attention, the infirmities and weakness of aging took their toll. There was not much sentimentalism about the process, but there were recollections. Documents in this section suggest how older people recalled their past and in some cases sought to recapture their youth.

Women's Roles

Women's roles in American society from the late eighteenth through the mid-nineteenth centuries changed little, except in urban areas, where the middle and upper classes were able to hire servants and redefine the places of women and men in society. The lives of most women in rural America remained more like they were before the Revolution, which meant daily demands of childrearing, home chores, gardening, and a host of other tasks such as cloth production. Some women played an integral role, beyond their own households, in many rural communities, especially serving as midwives in places where it was difficult to get a doctor and in those circumstances in which the pregnant woman preferred the care of another woman or could not pay the cost of a doctor. Before having children, a woman's role was to become a "good wife." Increasingly from the colonial period into the nineteenth century, marriage was becoming a matter of love and choice rather than parental dictation. Women thus had to weigh their prospects. As the letter from Emma Willard shows, advice on making the proper marriage, or marrying at all, was essential for women wanting to make the right choice. In some cases circumstances led to women taking on the roles of head of household and of a business. The excerpt from the diary of Samantha Barrett describes a woman who was forced by circumstances to run a farm and to carry out business that would normally have been taken care of by a man. The lives of slave women were subject to the power and even whims of their masters. The two documents on slave women show the different experiences that were attendant on the lives of slaves.

1. *Emma Willard, The Risks of Marrying (1815)*

As marriage changed from being an arrangement negotiated by parents for reasons of money, position, or conformity within a particular religion to being a love match between individuals, advice on marriage became more important. A literature of advice books and advice columns in women's magazines developed during the nineteenth century to speak to matters of marriage, childbearing, raising children, family and household management, and related concerns. But confidences among family members about the character of suitors and the consequences of marrying continued to be an important source of information and assurance. In this letter, Emma Willard, who ran a female academy in Middlebury, Vermont, and who had married a physician much older than herself, provides advice to her younger sister, Almira Hart, about the possible pitfalls of marriage. She suggests that a woman now responsible for her own happiness needs to inquire into the character and circumstances of her suitor and be realistic about the prospects for happiness. In a word, the woman needs to consider her own interests.

Middlebury, July 30, 1815.
Dear Sister:

You think it strange that I should consider a period of happiness as more likely than any other to produce future misery. I know I did not sufficiently explain myself. Those tender and delicious sensations which accompany successful love, while they soothe and soften the mind, diminish its strength to bear or to conquer difficulties. It is the luxury of the soul; and luxury always enervates. A degree of cold that would but brace the nerves of the hardy peasant, would bring distress or death to him who had been pampered by ease and indulgence. This life is a life of vicissitude. A period of happiness, by softening and enervating the soul, by raising a thousand blissful images of the future, naturally prepares the mind for a greater or less degree of disappointment, and unfits us to bear it; while, on the contrary, a period of adversity often strengthens the mind, and, by destroying inordinate anticipation of the future, gives a relish to whatever pleasures may be thrown in our way. This, perhaps you may acknowledge, is generally true; but you cannot think it applies to your case—otherwise than that you acknowledge yourself liable to disappointment by death. But we will pass over that, and we will likewise pass of over the possibility of your lover's seeing some object that he will consider more interesting than you, and likewise that you may hereafter discover some imperfection in his character. We will pass this over, and suppose that the sanction of the law has been passed upon your connection, and you are secured to each other for life. It will be natural that, at first, he should be much devoted to you; but, after a while, his business must occupy his attention. While absorbed in that he will perhaps neglect some of those little tokens of affection which have become necessary to your happiness. His affairs will sometimes go wrong, and perhaps he will not think proper to tell you the cause; he will appear to you reserved and gloomy, and it [will] be very natural in such a case for you to imagine that he is displeased with you, or is less attached than formerly. Possibly you may not in every instance manage a family as he has been accustomed to think was right, and he may sometimes hastily give you a harsh word or a frown. But where is the use, say you, of diminishing my present enjoyment by such gloomy apprehensions? Its use is this, that, if you enter the marriage state believing such things to be absolutely impossible, if you should meet them, they would come upon you with double force. We should endeavor to make a just estimate of our future prospects, and consider what evils, peculiar situations in which we may be placed, are most likely to beset us, and endeavor to avert them if we can; or, if we must suffer them, to do it with fortitude, and not magnify them by imagination, and think that, because we cannot enjoy all that a glowing fancy can paint, there is no enjoyment left. I hope I shall see Mr. L—. I shall be very glad to have you come and spend the winter with me, and, if he could with propriety accompany you, I should be glad to see him. I am involved in care. There [are] forty in our family and seventy in the school. I have, however, an excellent house-keeper and a very good assistant in my school. You seem to have some wise conjectures floating in your brain, but, unfortunately for your skill in guessing, they have no foundation in truth. . . .

Yours affectionately,
Emma Willard

Source: [Emma Willard to Almira Hart], July 30, 1815, in *The Life of Emma Willard*, by John Lord (New York: Appleton, 1873), 44–45.

2. Woman as Farmer and Businessman (1828)

Samantha Barrett lived on an eighty-five-acre farm in New Hartford, Connecticut, with her sister Zeloda, where they both operated the farm. Their father died in 1821, and the two girls had their elderly mother to take care of. When Samantha began keeping her diary in 1828, she was forty years old. When reading this excerpt, one notices that Samantha and her sister assumed many responsibilities and duties that were normally the province of a man. They kept track of the finances, hired men for tasks they were unable to carry out, sold cattle, and also did women's work in the house and the garden, such as making soap and weaving cloth. The rhythms of domestic life for such women were dictated by the constant need to tend animals and keep up the farm and household. There was little time for leisure.

1828
May

1 Pleasant and warm—making soap—Mr Hamlin calld—PM Loda visited Mrs Cowles—Leister came after some milk—evening read about the Greeks

3 Clouday—some rain—Loda carried four pounds 1/2 of butter to the store, one shilling a pound—thunder shower—raind hard—Mr Tyler, Mr Butler, Mr A Loomis, Mr Lyman—Cornelia cleared of worm—Roman and William came home—heard from Grove—evening—raind hard

6 Clouday—went to Mr Masons to borrow a trap—Abijah plowd our garden—fixd some fence—took down our hog pen—got out some manure—cut off our old cows tail—Mr Barnes workd in our garden—I went to Mr Butlers on an errand—Capt G Henderson had a barn raised—evening thundered and lightened and raind hard

10 Plesant—warpd and got in a piece—Loda planted peas and beans in the garden—Capt H calld to get some squash seeds—Mr Munson did a job for us. Emeline came from Mr Loomis, staid all night

13 Clouday—Mother and Loda rode out—I went to the store, carried nine 1/2 pounds butter, nine pence per pound—bought one pound tea—had our horse shod—wove—Mr B

calld—few drops of rain—a trunk pedler calld—put up some fence—evening Mrs Holcomb gone to John Hendersons wedding—I sat up till she came home 11 oclock—

15 Raind—carried Mrs Barnes bonnet home, gave her some pork—went to Mr Hunts, he gave me a order of ten shillings—visited the poor families—wove—Abijah, Mr Munson calld—evening visited Mrs H–

18 Sabbath—Clouday—Loda and myself attended meeting—Mr Yale preached—classed the scholars for sabbath school—Mrs Ruth Henderson, Mrs Sarah Lord, Delia Cook asked for a letter of dismission from this church—meeting Thursday evening at the center school house—

20 Plesant—washd—Abijah plowing potatoes ground—lost one of our sheep—Mr Hamlin calld—sold Mr Munson one of our calves for three dollars, eight weeks old—EL came to make a visit, staid all night—corner stone laid to NE meeting h [house].

25 Sabbath—AM plesant—Mother and Loda attended meeting—Mr Loomis rode with them—Mr Yale preached—Mr Chapin and Catherine M published—Mr Dawson very poor —evening read a little—hard shower of rains

29 Clouday and warm—carded wool—Mr Woodrull washd sheep—Loda went to see Mr Dawson, found him unable to speak—Mr Yale calld, gave him some apples—men to work on the road —Mrs Steel, Mrs Segar calld—evening Mrs H

June

2 Plesant—wove some—Alonson Spence calld wishing to by our lambs—PM Mrs Barnes made us a visit—evening Mr. Hamlin calld, sold him four pounds twelve ounces pork, paid 33 cents cash—wedding at Mr Marsh—began to make cheese

5 Clouday, very—growing time—washd and cleand our floors—Mr Barnes pold part of our peas—PM thundershower—rain hard—A trunk pedler calld—Huldah and Loda traded with him—Roman started for Boston—sent a letter to Grove

6 Very warm weather—Mr Woodruf sheard our sheep and Mr Steel sheard Groves—borrowed some tar to Mr Munsons to mark our sheep—finished weaving Mrs Segars piece, nine yards—PM Mrs Wheeler and Laura Steel visited here—lent Laura my 3 to reed—evening constant visiter calld

7 Plesant—finished picking wool—Levi cut wood for us, paid him in pork and bread. Mr Hamlin mended my shoes, price twenty cents—evening hard thunder shower—

10 Plesant—Mrs Holcomb and myself rode to ward lot, drove our sheep—drove our heifers home—went to Capt H—Indians called for cider—greast my wool—Lidia Fletcher calld and Mrs Cowles—Indian came again—evening Mr Hamlin

11 In the morning clouday—rode to the carding machine—had my wool carded, eight pounds—Mother visited sister Loomis—spun fifteen knots—Loda went after mother—PM calld

17 Clouday and very warm—Mr Barnes cut poles and pold our beans—let him have one gallon cider, some pork and cheese—Loda rode to Calvins—showers of rain—

19 Plesant and cool—drove our sheep to wardlot—Mrs Loomes and Mrs Coe calld—Mrs H, Loda and Myself rode to FH store—I bought me a silk shawl, price 11/6 , one fish, one pint wine, one pint rum, one pocket handkerchief, other things—Mrs Holcomb, Col Goodwin calld, wishing to get a piece wove—Pitts G calld—evening Levi calld for a drink of cider—

23 Another warm day—spun—Abijah plowing and hoeing potatoes—Mr Barnes came after a gallon of cider—PM Mrs Holcomb and myself took a walk, calld at Mr Barnes—found Mrs Filly sick—calld at Mr Loomis, Mrs N Cowles, Lynds and the poor house —found Del tied up, very much brused—how tired I was—retired

July

2 Plesant—finished spinning my wool, had 21 knots—washed it out—PM Mrs Holcomb and myself rode to ward lot—salted our creatures —drank tea at Capt Hendersons with the Widow Ruth and she that was Manerva Mather—evening Elmina Clark Nelson and Mr Hamlin here—sat up till most eleven

3 Very warm—Mrs Dowd very poor—spoold and warpd piece —Nath calld—PM Emeline made us a short visit—fixing for independence—went with her as far as Mr Munsons—raind—Abijah borrowed some grain of us, carried it to mill—evening Lucia Clee

5 Raind and sun shind—wove—thunder showers—Nelson calld—string beans for dinner—PM more thunder showers—Mr Cowles and George came to cover our shed

8 Clouday part of the day—turned and raked hay—Mr Hamlin helped—got in two loads—Grove helped—drove our heifers to wardlot—drove our sheep home—paid Mr Hamlin in pork—raind—evening a hard thunder shower with sharp lightening—Mr Dowd staid all night

11 Raind very hard—Mr Butler calld—Mr Hamlin came for his pay for work—let him have four pounds seven [ounces] of pork, three pounds butter, three of cheese—got in Mr Benhams piece —went to Mr Barnes on an errand—sun shind very warm—PM Major Johnson calld—raind—Loda rode to Mr Rogers

16 Clouday and rainey—finished weaving Mr Benhams piece, fifteen yards—Nath set a trap in our orcheard to cetch a wood chuck—PM Mr Cowles calld, let him have a quart of brandy to pay for making open shed

21 Very warm—Mr Gird came after Groves lambs, came before four, bought eleven, paid twelve dollars 37 cents—Loda rode to the carding mill, got our wool carded, returned half after eight—

29 Good hay weather—Mr Dowd began in our meadow, I turned and racked thirty two heaps—Emeline came here—evening Mr Pitkin, Langdon Nelson came here

31 In the morning a very hard thunder shower—lightened very sharp—clear of [off] pleasant—Loda and myself rode to Canton, bought at Mygots one fancy handkerchief, 6/9, sold two pairs of socks, four shillings—one pair thread stockings, 3/6—went to Mr Barbers, got two runit bags—bought at Mr Browns store half a bushel salt, forty cents cash, one vinegar cruise , twelve cents—Cornelia came to make a visit

Source: *Diary of Samantha Barrett, New Hartford, Conn., 1811 to 1829*, selected entries, ed. Old Sturbridge Village (Hartford, CT: Connecticut Historical Society [n.d.]), http://www.osv.org/school/lesson_plans/ShowLessons.php?PageID=P&LessonID=34&DocID=1164&UnitID= (accessed May 2011).

3. *Roles of Female Slaves (1855–1865)*

During the Great Depression, in an effort to give unemployed writers work, the Works Project Administration (WPA), established in 1935, employed writers and researchers to interview and document the stories of former slaves. More than 2,300 former slaves were interviewed, and their stories have left an invaluable record of slavery in America. The narratives were a mix of folklore and cautious comments about life in bondage and after it. The following is taken from the narratives of former slaves living in Oklahoma at the time of their interview but who had been slaves elsewhere. It details the varying experiences of female slaves in the South. Sina Banks recalled the benevolence of a felicitous master, while Annie Hawkins remembered a master who was cruel and uncaring.

Sina Banks, Age 86, McAlester, Oklahoma

Old Master let all his slaves know that the harder they worked and the more they raised the more they and their families would have to eat and wear. He always divided with them and none of them minded the hard work and never let nothing go to waste.

He never let any of his women work in the field as he always said they had plenty to do to look after work at the house, spinning weaving, sewing, cooking, mending, and looking after the white folks and the children. Everybody was always busy. All the women did the spinning and weaving but they divided the rest of the work. All the food was cooked at the big house. They had big pots that hung over the fire on racks and big ovens with lids to bake bread and cakes. They had a big cook stove but hardly ever used it as they had rather cook on the fireplace. Two of the women done the cooking and two others dished it up and served the white folks and others to[ok] part of it to their cabins for they men and children. Everybody et at the same time, and the same kind of food. . . .

When the women had plenty of cloth woven they would go to work and make it up into clothes. The men were looked after first. Mother done all the cutting. She would take her lapboard in her lap and cut out pants, coats, shirts, and underwear. Another job the women had was to make hats for the men. They would plait wheat and rye straw and weave it into hats. They would line the hats with green material so it would shade their eyes.

Annie Hawkins, Age 90, Colbert, Oklahoma

I never had no whitefolks that was good to me. We all worked jest like dogs and had about half enough to eat and got whupped for everything. Our days was a constant misery to us. I know lots of niggers that was slaves had a good time but we never did. Seems hard that I can't say anything good for any of 'em but I sho' can't. When I was small my job was to tote cool water to the field to the hands. It kept me busy going back and forth and I had to be sho' my old mistress had a cool drink when she wanted it, too. Mother and my sister and me worked in the field all day and come home in time to clear away the things and cook supper. When we was through in the kitchen, we would spin fer a long time. Mother would spin and we would card.

Source: *WPA Slave Narrative Project, Oklahoma Narratives*, Vol. 13. Federal Writer's Project, United States Work Projects Administration (USWPA); Manuscript Division, Library of Congress [1941].

Children

Our memories of childhood are shaped by our domestic environment: our home, parents, brothers and sisters, extended family, and playmates and schoolmates, as the case may be. The lives led by children in America during the period of the Revolution to the eve of the Civil War were varied by circumstance. In the first document, Frederick Douglass recalls his childhood as a slave, showing how the nuclear family was destroyed by the institution of slavery. Douglass was denied the opportunity to be nurtured by a mother and a father, which was considered to be crucial in the development of children. This is contrasted with the experience of Caroline Cowles Richards, who, although she lost her mother and was required to live with her grandparents, grew up in a loving household in the care of her grandparents. The document tells of the chafing of youth against restrictions, curiosity about the adult world, and the consequences of their actions. Mary Ella Grandberry's experience as a slave child is an example of how children of later generations are unappreciative of the hardships their parents or grandparents endured and how their lives shaped their views of childhood.

4. Frederick Douglass on the Life of a Slave Child (1820s)

Frederick Douglass was America's most famous African American in the nineteenth century. Born a slave in Maryland, he escaped to Massachusetts and spent his life speaking, traveling, and publishing about the abolition of slavery and the rights of various oppressed groups. In this excerpt, which begins his 1845 autobiography, the book that made him famous and in many ways provided the structure and themes of the slave narrative genre, Douglass tells little of his daily life as a child, but gives a fascinating account of the endemic contradictions of slavery and its tragic effects on children and families. In a culture where maternal care was considered paramount and family integrity a Christian responsibility, Douglass describes being intentionally separated from his mother by his owners. He claims his father might have been a white man, perhaps even his master.

The description of Douglass's relationship to his mother is designed to be touching—she would at times walk twelve miles each way after work to lie down with him for a few hours before she had to leave to make it back to the fields at dawn the next day, and he never saw her in daylight. However, he also insists he was not attached to her, which makes the whole situation and her extraordinary efforts to see her child all the more tragic and ironic.

Whether Douglass's father was a white man or not, the relationship of a mixed-race slave to his father, if his or her father was the master, was even more conflicted. Douglass points out the jealousy of slave owners' wives when confronted with their husbands' illegitimate children and how owners whipped, beat, and even sold their own children; had siblings torture one another; separated their children from their mothers; and deprived their children of any family and the affection and support that comes with it.

Douglass raises the important issue of interracial relationships. Such relationships were not only taboo to many whites, but also illegal in some states until 1967, when the U.S. Supreme Court overturned racial purity laws. The natural distinction between races was a staple argument of proslavery whites, who used pseudoscientific theories and, as Douglass mentions, biblical support to conclude that blacks were inferior to whites and were not intended by God to intermarry or have these children.

If Douglass was a mixed-race child (he himself admitted he did not know for certain who his father was), his having a white father and a black mother made him in some sense at least as much white as black. The differences he points out between himself and his African ancestors indicates the changing nature of race in the United States well before the Civil War and the resulting emancipation of all slaves in the 1860s, and race continues to be a central but changing issue in American society today.

I was born in Tuckahoe, near Hillsborough, and about twelve miles from Easton, in Talbot county, Maryland. I have no accurate knowledge of my age, never having seen any authentic record containing it. By far the larger part of the slaves know as little of their ages as horses know of theirs, and it is the wish of most masters within my knowledge to keep their slaves thus ignorant. I do not remember to have ever met a slave who could tell of his birthday. They seldom come nearer to it than planting-time, harvest-time, cherry-time, spring-time, or fall-time. A want of information concerning my own was a source of unhappiness to me even during childhood. The white children could tell their ages. I could not tell why I ought to be deprived of the same privilege. I was not allowed to make any inquiries of my master concerning it. He deemed all such inquiries on the part of a slave improper and impertinent, and evidence of a restless spirit. The nearest estimate I can give makes me now between twenty-seven and twenty-eight years of age. I come to this, from hearing my master say, some time during 1835, I was about seventeen years old.

My mother was named Harriet Bailey. She was the daughter of Isaac and Betsey Bailey, both colored, and quite dark. My mother was of a darker complexion than either my grandmother or grandfather.

My father was a white man. He was admitted to be such by all I ever heard speak of my parentage. The opinion was also whispered that my master was my father; but of the correctness of this opinion, I know nothing; the means of knowing was withheld from me. My mother and I were separated when I was but an infant—before I knew her as my mother. It is a common custom, in the part of Maryland from which I ran away, to part children from their mothers at a very early age. Frequently, before the child has reached its twelfth month, its mother is taken from it, and hired out on some farm a considerable distance off, and the child is placed under the care of an old woman, too old for field labor. For what this separation is done, I do not know, unless it be to hinder the development of the child's affection toward its mother, and to blunt and destroy the natural affection of the mother for the child. This is the inevitable result.

I never saw my mother, to know her as such, more than four or five times in my life; and each of these times was very short in duration, and at night. She was hired by a Mr. Stewart, who lived about twelve miles from my home. She made her journeys to see me in the night, traveling the whole distance on foot, after the performance of her day's work. She was a field hand, and a whipping is the penalty of not being in the field at sunrise, unless a slave has special permission from his or her master to the contrary—a permission which they seldom get, and one that gives to him that gives it the proud name of being a kind master. I do not recollect of ever seeing my mother by the light of day. She was with me in the night. She would lie down with me, and get me to sleep, but long before I waked she was gone. Very little communication ever took place between us. Death soon ended what little we could have while she lived, and with it her hardships and suffering. She died when I was about seven years old, on one of my master's farms, near Lee's Mill. I was not allowed to be present during her illness, at her death, or burial. She was gone long before I knew any thing about it. Never having enjoyed, to any considerable extent, her soothing presence, her tender and watchful care, I received the tidings of her death with much the same emotions I should have probably felt at the death of a stranger.

Called thus suddenly away, she left me without the slightest intimation of who my father was. The whisper that my master was my father, may or may not be true; and, true or false, it is of but little consequence to my purpose whilst the fact remains, in all its glaring odiousness, that slaveholders have ordained, and by law established, that the children of slave women shall in all cases follow the condition of their mothers; and this is done too obviously to administer to their own lusts, and make a gratification of their wicked desires profitable as well as pleasurable; for by this cunning arrangement, the slaveholder, in cases not a few, sustains to his slaves the double relation of master and father.

I know of such cases; and it is worthy of remark that such slaves invariably suffer greater hardships, and have more to contend with, than others. They are, in the first place, a constant offence to their mistress. She is ever disposed to find fault with them; they can seldom do any thing to please her; she is never better pleased than when she sees them under the lash, especially when she suspects her husband of showing to his mulatto children favors which he withholds from his black slaves. The master is frequently compelled to sell this class of his slaves, out of deference to the feelings of his white wife; and, cruel as the deed may strike any one to be, for a man to sell his own children to human flesh-mongers, it is often the dictate of humanity for him to do so; for, unless he does this, he must not only whip them himself, but must stand by and see one white son tie up his brother, of but few shades darker complexion than himself, and ply the gory lash to his naked back; and if he lisp one word of disapproval, it is set down to his parental partiality, and only makes a bad matter worse, both for himself and the slave whom he would protect and defend.

Every year brings with it multitudes of this class of slaves. It was doubtless in consequence of a knowledge of this fact, that one great statesman of the south predicted the downfall of slavery by the inevitable laws of population. Whether this prophecy is ever fulfilled or not, it is nevertheless plain that a very different-looking class of people are springing up at the south, and are now held in slavery, from those originally brought to this country from Africa; and if their increase do no other good, it will do away the force of the argument, that God cursed Ham, and therefore American slavery is right. If the lineal descendants of Ham are alone to be scripturally enslaved, it is certain that slavery at the south must soon become unscriptural; for thousands are ushered into the world, annually, who, like myself, owe their existence to white fathers, and those fathers most frequently their own masters.

Source: Frederick Douglass, *Narrative of the Life of Frederick Douglass, an American Slave, Written by Himself* (Boston: The Anti-Slavery Office, 1845).

5. Childhood and Breaking the Bonds of Home (1853)

Caroline Richards was a ten-year-old girl when she began her diary in November 1852, and she would continue to write in it for the next twenty years. The death of her mother led to her and her sister Anna being sent to live with her mother's parents in Canandaigua, New York. Her writings give us a glimpse into the life of a young girl growing up in a rural community in the mid-nineteenth century. The passages excerpted below, from May 1 and July 1853, show the influence of her grandfather and father, both Presbyterian ministers, as she reads the Bible every morning, and also point to the punishments meted out by parents to recalcitrant children. Her experience is in stark contrast to the lives of slave children. Here she notes how three boys in the neighborhood sought to leave home to experience life outside their home, and the consequences of their actions. Her interests, and ambition, reflected those of other white children of her day.

May I.—I arose this morning about the usual time and read my three chapters in the Bible and had time for a walk in the garden before breakfast. The polyanthuses are just beginning to blossom and they border all the walk up and down the garden. I went to school at quarter of nine, but did not get along well because we played too much. We had two new scholars today, Miss Archibald and Miss Andrews, the former about seventeen, and the latter about fifteen. In the afternoon old Mrs. Kinney made us a visit, but she did not stay very long. In dictionary class I got up sixth, although I had not studied my lesson very much.

July.—Hiram Goodrich, who lives at Mr. Myron H. Clark's, and George and Wirt Wheeler ran away on Sunday to seek their fortunes. When they did not come back every one was frightened and started out to find them. They set out right after Sunday School, taking their pennies which had been given them for the contribution, and were gone several days. They were finally found at Palmyra. When asked why they had run away, one replied that he thought it was about time they saw something of the world. We heard that Mr. Clark had a few moments private conversation with Hiram in the barn and Mr. Wheeler the same with his boys and we do not think they will go travelling on their own hook right again right off. Miss Upham lives right across the street from them and she was telling little Morris Bates that he must fight the good fight of faith and he asked her if that was the fight Wirt Wheeler fit. She probably had to make her instructions plainer after that.

Source: Caroline Cowles Richards, *Village Life in America, 1852–1872, Including the Period of the American Civil War as told in the Diary of a School-Girl* (New York: Henry Holt & Company, 1913), 13–14.

6. The Childhood of a Slave (1850s)

Mary Ella Grandbury was one of the former slaves interviewed by the Federal Writers' Project during the Great Depression. Her narrative on the experiences of her childhood as a slave contrasts greatly with the experiences of free white children, and, as Mary Grandbury states, the children of both races after slavery. She represents the children who never had the opportunity to play as free children were able to do; she was never able to be a child. She notes that young children in the 1930s had no appreciation of how difficult life was for their elders.

I don't know jes' how old I is', but I knows dat I some' ers nigh ninety yars ol'. I was borned in Barton, Alabama. My Father an' mother come from Richmond, Virginny. My mammy was name Margaret Keller an' my pappy was Adam Keller. My five sisters was Martha, Sarah, Harriet, Emma, an' Rosanna, an' my three brothers was Peter, Adam Jr., an' William.

Us all live in a li'l log cabin jes' off the Big House. Life wan't ver' much for us 'caze we had to work an' slave all de time. Massa Jim's house was a little ol' frame buildin' lack an ord'nary house is now. He was a single man an' didn't hab so terrible much, it seem. He had a whole lot too, jes' to look at him you'd thank he was a po' white man. Dere was a lot o' cabins for de' slaves, but dey wasn't fettin' for nobody to lib' in. We jes' had to put up wid 'em.

I don' member' much about when I was a chil'. I disremembers ever playin' lack chillums do today. Ever since I kin' 'member I had a water bucket on my arm totin' water to da han's. Iffin I wan't doin' dat, I was choppin' cotton. Chilluns nowadays see a good time to w'at we did den. Ever' mornin' jes about hip of day de oberseer was' roun' to see that we was ready to git to di fiels. Plent times us had to go widouten' breakfas', 'caze we didn' git up in time to git it 'fo' de man done come git us on de way to de fiel'. Us walked twell dinner time jes de same before we got anythang to eat.

Source: Mary Ella Grandberry, "Slave Narrative, Today's Folks Don't Know Nothin'," in WPA Slave Narratives, *Born in Slavery: Slave Narratives from the Federal Writers' Project, 1936–1938, Alabama Narratives,* Vol. I. Library of Congress [1941], 157.

Old Age

The onset of old age often prompts people to become retrospective. Some look upon their youth and lament lost opportunities, while others recall a life well lived. In antebellum America, even with the dramatic developments in manufacturing and transportation, life expectancy was low. Disease, injury, and wars took their toll. Living beyond sixty years of age was considered exceptional, so it is not surprising that people during this period would dwell on their lives as they moved closer to death. This section looks at varying views of those who were elderly and how they recalled the lives they had lived. George Washington reminisces about his youth through his friend Marquis de Lafayette, and although his tone is melancholy, he still thinks he has led a very full life. The changes that people experience as they proceed through life and how those changes have colored them are the subject of a lament from *The New-England Magazine*, a very doleful expression of the loss of youthful exuberance and joy in life. The enjoyment of rest at the close of an active life was welcomed by some. Rather than see old age as a time to prepare for death, many looked forward to a period when they could enjoy the fruits of their labors, relax, and even still revel in life. And people who had come to believe in salvation and a heavenly reunion with loved ones did not fear death.

7. *George Washington to the Marquis de Lafayette* (1784)

George Washington, general of the Continental Army in the American Revolution and first president of the United States, had developed a strong friendship with his onetime subordinate, the Marquis de Lafayette, during the American Revolution, much like that of a father to a son. When Lafayette came to visit Washington at his estate at Mount Vernon in Virginia following the war, the two renewed their close friendship. Washington had seen both his father Augustine and his stepbrother Lawrence, who was like a surrogate father to him, die at an early age. As he parts from his friend Lafayette, Washington reflects on the parting, noting his age (he was fifty-two), that he does not expect to live much longer, and that he might not see his friend again, but he also notes that he has led a full life and has no regrets about missed opportunities. Sadly, Washington's premonition was correct; Lafayette would not return to the United States until 1825, by which time Washington had already been dead for twenty-six years.

Mount Vernon, December 8, 1784

My Dr. Marqs: The preregrination of the day in which I parted from you, ended at Marlbro': the next day, bad as it was, I got home before dinner.

In the moment of our separation upon the road as I travelled, and every hour since, I felt all that love, respect and attachment for you with which length of years, close connexion and your merits have inspired me. I often asked myself, as our carriages distended, whether that was the last sight, I ever should have of you? And tho' I wished to say no, my fears answered yes. I called to mind the days of my youth, and I found they had long since fled to return no more; that I was now descending the hill, I had been 52 years climbing, and that tho' I was blessed with a good constitution, I was of a short lived family, and might soon expect to be entombed in the dreary mansions of my father's. These things darkened the shades and gave a gloom to the picture, consequently of my prospects of seeing you again: but I will not repine, I have had my day.

Source: George Washington, *The Writings of George Washington: from the Manuscript Resources, 1745–1799,* Vol. 28, *December 5, 1784–August 30, 1786,* ed. John C. Fitzpatrick (Washington, DC: United States Government Printing Office, 1938), 6–7.

8. *Sports of Childhood (1832)*

The following lament, from The New-England Magazine *in July 1832, remarks on the passage of youth and the onset of age and reflects on the feelings that many have when they reminisce about their lives, particularly how life has made them lose the exuberance of their youth. Such topics were common fare in American literature, poetry, and even art, an ironic turn for a people and republic that also boasted of their youth and destiny.*

I have been young, and now am old.

WHEN a happy child, I longed for manhood, and I am now a careworn man. Reason and reality sway their stern sceptre over me, and their domination may be traced in my furrowed brow. Wisdom has scattered snows on my temples, and Prudence shot ice to my soul; the sports of the child have long been lost in the pursuits of the man. We should be too happy to die with resignation, could we retain amidst our experience and later knowledge, the buoyancy of youthful spirits, and continue to hope boldly and blindly in spite of disappointment.

That the boy is father to the man may be good poetry, but it is no true philosophy. The soul, indeed, is sexual, for how early does the feminine attach itself to finery and to dolls. I, who am of the less graceful sex, should have been an equestrian of note, were the indications of character, in childhood to be trusted. A centaur was my type; before I was clad in trowsers, I was to be seen prancing in the garden, on a willow twig, like a witch upon a broomstick, and Sancho upon Clavileno, could not, in imagination move more swiftly. I was carried away by the impulse and the twig, and Orlando, mounted on Boyardo, felt less pride than I.

My next aspirations were for arms; and Bellona, in spite of my zeal, would have smiled at my equipments. Bows and arrows, that ex-cited the mirth of Captain Dalghetty, before they stretched him on the earth, were my first arms. I could not use them with the skill of Tell, or even of the primitive archer A. Had a pumpkin been placed at two yards, on the head of an ox, I should have hit neither the one nor the other. Robin Hood and Little John, though derided by Dalghetty, were to me the most honorable persons in history. Our youthful band, however, adopted or imitated some of the improvements in the art of war. We marched in paper caps, surmounted with a goose-quill; we girded ourselves with a belt of twine from which dangled a blade of wood. I have seen companies in the militia with no better discipline or equipments.

All the sons of New-England have a tendency to mechanics; their aim is not to save labor, but to double the product. I was therefore early indoctrinated in the mystery of a mill, and soon built one, with no other tools than a jack-knife and a broken fork; it was what we called a trip-hammer, moved by water, to strike upon a wooden anvil. The dam was the work of days, and I conducted the water of Goose Creek to a new channel, and a fall of seven feet. The dam remains one of the monuments of my childhood. Few others exist, except those of memory and thought, which are deeply engraven on my soul. I forget the conversations and occurrences of yesterday, while I remember, freshly, the most trifling occurrences, or passing thoughts of childhood.

It was but lately that I went by the place of the mill, in which if you should ask for the edifice, echo might answer, where! And it afflicted me to feel how little I have found in what others call a prosperous life, that has proved as satisfactory and innocent as the pursuits of early youth. Had I been a lachrymose poet, I could have wept; but, being only a foolish elderly man, I doffed coat, and worked an hour in clearing the channel and repairing the dam. Two of my nephews came up and caught me in the fact; but they were children, and loved me the better for having with them this community of feeling.

Is it I who am changed, or has nature changed around me? The birds are no longer cheerful to me, the morning air in a south-west wind no longer breathes of flowers, as when I was a child. I have lost, like Macbeth, that alacrity, and cheer of mind.

I mourn, but ye woodlands, I mourn not for you.

Ye are waving and green, and your dews are as brilliant as when I brushed them away; but I have no longer the sense of enjoyment. I am changed. Novelty and freshness no longer charm me; I am all habit. I have a course, not of pleasures, but of life, like that of the horse in his mill, and which he enjoys not, though custom renders it endurable. Admit the worn-out animal to the green pastures, and he no longer frisks and plays; but from habit, he still continues to walk round in a circle, even in cropping the clover. Where is my taste for the beautiful and the sublime? Yet is nature full of sublimity and beauty. Would that I were again a child, though the most ragged and bronzed, that ever climbed for a crows nest, and made loaves of mud by the way-side. Farewell! I may say with Madame Roland, splendid chimeras of youth, from which I have reaped so much de-light! sublime illusions, generous sacrifices, hope and happiness, farewell! P.

Source: "Sports of Childhood," *The New-England Magazine* 3, no. 1 (July 1832): 7–8.

9. *Nathan Parker Willis on Aging Gracefully (1849)*

The author of this selection, Nathan Parker Willis, was a successful U.S. writer, publisher, and editor in the first half of the nineteenth century. Among his friends was Edgar Allan Poe, and it was Willis who first published Poe's famous poem, "The Raven," in 1845. In the document below Willis is writing to a friend about his old age. He wants to look at the life of others from the outside; enjoy the company of friends; and live a quiet, slow, and peaceful retirement. Willis is trying to convince a friend of his, a doctor, to retire in the company of like-minded friends to the country near his own retirement home on the Susquehanna River in upstate New York, luring him with promises of leisure and companionship. The natural environment was one of the main attractions for Willis, as it was for an emerging group of American writers and artists, and he assures his friend that he is even attending to the placement of trees and shrubbery. It bears remembering that cities in the 1840s were smaller than today, but growing rapidly and becoming crowded, dirty, and more prone to disease. Retired life in the country was potentially a more pleasant and viable prospect. Willis definitely seems to be looking forward to a life without the business and pressures of what had been his professional life, although he is not interested in giving up intellectual pursuits. Certainly neither money nor health seems to be a problem. He does not seem to have unsatisfied ambitions. He anticipates a stimulating social and intellectual life being more pleasurable without other motivations or concerns.

. . . You can scarce understand, dear Doctor, with what pleasure I find this new spring in my path—the content with which I admit the conviction, that, without effort or self-denial, the mind may slake its thirst, and the heart be satisfied with but the waste of what lies so near us. I have all my life seen men grow old, tranquilly and content, but I did not think it possible that *I* should. I took pleasure only in that which required young blood to follow, and I felt that, to look backward for enjoyment, would be at best a difficult resignation.

Now, let it be no prejudice to the sincerity of my philosophy, if, as a corollary, I beg you to take a farm on the Susquehannah, and let us grow old in company. I should think Fate kinder than she passes for, if I could draw you, and one or two others whom we know and "love with knowledge," to cluster about this—certainly one of the loveliest spots in nature, and, while the river glides by unchangingly, shape ourselves to our changes with a helping sympathy. Think of it, dear Doctor! Meantime, I employ myself in my rides, selecting situations on the river banks which I think would be to yours and our friends' liking; and in the autumn, when it is time to transplant, I intend to suggest to the owners where trees might be wanted in case they ever sold, so that you will not lose even a season in your shrubbery, though you delay your decision. Why should we not renew Arcady? God Bless you. . . .

And I will allow that I can scarce write a letter to you without shaping it to the end of attracting you to the Susquehannah. At least, watch when you begin to grow old, and transplant yourself in time to take root, and then we may do as the trees do—defy the weather until we are separated. The oak, itself, if it has grown up with its kindred thick about it, will break if left standing alone; and you and I dear Doctor, have known the luxury of friends too well to bear the loneliness of an unsympathizing old age. Friends are not pebbles, lying in every path, but pearls gathered with great pain, and rare as they are precious. We spend our youth and manhood in search and proof of them, and, when Death has taken his toll, we have too few to scatter—none to throw away. I, for one, will be a miser of mine. I feel the avarice of friendship growing on me with every year—tightening my hold and extending my grasp. Who, at sixty, is rich in friends? The richest are those who have drawn this wealth of angels around them, and spent care and thought on the treasuring. Come, my Doctor! I have chosen a spot on one of the loveliest of our bright rivers. Here is all that goes to make an Arcadia, except the friendly dwellers in its shade. I will choose you a hillside, and plant your grove, that the trees, at least, shall lose no time by your delay. Set a limit to your ambition, achieve it, and come away. It is terrible to grow old amid the jostle and disrespectful hurry of a crowd. The Academy of the philosophers was *out* of Athens. You can not fancy Socrates run against, in the market-place. Respect, which grows wild in the fields, requires watching and management in the cities. Let us have an old man's Arcady—where we can slide our "slippered shoon" through groves of our own consecrating, and talk of the world as *without*—ourselves and gay philosophy within. I have strings pulling upon one or two in other lands, who, like ourselves, are not men to let Content walk unrecognized in their path. Slowly, but, I think, surely, they are drawing hitherward; and I have chosen places for *their* hearthstones, too, and shall watch, as I do for you, that the woodsman's axe cuts down no trees that would be regretted. If the cords draw well, and Death take but his tithe, my shady "Omega" will soon learn voices to which its echo will for long years be familiar, and the Owaga and Susquehannah will join waters within sight of an *old man's Utopia*.

Source: N. Parker Willis, *Rural Letters and Other Records of Thought at Leisure Written in the Intervals of More Hurried Literary Labor* (New York: Baker and Scribner, 1849).

Part III
ECONOMIC LIFE

The economic development of the United States in the eighty-five years after the beginning of the Revolution was driven by a significant expansion stretching to and even across the Mississippi River; the rise of a significant manufacturing sector, especially in textiles, ironworks, machine tools, and processing agricultural products; and significant improvements in transportation, especially canals and railroads. Communication also improved, with the invention of the telegraph and innovations in printing and paper making speeding up the movement of information and lessening its cost. All this led to the development of a "market revolution" that linked American producers and processes with an Atlantic economy, as it also led to the need for more sophisticated systems of credit and other business resources. It also played out in politics—for example, the Bank War of 1832—and in the daily lives of Americans as they considered what to do or make, where to go, and what to buy.

Urban Life

Cities in America during this time grew bigger as the country experienced economic growth. Cities were not only the focal point for development of business, trade, and industry, they were also centers of government and culture. Americans also witnessed an influx of many people entering the country looking for new opportunities that an expanding nation offered. In some instances they met with great success, prompting them to encourage others to come join them. But along with these opportunities there also came poverty and the prejudice that strangers are subject to when they go to a new land. The expansion of the nation led many to call for the government to invest in internal improvements. Henry Cogswell Knight's letter below describes a city that is a center for trade and how its growth has affected its appearance. Washington, D.C., is seen today as the great center of American power. Harriet Martineau's letter gives us an entirely different picture of America's seat of government during the mid-nineteenth century, one that we would not recognize. Although much of the South remained tied to an agrarian economy, many of its larger port cities became well-developed economic centers. Emily Burke's letter gives a view of the city of Savannah, Georgia, in the decade leading up to the Civil War. These letters point to the ways industry and commerce changed these cities, creating bustling metropolises that were the engines of a growing economy.

1. A Description of Philadelphia (1814)

Under the pseudonym Arthur Singleton, Esq., the Reverend Henry Cogswell Knight, an Episcopal minister and poet from Massachusetts, made a visit to Philadelphia in 1814. In a letter to his brother he describes one of the great cities of the United States in the early nineteenth century, a city that was a center for commerce and finance. Its ports on the Delaware River, and the road network that led into and out of the city, connected Philadelphia to a vast hinterland and the Atlantic maritime world. But "progress" had its costs. Cogswell decries how the city has become sterile as a result of the growth of industry.

DEAR BROTHER,

THIS city, which is the great metropolis of Penn's Woodland, and which was eulogized by Him of Tarsus . . . *Philadelphia forever!* a Greek compound, you perceive, signifying brotherly-love; is as level as a Quaker's broad brim. The day after my arrival, I ascended the almost only eminence in the city, one of the two shot-towers, to spy down upon it. It appears not unlike a horizontal Brodingnagian brick-kiln; long never-ending blocks of brick, with little holes at bottom to creep in at; and little holes at top to peep out at. At this altitude, the eager currents of human beings appear diminished into a small folk, like Lilliputians; all, like the armies of the grandson of Cyrus, in a hundred years, to be no more. The city, which is six score of miles from the sea by the channel, is spread upon the isthmus between the Delaware, and the Schuylkill, half a score of miles above their confluence. These two rivers, east and west of the city, are the one grand, the other picturesque; and the elegant light broad-spanned arch thrown over the latter by our townsman Palmer, recalls agreeable associations. The Delaware waters were, last winter, so consolidated, opposite the city, that a festive ox was roasted whole upon the ice. Although this river is now floating ships to and fro from all nations, once was the time, when, if a ship arrived from Europe, the citizens used to chime Christ-church bells. As this city is, in many respects, the metropolis of the states, I confess I was disappointed in its externals. The streets running south and north were, in olden prime, called after the trees in the vicinity:—cedar, mulberry, sassafras, vine, chesnut, walnut, spruce, and pine. The streets crossing east and west are numbered; and the whole, being divided into wards and squares spreads into an immense chequer-board. There is but one crooked street in the city; and that, which is crooked, cannot be made straight. After you have walked one square, you have seen the whole. Indeed, the houses are so thick, there is no room for land. No spires, no domes, few bells, few promenades; no any thing to relieve the eye, or arrest the fancy. There is nothing like the long marble-fronted, but too finical, City-Hall; or the irregular, but beautifully verdant Battery, of New-York. Every view is quakerfied. No marvel, that Paine said, though rather irreverently, if a Quaker had been consulted at the Creation, what a drab-coloured world we should have had. Still, it is a noble city; wealthy, substantial, convenient; with extending blocks of massy private tenements; and a very few publick edifices of simple Doric grandeur, as, in particular, the marble bank. Christ-church is rather of the Gothic structure, and elegant; the bricks of this, and also of many other ancient buildings in the city, are, one red, another black glazed, in alternation. The six stately Corinthian columns, which support the roof in front of the first Presbyterian Church, look majestically. The national mint, or money-mine, is in this city; and was formerly under the supervisorship of

Rittenhouse. Central in the city, is a spacious mansion-house, which was erected for the President, when Congress, in by-gone years, sat in this metropolis. The water-works, whose hydrants supply the city with water inducted for three miles in subterrean [subterranean] conduits, with their ponderous steam-enginery, are proofs of the resistless submission of vast mechanical power to human ingenuity. In the circular mall, which enclosed the former nucleus of these works, is a small *jet d'eau*, where the fluid is spouted upwards through the long snipe-bill of a sculptured water-fowl, which stands upon the shoulder of a water-nymph; and after rising about twenty feet into the air, spreads and falls in spray into a grassy-fringed fountain beneath. In the western part of the city, are Vauxhall-Gardens, included, with a Rotundo in the centre; and about four miles out of the city, on the border of the Schuylkill, are the beautiful botanical gardens of the Bartrams; the first ever in the country; and where once loved to stroll, and where first germinated the splendid idea of Wilson, the Ornithologist. From Market-street wharf, upon which Franklin first landed, one has a fine view of Jersey-shore opposite; and of the Mariner's Hotel, fitted from the hull of a large ship, with an ensign for a sign, and moored on the middle of the river. The Delaware is daily crossed by steam-boats, with their broad dusky pennons of steam trailing behind; and by team-boats, which wheel along the water, propelled by horses on board in circular motion. About four miles above the city, on the west banks of the river, are the almost forgotten ruins of the mansion of William Penn, upon whose top was once, it is said, a leaden fish-pond. It is a curious fact in Natural History, that the environs of this city, and of Jersey, are visited, once in *seventeen* years, with locusts in Egyptian multitudes. Most places this way, even if small, are chartered with their mayor, recorder, aldermen and common council; and I trust that Boston will soon persuade its honest township into a lordly city; inasmuch as green-turtles are plenty. Soon after my arrival, a report of peace convulsed the whole city into ecstacies. Illumination! illumination! Briareus, with his hundred hands, was wanted to light the flambeaux of rejoicing. Soon, however, a counter-report palsied the spirits, and extinguished the tapers.

Source: Henry Cogswell Knight, *Letters from the South and West; By Arthur Singleton, Esq.* (Boston, MA: Richardson and Lord; J.H.A. Frost, printer, 1824), 5– 8.

2. Harriet Martineau on Washington, D.C., in the 1830s

Harriet Martineau was a well-known English journalist, abolitionist, political economist, and feminist. In 1834–1835 she paid an extended visit to the United States and wrote about her experiences. Her description of Washington, D.C., in the mid-1830s showed it for what it was: a southern town, dominated by men working for or wanting favors from the government, and without much grandeur, except for the Capitol, then under construction. Expecting to find a city on the level of the great capitals of Europe, Martineau was very disappointed and noted that her stay there was the worst time she had during her visit to the United States. Martineau's criticism of the capital and of American manners elicited outcries from Americans, who resented even the slightest criticism, especially from an Englishwoman, and prided themselves on being the "freest" and "best" people in the world.

Washington is no place for persons of domestic tastes. Persons who love dissipation, persons who love to watch the game of politics, and those who make a study of strong minds under strong excitements, like a season at Washington; but it is dreary to those whose pursuits and affections are domestic. I spent five weeks there, and was heartily glad when they were over. I felt the satisfaction all the time of doing something that was highly useful; of getting knowledge that was necessary to me, and could not be otherwise obtained; but the quiet delights of my Philadelphia home (though there half our time was spent in visiting) had spoiled me for such a life as every one leads at the metropolis. I have always looked back upon the five weeks at Washington as one of the most profitable, but by far the least agreeable, of my residences in the United States.

Yet we were remarkably fortunate in our domestic arrangements there. We joined a party of highly esteemed and kind friends: a member of the House of Representatives from Massachusetts, his wife and sister-in-law, and a senator from Maine. We (the above party) had a drawing-room to ourselves and a separate table at Mrs. Peyton's boarding-house; so that we formed a quiet family group enough, if only we had had any quiet in which to enjoy the privilege.

We arrived at Washington on the 13th of January, 1835, the year of the short session of Congress which closes on the 4th of March, so that we continued to see the proceedings of Congress at its busiest and most interesting time.

The approach to the city is striking to all strangers from its oddness. I saw the dome of the Capitol from a considerable distance at the end of a straight road; but, though I was prepared by the descriptions of preceding travellers, I was taken by surprise on finding myself beneath the splendid building, so sordid are the enclosures and houses on its very verge. We wound round its base, and entered Pennsylvania Avenue, the only one of the grand avenues intended to centre in the Capitol which has been built up with any completeness. Our boarding-house was admirably situated, being some little way down this avenue, a few minutes' walk only from the Capitol, and a mile in a straight line from the White House, the residences of the heads of departments and the British legation.

In Philadelphia I had found perpetual difficulty in remembering that I was in a foreign country. The pronunciation of a few words by our host and hostess, the dinner-table, and the inquiries of visiters were almost all that occurred to remind me that I was not in a brother's house. At Washington it was very different. The city itself is unlike any other that ever was seen, straggling out hither and thither, with a small house or two a quarter of a mile from any other; so that, in making calls "in the city," we had to cross ditches and stiles, and walk alternately on grass and pavements, and strike across a field to reach a street. Then the weather was so strange; sometimes so cold that the only way I could get any comfort was by stretching on the sofa drawn before the fire up to the very fender (on which days every person who went in and out of the house was sure to leave the front door wide open); then the next morning, perhaps, if we went out muffled in furs, we had to turn back and exchange our wraps for a light shawl. Then we were waited upon by a slave appointed for the exclusive service of our party during our stay. Then there were canvass-back ducks, and all manner of other ducks on the table, in greater profusion than any single article of food, except turkeys, that I ever saw. Then there was the society, singularly compounded from the largest variety of elements foreign ambassadors, the American government, members of Congress, from Clay and Webster down to Davy Crockett, Benton from Missouri, and Cuthbert, with the freshest Irish brogue, from Georgia; flippant young belles, "pious" wives dutifully attending their husbands, and groaning over the frivolities of the place; grave judges, saucy travellers, pert newspaper reporters, melancholy Indian chiefs, and timid New England ladies, trembling on the verge of the vortex; all this was wholly unlike anything that is to be seen in any other city in the world; for all these are mixed up together in daily intercourse, like the higher circle of a little village, and there is nothing else. You have this or nothing; you pass your days among these people, or you spend them alone.

Source: Harriet Martineau, *Retrospect of Western Travel*, 2 vols. (New York: Harper & Brothers, 1838), I: 143–45.

3. *The City of Savannah (1840s)*

Emily P. Burke was a teacher in Savannah for eight years, and during that period she wrote many letters home to New England recounting her experiences living in a southern city. Her observations of Savannah in the mid-nineteenth century show a bustling port city that was important in the development of the southern economy. As she notes, Savannah was unusual in that it kept much of its original design from the days of James Oglethorpe, who had laid it out a century earlier. But as in all port cities, whether shipping cotton or wheat, the action was by the water's edge, where people made their livings loading and unloading, storing, and selling goods.

Before carrying my description into the country, which I design shortly to do, I must dwell a little longer in the city, in order to note a few particulars, in whose relation I hope you will be interested. And first, I could wish that my descriptive powers would enable me to give you a somewhat correct idea of the beauty of some of the streets in Savannah, as well as of some of those places of resort that lie beyond it. But, at the best I can do, my delineation will fall so far short of the reality, I almost shrink from the undertaking.

Running parallel with the Savannah river there are six, which are called the principal streets. The first lying adjacent to the river is called the Bay street. Upon this most of the business in the city is transacted. No respectable families reside there. The buildings on this street are mostly stores, besides a few dwellings for colored people and sailors' boarding houses. The seaman's chapel is on the south end of the street, and the Exchange about the middle way of it; besides these I do not recollect that there are any other buildings of note there. The Exchange is a fine new building, and has the only observatory in the city, and this is, at all seasons of the year much resorted to, by those who are anxiously waiting the arrival of some friend at sea. This street is always so thronged by sailors, slaves, and rowdies of all grades and color, that it is not safe for ladies to walk there alone, and it is considered very disreputable for them to be seen there unaccompanied by a gentleman, even if several ladies are together. I regretted much that this was the case, for nature has done more for this part of the city than any other. Savannah is built upon a high bluff, and this is the first street that lies upon it; so there is from that side of it nearest the river a sudden descent towards the water, of perhaps twelve or fifteen feet, which gives to one standing upon the highest part of the bluff a most delightful view of the broad river that rolls below. Bay street runs the whole length of the city, and the greater part of it is shaded by trees on both sides so tall, and having branches so broad, that in many places they overlap each other, making the cool arch-way beneath one of the most delightful retreats from the feverish air, and the hot, red brick walls of the inland streets. It was one of the greatest luxuries I could enjoy, to escape the burning sands of the city, and spend a few moments of pastime upon those shady banks, and while the soft cooling breezes from the ocean's bosom fanned our heated brows, to stand and view the busy world "who go down to the sea and do business in great waters." There the observing and reflective mind sees scenes so emblematical of human life, he can not fail to draw fresh instruction from what is passing around him. There, beyond the bar, the eye rests upon the noble ship that first was launched in British seas, lying at ease in all her proud majesty, unmoved and as little heeding the movements of all smaller barques, as the lordly nabob revelling in wealth and luxury, does the every day events of a laboring world. Still farther on, the eye just catches a glimpse of the powerful steamer, as it irresistibly ploughs its deep path in the great sea, and forces itself against wind and tide into the long sought for haven, reminding one of that class of persons on life's theatre, who, regardless of the rights and wrongs, lives and possessions of their fellow creatures, rush on through seas of blood to glory and to fame. Then again, nearer to the shore, the light skiff almost destitute of ballast, not venturing its frail timbers among the heavy waves of deeper seas, skims along so lightly and smoothly above the rocks and quicksands that lie below, one is at first almost ready to believe the situation of those thoughtless gay, and almost brainless people, to whom these light barques are slightly analogus, was far the most desirable of any; for while many, whose hearts are more capacious, and whose brains have more solidity, are constantly not only mourning over their own ills but also lamenting the woes of others, these careless, unconcerned beings seem to float along upon the surface of society far above human cares and sorrows; but like the little skiff which is suddenly capsized if only a squall strikes her sails, so let but the blast of adversity sweep over their fortunes, and having none of that ballast in the day of trouble, which is acquired only by cares and toils, and all their bright hopes and prospects for the future are wrecked forever.

At the bottom of the bluff there is quite a space of land, furnishing room for numerous store houses and for the unlading of ships and boats as well as for all the exports in cotton, corn, rice, and tobacco, brought there from the country. If the situation on the top of the bluff is one of the coolest and most desirable in a hot summer's day, the one at the foot is one of the hottest and most undesirable. There not a tree spreads out its branches to ward off a single ray from the scorching sun, neither does a spear of grass spring up there to protect the feet from the burning sands, yet here, through all the long tedious days of a Southern summer, where the height of the bluff forbids almost every current of air, not only colored people, but many white men, are compelled by the love of filthy lucre, to pass their hours from morning till evening in the vending and purchasing of goods.

Source: Emily P. Burke, *Reminiscences of Georgia* (Oberlin, OH: J.M. Fitch, 1850), 63–67.

Rural Life

America's shift from a rural to an industrial economy during the nineteenth century did not mean that everyone flocked to the city and abandoned their farms. The country still relied on agriculture to provide the foundation and stimulus for its economy. And the agrarian ideal of the simple yeoman republican farmer still ruled in popular culture and political rhetoric. Agricultural work was hard and uncertain, but to many it was God's work to toil in the "garden" and reap the harvest of honest labor. Even slaveholders spoke in such terms.

The rural areas of the country were beautiful and attracted many travelers for their scenery, if not their accommodations. By the mid-eighteenth century many people sought the refuge of the country to escape the hustle and bustle of city life and to work in utopian communities that sought to create a sense of order through toiling diligently at farm work. The general view of southern rural life is of the lush plantations of the great planters, but as the account by Frederick Law Olmsted shows, most farms were worked by simple people who were unable to purchase a slave and lived in difficult conditions.

4. Travels in New York State (1790)

William Loughton Smith was a Federalist congressman from South Carolina who later went on to serve as American minister to Spain during the presidency of John Adams. Smith traveled through New England and New York in 1790 and left behind a detailed record of his observations during that time. Here he describes a trip to Albany, New York, and gives the reader a glimpse of rural life in the last decade of the eighteenth century. Americans appreciated such travel accounts and reports as they tried to take stock of their new nation.

Tuesday, September 7th. Early in the morning we left the Pool for Albany, the distance about thirty miles. The road for about fifteen miles is bad, hilly, and rocky, and traveling in a wagon without springs was extremely rough and unpleasant. The first part of the road is through a wild country, where new settlements are just forming along the brow of wooded hills or in rich vales; the wildness of the mountains and the multitude of the stumps yet remaining on the cleared ground give a gloominess to the prospect of this country, which in a few years will doubtless be a beautiful one, for the land is good and it is fast settling. We passed by Schermerhorn's mills and soon after ascending a high hill enjoyed from its summit a prospect of very considerable extent, terminated to the left by the lofty Kaatskill Mountains. We dined at Tobias' tavern at Phillips-town, kept by an impudent woman, where we were badly entertained. Thence to Albany the road is good, the country becomes more level as you descend towards the river; we passed through several woods and I observed that the land did not appear so good and was more thinly settled than I should have expected at so short a distance from the river. When within a mile of the river, arriving at the edge of a hill, a most delightful view suddenly presents itself, consisting of the noble river of the Hudson gliding smoothly along and carrying on its surface several vessels, the city of Albany in the midst of a verdant and fertile country, several handsome mansions on the river side, particularly Gen. Schyler's, which makes a noble appearance and is delightfully situated; the sloping hills on each side of the river highly cultivated, and the scattered farms with cattle grazing in the meadows, the whole terminated by distant hills and a fine view of the Kaatskill mountains. We crossed the ferry and entered Albany early in the afternoon.

Wednesday. Albany is an ugly town when not viewed at a distance. Most of the houses are built in the old Dutch style, with the gable ends to the street; it is said to contain 4,000 inhabitants. There are several modern, handsome brick houses; from the battery there is a fine view of the river and adjacent country. I took a walk to General Schyler's; his house is a large, square brick one, with a flat roof; it stands on a rising ground above the river, and enjoys a commanding view. We rode to the Cahoos falls, ten miles from Albany; the road for six miles runs through a level meadow along the river, which in the time of freshets overflows it and renders it a very rich soil; it belongs to Mr. Stephen Rennselaer, son-in-law of Gen. Schyler; this gentleman is called the Patroon, which is the Dutch name for the Lord of the Manor, and he owns an immense estate on the banks of the North river, and running many miles back into the country. We past by his house at the end of the Town, it is an old-fashioned brick house. We were obliged to pass through several of his gates which shut up the road, for the road is on his land and he cannot keep up fences for his cornfields on account of the freshets. He has 3,200 tenants and his rental is £12,000 per annum, York currency. He makes himself very useful to his neighbors by his acts of benevolence, and is adored by his numerous tenants, he is void either of avarice or ambition, the latter is remarkable, as he is a young man of twenty-five.

Nothing can be more pleasant than the ride for six miles, all the way close to the river's edge, and on a smooth, level road, with rich meadows or well-cultivated fields on the other side of the road. On the opposite shore just at the point where we quitted the river, stands Troy, a new and flourishing town at the head of navigation for sloops; it enjoys over Albany the advantage of receiving with more convenience the produce from Vermont and the eastern shore. It is but a few years since the first store was built, and now there are forty or fifty houses. A few miles above Troy is the New City or Lansingburg, which only has the water for sloops in freshets, but then has the advantage of being higher up in the country. At the point where we left the North river the Mohawk river enters it by several mouths, all of which are visible from the road; coasting up the Mohawk river, a view of which is now and then had through the woods, we proceeded four miles of a bad road till, entering into a woody and rocky spot, we suddenly had a full view of the fall of the Cahoos, which is the fall of the whole Mohawk river over a ledge of rock thirty feet high and 200 yards wide; in some places the fall appears sixty feet, when standing just above it. A considerable spray is occasioned by this prodigious body of water falling with such violence over the rocks, and a tremendous roaring is heard. The scenery around, consisting of hills, woods, and rocks, is romantic, and the beauty and grandeur of the falls, with the pleasantness of the ride, rendered this excursion highly gratifying.

Source: *Journal of William Loughton Smith, 1790–1791*, ed. Albert Matthews (Cambridge, MA: Harvard University Press, 1917), 53–55.

5. *Nathaniel Hawthorne on Hard Farm Work (1841)*

Nathaniel Hawthorne, author of such works as The Scarlet Letter *and* The House of the Seven Gables, *as well as many other novels and short stories, often employed the theme of the inherent evil and sin of humanity in his works. In 1841 Hawthorne joined a utopian community organized by George Ripley, which sought to create harmony through intellectual pursuits and labor, in West Roxbury, Massachusetts. Although known as a very private individual, Hawthorne joined the community in April 1841 hoping that the combination of work and intellectual activity would stimulate his future writing. Hawthorne grew tired of the community, and he departed in November 1841, when he found that the combination of work and thought didn't stimulate him. In 1852 Hawthorne published* The Blithedale Romance, *which includes many elements of his experiences at Brook Farm. In a letter to his sister, Hawthorne describes the work he does in the fields during the day, providing insight into the life of a farmer.*

As the weather precludes all possibility of ploughing, hoeing, sowing and other such operations, I bethink me that you may have no objection to hear something of my whereabout and whatabout. You are to know then, that I took up my abode here on the 12th ultimo, in the midst of a snowstorm, which kept us all idle for a day or two. At the first glimpse of fair weather, Mr. Ripley summoned us into the cowyard and introduced me to an instrument with four prongs, commonly called a dung-fork. With this tool, I have already assisted to load twenty or thirty carts of manure, and shall take part in loading nearly three hundred more. Besides, I have planted potatoes and peas, cut straw and hay for the cattle, and done various other mighty works. This very morning, I milked three cows; and I milk two or three every night and morning. The weather has been so unfavorable, that we have worked comparatively little in the fields; but, nevertheless, I have gained strength wonderfully—grown quite a giant, in fact—and can do a day's work without the slightest inconvenience. In short, I am transformed into a complete farmer.

This is one of the most beautiful places I ever saw in my life, and as secluded as if it were a hundred miles from any city or village. There are woods, in which we can ramble all day, without meeting anybody, or scarcely seeing a house. Our house stands apart from the main road; so that we are not troubled even with passengers looking at us. Once in a while, we have a transcendental visitor, such as Mr. [Bronson] Alcott; but, generally, we pass whole days without seeing a single face, save those of the brethren. At this present time, our effective force consists of Mr. Ripley, Mr. Farley (a farmer from the far west), Rev. Warren Burton (author of various celebrated works), three young men and boys, who are under Mr. Ripley's care, and William Allen, his hired man, who has the chief direction of our agricultural labors. In the female part of the establishment there is Mrs. Ripley and two women folks. The whole fraternity eat together; and such a delectable way of life has never been seen on earth, since the days of the early Christians. We get up at half-past four, breakfast at half-past six, dine at half-past twelve, and go to bed at nine.

The thin frock, which you made for me, is considered a most splendid article; and I should not wonder if it were to become the summer uniform of the community. I have a thick frock, likewise; but it is rather deficient in grace, though extremely warm and comfortable. I wear a tremendous pair of cow-hide boots, with soles two inches thick. Of course, when I come to see you, I shall wear my farmer's dress.

We shall be very much occupied during most of this month, ploughing and planting; so that I doubt whether you will see me for two or three weeks. You have the portrait by this time, I suppose; so you can very well dispense with the original. When you write to me (which I beg you will do soon) direct your letter to West Roxbury, as there are two post offices in the town. I would write more; but William Allen is going to the village, and must have this letter; so good-bye.

Nath Hawthorne
Ploughman

Source: Nathaniel Hawthorne, "A Letter from Brook Farm, 1841," in *The Way We Lived: Essays and Documents in American Social History*, Vol. 1, *1492–1877*, 4th ed., ed. Frederick M. Binder and David M. Reimers (Boston, New York: Houghton Mifflin Company, 2000), 202–3.

6. Frederick Law Olmsted on Rural Life in South Carolina (1850s)

During his travels through the southern and western portions of the country, Frederick Law Olmsted made careful observations of the people and the environment that they lived in. What is important about his observations is that we get a clearer picture of what life was like in the South in the years leading up to the Civil War. It was not made up primarily of great plantations and slaveholders, but ordinary people going about their everyday lives, as we see in the document below.

At every tenth mile, or thereabout, we changed horses; and, generally, were allowed half an hour, to stroll in the neighborhood of the stable—the agent observing that we could reach the end of the staging some hours before the cars should leave to take us further; and, as there were no good accommodations for sleeping there, we would pass the time quite as pleasantly on the road. We dined at "Marion County House," a pleasant little village (and the only village we saw during the day), with a fine pine-grove, a broad street, a court-house, a church or two, a school-house, and a dozen or twenty dwellings. Towards night, we crossed the Great Pedee of the maps, the *Big* Pedee of the natives, in a flat-boat. A large quantity of cotton, in bales, was upon the bank, ready for loading into a steam-boat—when one should arrive—for Charleston.

The country was very thinly peopled; lone houses often being several miles apart. The large majority of the dwellings were of logs, and even those of the white people were often without glass windows. In the better class of cabins, the roof is usually built with a curve, so as to project eight or ten feet beyond the log-wall; and a part of this space, exterior to the logs, is inclosed with boards, making an additional small room—the remainder forms an open porch. The whole cabin is often elevated on four corner-posts, two or three feet from the ground, so that the air may circulate under it. The fire-place is built at the end of the house, of sticks and clay, and the chimney is carried up outside, and often detached from the log-walls; but the roof is extended at the gable, until in a line with its outer side. The porch has a railing in front, and a wide shelf at the end, on which a bucket of water, a gourd, and hand-basin, are usually placed. There are chairs, or benches, in the porch, and you often see women sitting at work in it, as in Germany.

The logs are usually hewn but little; and, of course, as they are laid up, there will be wide interstices between them—which are increased by subsequent shrinking. These, very commonly, are not "chinked," or filled up in any way; nor is the wall lined on the inside. Through the chinks, as you pass along the road, you may often see all that is going on in the house; and, at night, the light of the fire shines brightly out on all sides.

Cabins, of this class, would almost always be flanked by two or three negro-huts. The cabins of the poorest class of whites were of a meaner sort—being mere square pens of logs, roofed over, provided with a chimney, and usually with a shed of boards, supported by rough posts, before the door.

Occasionally, where the silvery sand was darkened by a considerable intermixture of mould, there would be a large plantation, with negro-quarters, and a cotton-press and gin-house. We passed half a dozen of these, perhaps, during the day. Where the owners resided in them, they would have comfortable-looking residences, not unlike the better class of New England farm-houses. On the largest one, however, there was no residence for the owner, at all, only a small cottage, or whitewashed cabin, for the overseer. It was a very large plantation, and all the buildings were substantial and commodious, except the negro-cabins, which were the smallest I had seen—I thought not more than twelve feet square, interiorly. They stood in two rows, with a wide street between them. They were built of logs, with no windows—no opening at all, except the doorway, with a chimney of sticks and mud; with no trees about them, no porches, or shades, of any kind. Except for the chimney—the purpose of which I should not readily have guessed—if I had seen one of them in New England, I should have conjectured that it had been built for a powder-house, or perhaps an ice-house—never for an animal to sleep in.

We stopped, for some time, on this plantation, near where some thirty men and women were at work, repairing the road. The women were in majority, and were engaged at exactly the same labor as the men; driving the carts, loading them with dirt, and dumping them upon the road; cutting down trees, and drawing wood by hand, to lay across the miry places; hoeing, and shoveling.

They were dressed in coarse gray gowns, generally very much burned, and very dirty; which, for greater convenience of working in the mud, were reefed up with a cord drawn tightly around the body, a little above the hips—the spare amount of skirt bagging out between this and the waist-proper. On their legs were loose leggins, or pieces of blanket or bagging wrapped about, and lashed with thongs; and they wore very heavy shoes. Most of them had handkerchiefs, only, tied around their heads, some wore men's caps, or old slouched hats, and several were bare-headed.

The overseer rode about among them, on a horse, carrying in his hand a raw-hide whip, constantly directing and encouraging them; but, as my companion and I, both, several times noticed, as often as he visited one end of the line of operations, the hands at the other end would discontinue their labor, until he turned to ride towards them again. Clumsy, awkward, gross, elephantine in all their movements; pouting, grinning, and leering at us; sly, sensual, and shameless, in all their expressions and demeanor; I never before had witnessed, I thought, anything more revolting than the whole scene.

At length, the overseer dismounted from his horse, and, giving him to a boy to take to the stables, got upon the coach, and rode with us several miles. From the conversation I had with him, as well as from what I saw of his conduct in the field, I judged that he was an uncommonly fit man for his duties; at least ordinarily amiable in disposition, and not passionate; but deliberate, watchful, and efficient. I thought he would be not only a good economist, but a firm and considerate officer or master.

If these women, and their children after them, were always naturally and necessarily to remain of the character and capacity stamped on their faces—as is probably the opinion of their owner, in common with most wealthy South Carolina planters—I don't know that they could be much less miserably situated, or guided more for their own good and that of the world, than they were. They were fat enough, and didn't look as if they were at all overworked, or harassed by cares, or oppressed by a consciousness of their degradation. If that is all—as some think.

Source: Frederick Law Olmsted, *The Cotton Kingdom: A Traveller's Observations on Cotton and Slavery in the American Slave States* (New York: Mason Brothers, 1861), 384–88.

Immigration

As the United States entered into the mid-nineteenth century, a great influx of immigrants came into the country. Many came to escape the oppression and poor living conditions of their native land; most came for work. All hoped that they would get a fresh start and find new opportunities in the growing nation. But many experienced the prejudice that was associated with the entry of so many foreigners into the United States. Some even protested against the stereotypes that limited their acceptance and opportunities in America, as one Chinese American does below. As the newcomers entered their new land, many faced an uncertain future. An article from the June 23, 1853, *New York Times* describes people entering New York, noting that some will continue out west, while others will fall victim to exploiters who will use them and leave them in squalor with no hope of escape. Then there are those who have already made the journey and settled in America. As the letter included below shows, they will urge their relatives to make the journey and experience the freedom they now have.

7. *A Protest against Prejudice (1852)*

The following letter was printed in the Daily Alta California *in an editorial on May 5, 1852. In it Norman Asing, a Chinese immigrant who came into New York in 1820 and then in 1850 moved to California, where he owned a restaurant, addresses the governor, John Bigler. Bigler was looking to put a stop to the immigration of Chinese into the United States. Asing questions the assertions made by Bigler that the Chinese are not worthy to enter the country and argues that they should be extended the same dignity as white European immigrants. Such prejudice against the Chinese led to racial segregation in Western territories and states and eventually to the federal Chinese Exclusion Act in 1882.*

Sir:

I am a Chinaman, a republican, and a lover of free institutions; am much attached to the principles of the government of the United States, and therefore take the liberty of addressing you as the chief of the government of this State.

Your official position gives you a great opportunity of good and evil. Your opinions through a message to a legislative body have weight, and perhaps none more so with the people, for the effect of your late message has been thus far to prejudice the public mind against my people, to enable those who wait the opportunity to hunt them down, and rob them of the rewards of their toil. You may not have meant that this should be the case, but you can see what will be the result of your propositions.

I am not much acquainted with your logic, that by excluding population from this State you enhance its wealth. I have always considered that population was wealth; particularly a population of producers, of men who by the labor of their hands or intellect, enrich the warehouses or the granaries of the country with the products of nature and art.

You are deeply convinced you say "that to enhance the prosperity and preserve the tranquility of this State, Asiatic immigration must be checked." This, your Excellency, is but one step towards a retrograde movement of the government, which, on reflection, you will discover; and which the citizens of this country ought never to tolerate. It was one of the principal causes of quarrel between you (when colonies) and England; when the latter pressed laws against emigration, you looked for immigration; it came, and immigration made you what you are—your nation what it is. It transferred you at once from childhood to manhood and made you great and respectable throughout the nations of the earth.

I am sure your Excellency cannot, if you would, prevent your being called the descendant of an immigrant, for I am sure you do not boast of being a descendant of the red man. But your further logic is more reprehensible. You argue that this is a republic of a particular race—that the Constitution of the United States admits of no asylum to any other than the pale face. This proposition is false in the extreme, and you know it. The declaration of your independence, and all the acts of your government, your people, and your history are all against you.

It is true, you have degraded the Negro because of your holding him in involuntary servitude, and because for the sake of union in some of your states such was tolerated, and amongst this class you would endeavor to place us; and no doubt it would be pleasing to some would-be freemen to mark the brand of servitude upon us. But we would beg to remind you that when your nation was a wilderness, and the nation from which you sprung barbarous, we exercised most of the arts and virtues of civilized life; that we are possessed of a language and a literature, and that men skilled in science and the arts are numerous among us; that the productions of our manufactories, our sail, and workshops, form no small share of the commerce of the world; and that for centuries, colleges, schools, charitable institutions, asylums, and hospitals, have been as common as in your own land.

That our people cannot be reproved for their idleness, and that your historians have given them due credit for the variety and richness of their works of art, and for their simplicity of manners, and particularly their industry. And we beg to remark, that so far as the history of our race in California goes, it stamps with the test of truth the fact that we are not the degraded race you would make us. We came amongst you as mechanics or traders, and following every honorable business of life. You do not find us pursuing occupations of degrading character, except you consider labor degrading, which I am sure you do not; and if our countrymen save the proceeds of their industry from the tavern and the gambling house to spend it on farms or town lots or on their families, surely you will admit that even these are virtues.

You say "you desire to see no change in the generous policy of this government as far as regards Europeans." It is out of your power to say, however, in what way or to whom the doctrines of the Constitution shall apply. You have no more right to propose a measure for checking immigration, than you have the right of sending a message to the Legislature on the subject. As far as regards the color and complexion of our race, we are perfectly aware that our population have been a little more tan than yours.

Your Excellency will discover, however, that we are as much allied to the African race and the red man as you are yourself, and that as far as the aristocracy of skin is concerned, ours might compare with many of the European races; nor do we consider that your Excellency, as a Democrat, will make us believe that the framers of your declaration of rights ever suggested the propriety of establishing an aristocracy of skin.

I am a naturalized citizen, your Excellency, of Charleston, South Carolina, and a Christian, too; and so hope you will stand corrected in your assertion "that none of the Asiatic class" as you are pleased to term them, have applied for benefits under our naturalization act. I could point out to you numbers of citizens, all over the whole continent, who have taken advantage of your hospitality and citizenship, and I defy you to say that our race have ever abused that hospitality or forfeited their claim on this or any of the governments of South America, by an infringement on the laws of the countries into which they pass. You find us peculiarly peaceable and orderly. It does not cost your state much for our criminal prosecution. We apply less to your courts for redress, and so far as I know, there are none who are a charge upon the state, as paupers.

You say that "gold, with its talismanic power, has overcome those natural habits of non-intercourse we have exhibited." I ask you, has not gold had the same effect upon your people, and the people of other countries, who have migrated hither? Why, it was gold that filled your country (formerly a desert) with people, filled your harbours with ships and opened our much-coveted trade to the enterprise of your merchants.

Source: Norman Asing, "To His Excellency Gov. Bigler," *Daily Alta California* (San Francisco), May 5, 1852.

8. *An Uncertain Future: Immigrants Arriving in New York City (1853)*

The following article from the New York Times *on June 23, 1853, describes the arrival of new immigrants in New York City and the hopeful faces of many as they enter upon a new life. Also related is the seedy side of their existence, victimized by those who come to take advantage of them for their own gain; many of these people will end up living in squalor in the poor section of the city without hope of getting out, and further adding to the numbers of the poor there.*

If you would see, for a moment, one of the streams in the great current which is always pouring through New-York, go down a summer afternoon to the North River Wharves. A German immigrant ship has just made fast. The long wharf is crowded full of trucks and carts, and drays, waiting for the passengers. As you approach the end you come upon a noisy crowd of strange faces and stranger costumes. Mustached peasants in Tyrolese hats are arguing in unintelligible English with truck-drivers; runners from the German hotels are pulling the confused women hither thither; peasant girls with bare heads, and the rich-flushed, nut brown faces you never see here, are carrying huge bundles to the heaps of baggage; children in doublets and hose, and queer little caps, are mounted on the trunks, or swung off amid the laughter of the crowd with ropes from the ship's sides. Some are just welcoming an old face, so dear [in] this strange land, some are letting down the huge trunks, some swearing in very genuine low Dutch, at the endless noise and distractions. They bear the plain marks of the Old World. Healthy, stout frames, and low, degraded faces with many stamps of inferiority; dependents, servitude, on them; little graces of costume too—a colored headdress or fringed coat—which never could have originated here; and now and then a sweet face, with the rich bloom and the dancing blue eye, that seem to reflect the very glow and beauty of the vine hills of the Rhine.

It is a new world to them—oppression, bitter poverty behind—here, hope, freedom, and a chance to work, and food to the laboring man. They may have the vaguest ideas of it all—still, to the dullest some thoughts come of the New Free World.

Every one in the great City, who can make a living from the freshly arrived immigrant is here. Runners, sharpers, peddlers, agents of boarding-houses, of forwarding-offices, and worst of all, of the houses where many a simple immigrant girl, far from friends and home, comes to a sad end. Very many of these, who are now arriving, will start tomorrow at once for the far West. Some will hang about the German boarding-houses in Greenwich-street, each day losing their money, their children getting out of control, until they at last seek a refuge in Ward's island, or settle down on the Eleventh Ward, to add to the great mass of the poverty and misery there gathered. From there we shall see their children sallying out these early mornings, as soon as light, to do the petty work of the City, rag-picking, bone-gathering, selling and peddling by the thousands, radishes, strawberries and fruit through every street.

Source: "Walks Among the New York Poor," *New York Times*, June 23, 1853.

9. *A Letter Home (1855)*

The following letter from Peter Klein to his parents is an example of the networks that developed that brought many immigrants to America. Coming from the town of Güchenbach, six miles north of Saarbrüchen, in a region known for coal production, Klein and those with similar experience were drawn to jobs where their skills and experience would pay off. Klein settled in Pottsville, Pennsylvania, with his cousin Peter Büch, and worked in the mines there until 1856, when he, Büch, and a few friends set off for California to work in the gold fields. Klein eventually worked as a laborer in a quartz mine in California. Such movement from place to place was common, especially in mining.

Pottsville, May 21st, 1855

Dear Parents,

I received your letter in the best of health and see from it that you are all well, which pleases me. You write that my sister Elisabeth wants to come here, which I would very much like, for let me tell you, a good woman can have a much, much better life here in this country than in Germany.

You write in your last letter that you want to know how coal is worked here. I can tell you that most of the work is done with powder, and shifts are 10 hours, and the piece rates are like in Germany, and one man digs as much coal as six in Germany.

Then you should know that they have coal here that is from 4 feet up to 20 and 30 and 40 feet high. That's to let you know there's only a handful of coal in Germany, compared to here.

You also wanted to know why Peter Büch and I are no longer together. When Peter Krebs got here, the two of them worked together, and then they left this place and we get together every 3 or 4 weeks.

You also write in Peter Krebs's letter that Peter Büch's family wants to come here, I'll tell you, if they want to work in coal they can do much better here than in Germany. And when they leave for the journey, they shouldn't bring any cloth and only a little clothing along.

The best thing is a good bed, and not too little food, just a lot of potatoes, that's the best at sea.

I should also say be careful on the trip and don't be too good-hearted, so you won't get cheated.

Get yourselves good passports, so you don't get into a mess that costs you a lot of money.

Friedriech Klickert asked me to write what a pair of boots costs, so tell him 4 to 5 dollars, and leather isn't more expensive than over there.

That's all I can think of to write now. The gold dollar under the seal is for godson Peter/ your son, Peter Klein.

My wife and I send you our regards and best wishes. Johann Gothie

Source: *Briefe aus Amerika. Deutsche Einwanderer schreiben aus der Neuen Welt*, Walter Kamphoefner, Wolfgang Helbich, Ulrike Sommer; Verlag C.H. Beck, München 1988, translated by Susan Carter Vogel (Ithaca & London: Cornell University Press, 1991), 389–90.

Trade

As the United States emerged from the War of 1812, there were many who believed that the government should take an active role in promoting internal improvements that would help the nation develop a stronger economy. The building of canals was the first focus of facilitating internal trade and for getting goods from the interior of the country to the cities for local distribution or export. The report of the Ohio Board of Canal Commissioners is an example of this effort. In the competition to finance the many internal projects that the states sought to make, many turned to overseas investors for funding. As a result, expenses increased and foreign debt became a problem for many states and investors. Charles Francis Adams proposes a solution for this problem in an article in the *North American Review* in October 1840.

10. Canals for a Growing Nation (1828)

The success of the Erie Canal, and the money that it brought into New York State, became a blueprint for other states to build canals in the first forty years of the nineteenth century. This report of the Ohio Board of Canal Commissioners uses the example of the Erie Canal as a reason for investing money in the building of a canal. The money that would be gained would far outweigh the money expended on it. The planning and building of canals became an obsession until the advent of railroads in the 1830s. The canal boom outpaced the traffic necessary to make it pay, and several states defaulted on obligations from failed "internal improvements" projects. But the canals were part of the transportation revolution that knitted together the regions and made possible the market revolution. Building the canals also provided many jobs, which attracted Irish immigrants.

Though the construction of the great [Erie] canal of New York is a work so grand and imposing, its advantages to the public are not less apparent. The benefits of which have already resulted from that work, although it is not yet completed, are so great as to stagger belief, if they are not capable of proof amounting almost to mathematical demonstration.

That every saving in the expense of transporting the surplus productions of a country to market, is just so much added to the value at home, is a proposition to [too] evident to require proof, and too plain to need illustration. We accordingly find that any article designed for distant market, increases in price, where it is produced, in exact proportion to the diminution in the expense of conveying it to its place of destination, unless affected by accidental circumstances. Taking this rule as a criterion, it is ascertained from information derived from authentic sources, that on the productions of the country exported from the single county of Monroe, situated on the Genesee river in New York, and the property received in return, more than 275,000 dollars was saved during the last season; in other words, so much money was put into the pockets of those who raised that produce for market and those who received such articles as they needed in return. This benefitted soley from the Erie canal, and the sum thus saved to a small section of country, would more than pay the interest for one year on all moneys expended in the construction of all the canal lines in that state, which were then completed. This fact alone, speaks volumes in favor of canal navigation, and ought to carry conviction to the mind of every reflecting man.

Source: Ohio Board of Canal Commissioners (1824), *Second Annual Report, Civil Engineer* (January 19, 1828), 75–79.

11. Charles Francis Adams on Financing Internal Improvements (1840)

Charles Francis Adams was the son of President John Quincy Adams and the grandson of President John Adams, both of whom believed in funding internal improvements to facilitate the growth of America's economy, so he was uniquely qualified to address the problems that had led to the increasing debt to foreign investors because of the competition between the states. What he suggests is a comprehensive, orderly government program that would support these projects and keep the money out of the hands of foreign investors. His prejudice against dependence on foreign investment, however unwise as policy given the enormous credit needs of an expanding American economy, fit with the common American concern about maintaining "independence."

In consequence of the applications for loans, that are perpetually making by the states to the capitalists of Europe, and particularly of London, an obvious necessity arises for the information necessary to estimate properly the ability of the respective applicants to fulfill the engagements they are disposed to make. Hitherto, it would certainly seem as if a suitable degree of attention had not been paid to the duty of collecting this, and as if money had been advanced at hap-hazard, with more reference to the tempting nature of the terms offered, than to the resources of the parties offering them. It is high time that this mode of proceeding should be changed; for it will inevitably lead to disappointment upon one side, and irritation upon both. The more usurious the contract is, the more oppressive it will be felt by the borrower; and, if ultimately there should be found an unwillingness to comply with its conditions, amounting in fact to inability, the greater will be the disposition to seek in the severity of those conditions an excuse for non-performance. This is the nature of man whether taken individually or in society; and when we hear of some of the agreements which have been made in London, it is, we confess, with no small surprise, that we perceive how far the ordinarily shrewd and careful citizens of that great metropolis appear to have overlooked or forgotten it.

Nineteen states out of the twenty-six, and one territory, have authorized the contracting of a debt, which in the aggregate may now be estimated as equal to two hundred millions of dollars. A very large part of this is actually due to foreigners, and consequently subjects the country to a heavy annual drain of money in the form of interest, which must, in most cases, be remitted to Europe at the hazard and expense of the borrowers. It is, therefore, highly incumbent upon every citizen of the United States, if he does not now know, directly to set about understanding, what he has got to represent [show for] the debt thus created, and how far his industry and his capital have been assisted or hazarded by the mode in which the money raised has been spent . . . .

Of the large amount that has been borrowed within a few years by the states, considerably more than half has been expended in works of internal improvement, such as canals, railways, turnpike roads &c.; the rest has been made the basis of banking institutions. Of the large amount that has been borrowed within a few years by the States, considerably more than half has been expended in works of internal improvement, such as canals, railways, turnpike roads, & c.; the rest has been made the basis of banking institutions. The first mode of appropriation has been that most generally adopted in the free States of the Union; the second has been confined in a great degree, though not entirely, to the slaveholding States. Both of them have been productive of very important immediate effects upon the industry of the community. Yet it remains to be seen, whether the disadvantages that may be experienced hereafter from the manner in which the works have been carried on, will not require a great deduction from the benefits derived.

There was, no doubt, much weight in the objections made to the adoption of the policy of internal improvements by the national government, when it was agitated. The principal ones were, that the system could not be carried on with a proper regard to economy, and that it would be the means of creating an army of dependents upon the administration, whose votes could be influenced to settle the popular elections.

There were other arguments drawn from the jealousy of encroachment upon State rights, which showed more narrowness of mind, than solidity of judgment or comprehensiveness of policy; we therefore do not state them. Of the two objections enumerated, the first appears to us to have been far the stronger. The tendency of the members of our national legislature to regard measures rather in the light of instruments with which to advance their popularity within their districts at home, than as modes of promoting the general prosperity, would inevitably have given rise to much contention, and to the proposal of many schemes of no great national benefit, the adoption of which it would nevertheless have been difficult successfully to resist. And the execution of the system might have made an opening to much favoritism and jobbing, which would have put the country to great expense with little benefit.

Admitting these objections to a national system of internal improvements to have very great weight, it is nevertheless much to be doubted whether those, which lie against the one adopted as a substitute for it, do not more than counterbalance them. In the first place, the tendency to improvements of a local arid wholly useless character, instead of being counteracted by the separate action of the States, has been infinitely increased. The competition from being between great sections of country, the West, the East, the South, and the North, as it was in Congress, has been between the several states, and in some cases has degenerated into a contest between the different counties in the same states. In addition to this, there has been no system adopted to make the works executed to conduce to the common benefit. The utter want of general plan has led to a hurtful emulation, by which each state tries to secure to itself whatever it may gain from trade from one point and to another, which if carried on, must in the end absorb all the profits attending even the most judiciously executed ones. There can be little help of permanent profit in any one quarter, where success becomes the signal for new efforts in other to diminish if not destroy it. Moreover, the extraordinary expense at which all this is carried on by the states would have covered the many fat jobs given to favorites of the national government, even if we are to suppose such things do not also happen with the states themselves. Most of the money which has been raised to pay for these state undertakings, has been borrowed upon terms much less advantageous than it would have been, had the United States been the applicant. The wealthy capitalists of Europe, who would have been glad to advance to the national government the whole of which has been actually procured, at a very low rate of profit, on account of the general confidence in the security of the loan, have been induced to do the same thing to the separate states only by extraordinary appeals to their avarice, and the offer to them of terms, which, in many cases, if they had been made in private among individuals at home, would have been reckoned to be highly usurious.

On the whole, therefore, if we strike the balance between centralism and consolidation on the one side, and state pride on the other, we shall perhaps discover that the latter, however good in itself, is apt, when carried to an extreme, to prove, like all other pride, equally expensive and inconvenient. And we may also find, that the very moment, when it appears to have most firmly established its preponderance in the national councils, is the one from which the heaviest counterpoise begins to make itself felt. The Americans are proverbial for never being discouraged. If they cannot carry a point directly, they will manage to do it by some roundabout way.

Source: Charles Francis Adams, "[Review of] 'Observations on the Financial Position and Credit of Such of the States of the North American Union as Have Contracted Public Debts,' by Alexander Trotter," *North American Review* 51 (October 1840): 317–21.

12. Funding the Railroads (1851)

In an article in the American Railroad Journal, an anonymous contributor discusses the advantages of railroads, as well as detailing the need to allow private interests to finance the building of the railroads. The writer believes that private interests would be more likely to carry out the project better than corrupt legislatures, which would drive up costs and delay the completion of the railroads. The dream of railroads providing transportation and the movement of goods across the nation would be realized after the Civil War, achieved through both private and government funding.

Our capacity for production is unlimited, but much of our most fertile lands are worthless, simply because there exists no means of sending their productions to a market. In very many parts of this country corn may be raised at a profit at 20 cents a bushel, while the same article is worth 70 cents in New York. If it could be forwarded for 10 cents a bushel, the producer would make 40 cents additional profit. The reduced cost of transportation (the price remaining the same) measures the increased profits of the seller. But it often happens in many parts of the country, that all surplus beyond the wants of the consumer is *worthless*. A railroad, therefore, gives a value to articles that had no commercial value before, and in this respect, creates wealth where none for practical purposes existed.

It is in this view, that we must estimate, the importance of railroads to the West, and the value of their securities. The producing portion of the country is far removed from the consumers. All the surplus products of the West require to be exported, and the capacity to produce is only measured for the means of transportation. The fact, too, that our present agriculture engrosses almost the entire attention of our western people, and compels them to *import* all that their own farms and industry do not supply. Facilities for transportation, therefore, are what give the ability to purchase. Exports and imports bear the same ratio to each other, because the amount that a farmer can produce is limited by the amount he can sell. Western railroads, therefore, produce in this way a double result, and create an *import*, while their original and primary object was to facilitate the export trade.

* * *

We go for free railroading, and think that there is less danger in entrusting to people the management of their own affairs, than to commit them to the control of a corrupt legislature. But if we are going to have rival roads, let us build these rivals where they can be made the means of a positive good to some, as well as harm to others. Let the rival occupy if possible a *different* route; where it can be the means of a *local* and *public* good, as well of private pique or spleen . . . .

Rival lines gave the death blow to English railroads. Millions upon millions were thrown away in the same manner in Massachusetts. We do not like to witness the commencement of such schemes in New York. We have not money enough to throw away on them. Such as are based upon ill will or upon speculation are always dangerous, not only in results, but in the influence they exert upon the community, in fostering the same spirit that gave birth to the first. A scheme that has not a legitimate object should never be trusted. Its getters up are looking after their own ends, and the public will find that when these ends are accomplished, that they will be left to shift for themselves. . . .

It may not be inappropriate to state here the usual manner in which securities are negotiated. We have already spoken of sales at auction. These are considered safe to be tried only under peculiar circumstances. If one man is seen running through the streets, no person would think of following him. But let ten start together, and every person in sight will join in the chase. If these ten halloo, the rest will hallo in sympathy; and if the leaders act in concert, they will acquire such an influence over the feelings of those following, as to have them almost entirely under their control, and ready for any dare-devil exploit that may have been planned. Persons are in this way easily brought into a state, when they "go it blind," indifferent, unconscious even, of any blows or contusions they may receive. So with selling railroad securities at auction. The great mass of operators will of course unite to break down the sale; and will do so, unless it is strongly supported. A few strong names must be selected to lead off, to puff and blow, and manufacture a public sentiment in favor of the what to be sold; to form the nucleus, and start off in the race, and the number and spirit of that that will follow, will bear an exact proportion to the apparent zeal and confident assertion of the leaders. After the public sentiment is brought up to the proper point, and take for the sellers what cannot be disposed of *bona fide*. All this process, as well may be supposed, costs something; so much that sales made in this manner, are only resorted to where a large amount is to be disposed of. Securities at auction often bring more than those sold at private sale, but the expense is great, and the risk still greater. If the parties fail to make a good *hit*, the security loses *caste*, and then must be disposed of as a second hand article.

When securities are disposed of at *Private* sale, the broker or operator to whom they are committed, makes up a *party* of his friends, among whom they are divided, each taking 5, 10, or $20,000; for, notwithstanding we have some pretty capacious maws on Wall Street, it can boast of a few individuals who severally could comfortably digest a mass of bonds of $500,000, without having the functions of his business stomach somewhat deranged.

. . . As soon, therefore, as the seller with the greatest secrecy and confidence, imparts his scheme to the money lender or broker, he communicates with an electric dispatch with the same to some twenty or thirty others. The whole party must know and discuss the matter, as much as the principle [principal] who stands between them and the seller. If the seller, for the purpose of trying the market, and finding out what he can expect to sell for, goes to other operators, he strikes the wires which carry his secrets around another circuit, composed of an equal number of names. In this manner, a person mat [may] have been a day in Wall Street before every important man on 'change [the exchange] will understand his whole scheme as well as the seller does himself. He has thus shown his whole hand, without knowing a card held on the other side. . . .

No person wishes to invest his money in a security that is not popular with *all* parties—that will not always sell without requiring any efforts on his part to give it credit. The frowns of a half-dozen leading operators are often sufficient to damn a good security, which would at once have gone into public favor under the smiles of the same persons. So long, therefore, as purchasers have plenty of room for choice, they prefer securities that are well known to those which must be pushed and crowded into favor by efforts of their own. Another evil which results from the exposure of a scheme in the manner stated is the fact, that unless securities are "placed" soon after they come into the market, the inference is, that there is some intrinsic defect in them which has prevented a sale. The securities in this way become *shop-worn*, and must be sold as second-hand goods. . . .

When a person comes here for money, he must bear in mind that $400,000 or $500,000 is no small sum. . . . He must remember that money is power and that the holder can dictate to a great extent his own terms, and above all, he must bear in mind, that he is liable to encounter the opposition of parties he never heard or dreamed of before, and that he will come in contact with those who, for life have made man a study, who, at a glance almost, detect his weak points, and lay their plans accordingly. Life in Wall Street is a constant contest, and he who would sustain himself in it must prove himself superior to those he meets in their own way.

Source: "Western Securities," *American Railroad Journal* (January 25, 1851): 56–57, reprinted in *Antebellum American Culture: An Interpretive Anthology*, ed. David Brion Davis (Lexington, KY, and Toronto: D.C. Heath and Company, 1979), 176–79.

Part IV

INTELLECTUAL LIFE

The development of intellectual life in America from the Revolution to the Civil War was centered on the growth of the nation. The education of American youth became central to the ideas of the republic, which looked to distinguish its schools from those of Europe, while also providing an education that was as well developed as their European counterparts. With the expansion of the nation, there was a need to explore its vast reaches to discover the unknown plants, wildlife, and climate conditions of the regions that lay beyond the horizon. Explorers and amateur scientists encountered terrible conditions while carrying out their work, but they marched on, recording their observations; making maps; and gathering specimens of flora, fauna, and minerals for study. In doing so they helped make the West knowable and accessible. They found uses for it. They also pointed the way for others to follow.

The field of medicine dealt with the many problems encountered by people in the United States and laid the groundwork for the diagnosis of alcoholism and better treatment of the mentally ill. Medical practitioners were perplexed by older diseases such as yellow fever, which would remain a scourge in the United States into the twentieth century.

In writing fiction, poetry, and history—the principal forms of "literature" during this period—Americans continued to look to Europe for forms. But some Americans were already experimenting with stories drawn from local lore and were shaking off their dependence on older forms. Books published in England, especially, continued to sell well in the United States. But American writers were finding their own voice and an American market. Increased literacy and improvements in printing and papermaking also made publishing more widespread; there were more readers and more ways to reach them. By the eve of the Civil War American literature began to take on an independence that would be its hallmark in the second half of the nineteenth century. Although poems like "The Raven" borrowed their structure from English poetry, American poetry was beginning to develop its own style, which gained popularity throughout the country. Edgar Allan Poe, with his stories of "ratiocination" and other tales, was also developing new forms of prose. Writers were not shying away from social issues like slavery, factory life, and the crime and worries of urban life.

Education

The education that was developed in the wake of the Revolution was reflective of the schools of Europe. The curriculum was based on mathematics, grammar, and reading during the period of primary education and moved into areas such as languages (mainly Latin) and science as students moved on to high school. If a member of the upper class, the (male) student was expected to go on to study at college, though more for social connections than serious scholarship. Many students chose to study law or looked to become preachers, so Latin and theology took on a prime importance, as well as science and philosophy. Many believed that the best education available was in Europe, but in the first document, Thomas Jefferson points to a need to keep students in America so that they will not be poisoned against republican ideology in European schools. The development of American schools during the nineteenth century can be seen in the accounts of two European observers of American schools, Sir Charles Lyell and the Reverend Jean Henri Grandpierre. Both comment on how well the students in an American classroom performed as opposed to those in schools in their native countries and found that American students did very well.

1. *Thomas Jefferson on the Advantages of an American Education (1785)*

In 1785 Thomas Jefferson wrote this letter warning against sending American youths to Europe for their education. He argues that education abroad puts a student at a disadvantage because the "objects of a useful American culture" are not universal. During and because of the American Revolution, Americans insisted they were a more virtuous people than the corrupt, contaminated Old World, and sought to create their own institutions to ensure their "independence." Even an "American" English became part of this desire for a republican character, as Noah Webster later argued and then provided with his dictionary.

I should sooner have answered the paragraph in your letter of September 19, respecting the best seminary for the education of youth in Europe, but that it was necessary for me to make inquiries on the subject. The result of these has been to consider the competition as resting between Geneva and Rome.

They are equally cheap and probably are equal in the course of education pursued. The advantage of Geneva is that students acquire there the habit of speaking French. The advantages of Rome are the acquiring a local knowledge of a spot so classical and so celebrated; the acquiring the true pronunciation of the Latin language; a just taste in the fine arts, more particularly those of painting, sculpture, architecture, and music; a familiarity with those objects and processes of agriculture, which experience has shown best adapted to a climate like ours; and lastly, the advantage of a fine climate for health. It is probable, too, that by being boarded in a French family, the habit of speaking that language may be obtained.

I do not count on any advantage to be derived in Geneva, from a familiar acquaintance with the principles of that government. The late revolution has rendered it a tyrannical aristocracy, more likely to give ill than good ideas to an American. I think the balance in favor of Rome. Pisa is sometimes spoken of as a place of education. But it does not offer the first and third of the advantages of Rome.

But why send an American youth to Europe for education? What are the objects of a useful American education? Classical knowledge; modern languages, chiefly French, Spanish, and Italian; mathematics; natural philosophy; natural history; civil history; and ethics. In natural philosophy, I mean to include chemistry and agriculture, and in natural history, to include botany, as well as the other branches of those departments. It is true that the habit of speaking the modern languages cannot be so well acquired in America; but every other article can be as well acquired at William and Mary College as at any place in Europe. When college education is done with and a young man is to prepare himself for public life, he must cast his eyes (for America) either on law or physic [medicine]. For the former, where can he apply so advantageously as to Mr. Wythe? For the latter, he must come to Europe. The medical class of students, therefore, is the only one which need come to Europe.

Let us view the disadvantages of sending a youth to Europe. To enumerate them all would require a volume. I will select a few. If he goes to England, he learns drinking, horse racing, and boxing. These are the peculiarities of English education. The following circumstances are common to education in that and the other countries of Europe. He acquires a fondness for European luxury and dissipation, and a contempt for the simplicity of his own country; he is fascinated with the privileges of the European aristocrats, and sees with abhorrence the lovely equality which the poor enjoy with the rich in his own country; he contracts a partiality for aristocracy or monarchy; he forms foreign friendships which will never be useful to him, and loses the seasons of life for forming in his own country those friendships which, of all others, are the most faithful and permanent. He is led by the strongest of all the human passions into a spirit for female intrigue, destructive of his own and others' happiness, or a passion for whores, destructive of his health; and, in both cases, learns to consider fidelity to the marriage bed as an ungentlemanly practice and inconsistent with happiness. He recollects the voluptuary dress and arts of the European women, and pities and despises the chaste affections and simplicity of those of his own country; he retains through life a fond recollection and a hankering after those places which were the scenes of his first pleasures and of his first connections.

He returns to his own country a foreigner, unacquainted with the practices of domestic economy necessary to preserve him from ruin, speaking and writing his native tongue as a foreigner, and therefore unqualified to obtain those distinctions which eloquence of the pen and tongue insures in a free country; for I would observe to you that what is called style in writing or speaking is formed very early in life, while the imagination is warm and impressions are permanent. I am of opinion that there never was an instance of a man's writing or speaking his native tongue with elegance who passed from fifteen to twenty years of age out of the country where it was spoken. Thus, no instance exists of a person's writing two languages perfectly. That will always appear to be his native language which was most familiar to him in his youth.

It appears to me, then, that an American coming to Europe for education loses in his knowledge, in his morals, in his health, in his habits, and in his happiness. I had entertained only doubts on this head before I came to Europe; what I see and hear since I came here proves more than I had even suspected. Cast your eye over America. Who are the men of most learning, of most eloquence, most beloved by their countrymen and most trusted and promoted by them? They are those who have been educated among them, and whose manners, morals, and habits are perfectly homogeneous with those of the country.

Did you expect by so short a question to draw such a sermon on yourself? I dare say you did not. But the consequences of foreign education are alarming to me as an American. I sin, therefore, through zeal, whenever I enter on the subject. You are sufficiently American to pardon me for it.

Source: *Memoirs, Correspondence, and Private Papers of Thomas Jefferson*, vol. 1, ed. Thomas Jefferson Randolph (London: Henry Colburn and Richard Bentley, 1829), 345–47.

2. Sir Charles Lyell Describes a Boston School (1845)

Sir Charles Lyell was a Scottish-born geologist whose book Principles of Geology *brought him world renown. Lyell was also a friend of Charles Darwin and became the first scientist to support Darwin's* On the Origin of Species, *although he didn't endorse all its ideas. Lyell traveled twice to the United States and published his experiences from both trips. In the following excerpt, Lyell discusses his visit to a Boston school, and the performance of its students as opposed to those in England, on his second visit to the United States in the late 1840s.*

Nov. 27, 1845

The population of Boston, exclusive of Charlestown, Roxbury, and Cambridge (which may be regarded as suburbs), is at present about 115,000, of which 8000 are Roman Catholics, chiefly of Irish extraction; but there are besides many Scotch and English emigrants in the city. In order to prove to me how much may be done to advance them in civilization in a single generation, I was taken to a school where nine-tenths of all the children were of parents who had come out from England or Ireland. It was not an examination day, and our visit was wholly unexpected. We entered a suite of three well-aired rooms, containing 550 girls. There were nine teachers in the room. The pupils were all between the ages of nine and thirteen, the greater portion of them the daughters of poor laborers, but some of them of parents in good circumstances. Each scholar was seated on a separate chair with a back to it, the chair being immovably fixed to the ground to prevent noise. There was no uniformity of costume, but evidently much attention to personal neatness, nearly all of them more dressed than would be thought in good taste in children of a corresponding class in England. They had begun their studies at nine o'clock in the morning, and are to be six hours at school, studying fifty minutes at a time, and then being allowed to ten minutes for play in a yard adjoining. I observed some of the girls very intent on their task, leaning on their elbows and in other careless attitudes, and we were told by the masters that they avoid as much as possible finding fault with them on minor points when they are studying. The only punishments are a reprimand before the class, and keeping them back after school hours.

The look of intelligence in the countenances of the greater number of them was a most pleasing sight. In one of the upper classes they were reading, when we went in, a passage from Paley "On Sleep," and I was asked to select at random from the school-books some poem which the girls might read each in their turn. I chose Gray's Elegy in a Churchyard, as being none of the simplest for young persons to understand. They each read a verse distinctly, and many of them most gracefully, and explained correctly the meaning of nearly all the words and allusions on which I questioned them.

We afterward heard the girls of the arithmetic class examined in algebra, and their answers showed that much pains had been taken to make them comprehend the principles on which the methods of calculation depended. We then visited a boy's grammar school, and found there 420 Protestant and 100 Catholic boys educated together. We remarked that they had a less refined appearance and were less forward in their education than the girls whom we had just seen, of the same age, and taken from the same class in society. In explanation I was told that it is impossible to give the boys as much schooling, because they can earn money for their parents at an earlier age.

Source: Sir Charles Lyell, *A Second Visit to the United States of North America*, 2 vols. (New York: Harper & Brothers, 1849), 147–48.

3. *A Frenchman's Views of the American School System (1853)*

The Reverend Jean Henri Grandpierre was one of the most influential Protestant leaders in France during the nineteenth century. He was the principal editor of a journal, L'Espérance, *devoted to the interests of the Protestant churches. He wrote about his experiences during a trip to the United States in 1853; the account was published in the states a year later. He compares his observations of American society to that of France, and not unfavorably. In this section he discusses the education system in Massachusetts and notes its organization and ability to provide a superior education to its students.*

In America, as it is well known, government has nothing to do either with the support, or the discipline of the churches, universities, and theological faculties. These are left entirely and exclusively to private management. But, on the other hand, the administration takes the direction of the system of primary instruction, which it has most successfully conducted. This is thought of too great importance to be left to individual effort. Every town is obliged to levy taxes and contributions for the foundation and support of a school. There is no village, however small, that has not its schoolmaster or mistress. A Board of Education, composed of the most eminent men, chosen from all religious denominations, is charged with the general supervision of these schools. This board selects properly qualified teachers, presents them to the school districts, and sees that the local committees fulfil their duties with regard to their respective schools. The attendance on these schools is not obligatory, but such is the force of opinion, that a parent who should neglect to send his children either to the public or to a private school would become the object of public animadversion. Every citizen of the United States should be able at least to read and write.

Infant schools are very numerous in America; there are, besides, free schools of three grades, the primary school, the grammar school, and the high school. On leaving the high school, a young man possesses all the attainments necessary to him, except such as are required in order to enter the schools of theology, law or medicine; and a young woman, having received no other instruction than that given in the school of the third degree, may be considered as well educated as one who, in France, should have passed several years in the best boarding-schools.

An active, studious, and intelligent schoolmaster or mistress may rise successively from the lower to the higher school, and thus receive a salary increased from three hundred to fifteen hundred dollars.

There are no less than from four thousand to five thousand teachers of both sexes employ[ed] in the common schools of Massachusetts alone.

To foster a professional spirit in those persons charged with the education of youth, and at the same time to keep them much improved in scientific progress, the Board of Education in Massachusetts has founded Teachers' Institutes, of which there are now about twenty in operation in the State. The following statement will explain their character. Once a year, on a given day, the one hundred, two hundred, or three hundred teachers employed within certain districts, are invited to meet and spend a week in some central town, which is designated. There they find the secretary of the department of public instruction, with seven or eight professors, the most eminent in their several branches. During this week, from morning till night, the teachers attend lectures on natural history, physical geography, profane history, mathematics, elocution, recitation, &c. They are far from finding irksome the time thus fully occupied; indeed, I am told by one of their professors, that often, after having finished the six or seven lessons required of him, he has been obliged to read two or three more by way of supplement, in order to satisfy their earnest entreaties. Thus encouraged in their career, and aided in their studies, they return with new ardor to take the direction of their respective schools.

In all the public schools the Bible is read and taught, without reference to the differences between the various religious sects. It has been the more easy to come to an understanding upon the nature of this instruction, as all the communions in the United States, with the exception of a few Unitarian congregations, are *Orthodox*, and differ only upon certain points of doctrine and observances. Religious instruction of a *special* character, is reserved for the Sunday schools, which are held in the church to which the parents of the children belong. It would be difficult to find in the United States, a single church that has not its Sunday school, conducted by pious laymen, well versed in the knowledge of sacred history, and of the dogmas and ethics of Christianity. So thoroughly qualified, indeed, are they for this work, that a Swiss professor, established in a small town in the State of New York, remarked, in speaking of the instruction they give, "I assure you that I myself learn much in preparing my children for the Sunday school," and he added, "I am not sure that there could not be found more than one child in our Sunday schools in America, who understands his Bible better than some of our pastors in Europe."

We have received the greater part of the above information from Dr. Sears, the Secretary of the Board of Education of the State of Massachusetts, whom we had the pleasure of meeting on board the "Empire State"—a magnificent steamboat—on our way from Boston to New York.

From the common schools we pass to the colleges. All the colleges in the United States are arranged on the same plan, and comprise four classes of students—the Freshmen, or new comers, the Sophomore, the Junior and the Senior. These singular designations are used not only by the students, but by the college governments in their catalogues and publications. The young men who attend the colleges are lodged and boarded for about one hundred and sixty or two hundred dollars a year, in buildings belonging to the university, and are subjected to a rigid discipline with regard to their hours of rising, of going out, &c. They are required, moreover, to attend morning and evening prayers held daily in the chapel, besides the public services of the Sabbath, and even services held during the week. Those among them who obtain permission to lodge outside the college walls, can only do so in houses approved of by the faculty, where the same discipline is in some measure observed.

Each year, at the close of the terms, the senior class graduates—that is to say, the students who compose it, receive a diploma which holds the middle place between the diploma of *Bachelier ès-lettres* and that of *Bachelier ès-sciences*. The degree is conferred publicly, and the assembly on the occasion is always held in some church, and opened invariably with prayer. This ceremony attracts a crowd of spectators, not only among the relatives and friends of the students, but from the town and surrounding country. The Governor of the State of Massachusetts never fails to attend with his staff at Harvard College on these occasions.

Before receiving their diplomas, the most distinguished of the graduates are obliged to pronounce a public discourse. These discourses are in prose or verse, some in Latin, some even in Greek. Popular confidence in any institution in America, is bestowed only in the degree in which that institution is submitted to popular control. The American public recognises willingly that the professors have the capacity and the right of judging as to the merit of those on whom academical honors are bestowed, but at the same time it likes to verify for itself that these honors have been awarded to real merit. If the senior class which is to graduate, be composed of eighty-seven members, as was the case the 20th of July last, at Cambridge, the first half of the class will be called upon to speak, the crowd that fills the church comes prepared to listen to the same number of discourses, excepting, indeed, some few which are omitted by special favor in cases of sickness or unavoiddable absence. These discourses are all written, committed to memory, and recited. The college gown and cap are required to be worn on these occasions, as they are pronounced before the President of the University, and a circle of professors, and other dignitaries.

Source: Rev. Jean Henri Grandpierre, *A Parisian Pastor's Glance at America* (Boston: Gould and Lincoln, 1854), 27–33.

Science: Exploration

The Louisiana Purchase in 1803 opened up a vast unexplored land to Americans. The only people who had any knowledge of this region, which stretched from the Mississippi to the present state of Oregon, were fur trappers and Native American Indians. To find out what lay in this region, two expeditions were sent into the territory to gather as much information as possible on this mysterious land. Not only were the explorers to map out a route for future travelers; they were also to gather as much scientific knowledge as they could find along the way. The first expedition was led by Captains Meriwether Lewis and William

Clark. Their route took them into the northwest, where it was hoped they would find the fabled Northwest Passage. Along the way they noted every feature of terrain they encountered, so that scientists would have a record of what could be found in this new land. The second expedition was led by Lieutenant Zebulon Pike and sought to explore the southern region of the Louisiana Purchase and its borders, including land claimed by Spain. Pike's expedition was beset by difficult conditions, and these are noted in his report on his exploration into the region. Later in the nineteenth century, further explorations were carried out to find an overland route to California. Lieutenant John C. Frémont led several expeditions in an attempt to find the best route to California, and his reports on the plant life, geology, and physical terrain were invaluable to researchers in Washington and prospective settlers and miners.

4. Meriwether Lewis, The Lewis and Clark Expedition (1804)

The Louisiana Purchase increased the size of the United States from the Mississippi River to the present states of Oregon and Washington. The land was a mystery to everyone except the Indian tribes who lived there and individual fur trappers who plied their trade there, and nobody yet knew its expanse or resources. After the acquisition of this vast territory, President Thomas Jefferson assigned his personal secretary, Captain Meriwether Lewis, to lead an expedition into this new land to gather scientific and geographic information for study, to make contact with native peoples and learn about their interests and alliances, and to find the fabled Northwest Passage. Most especially he wanted to collect useful information on the land, climate, natural resources, geography, and people—all with an eye to future trade and settlement. Lewis and his friend Captain William Clark led a group of forty men on a two-year journey that led them to the Pacific Ocean. The information they obtained along the way led to greater study of the territory and a better understanding of all that lived and might be exploited in this new land. The following is an excerpt from Lewis's diary of the expedition as they made their way up the Missouri River in July 1804. The later publication of the maps and some of the reports from the journey encouraged further exploration and later settlement and development. Such expeditions and their maps and reports excited American migration and ambition and also charted the way west for many people.

Wednesday, July 18. The morning was fair, and a gentle wind from southeast by south carried us along between the prairie on the north, and Bald Island to the south: opposite the middle of which, the Nishnahbatona approaches the nearest to the Missouri. The current here ran fifty fathoms at 41". At thirteen and a half miles, we reached an island on the north, near to which the banks overflow; while on the south the hills project over the river and form high cliffs. At one point a part of the cliff, nearly three quarters of a mile in length, and about two hundred feet in height, has fallen into the river. It is composed chiefly of sandstone intermixed with an iron ore of bad quality; near the bottom is a soft slatestone with pebbles. We passed several bad sandbars in the course of the day, and made eighteen miles, and encamped on the south, opposite to the lower point of the Oven islands. The country around is generally divided into prairies, with little timber, except on low points, islands, and near creeks, and that consisting of cottonwood, mulberry, elm, and sycamore.

The river falls fast. An Indian dog came to the bank; he appeared to have been lost and was nearly starved: we gave him some food, but he would not follow us.

Thursday, July 19. The Oven islands are small, and two in number; one near the south shore, the other in the middle of the river. Opposite to them is the prairie, called Terrian's Oven, from a trader of that name. At four and a half miles we reached some high cliffs of a yellow earth, on the south, near which are two beautiful runs of water, rising in the adjacent prairies, and one of them with a deerlick, about two hundred yards from its mouth. In this neighbourhood we observed some iron ore in the bank. At two and a half miles above the runs, a large portion of the hill, for nearly three quarters of a mile, has fallen into the river. We encamped on the western extremity of an island, in the middle of the river, having made ten and three quarter miles. The river falls a little. The sandbars which we passed to-day, and [are] more numerous, and the rolling sands more frequent and dangerous, than any we have seen; these obstacles increasing as we reach the river Platte. The Missouri here is wider also than below, where the timber on the banks resists the current; while here the prairies which approach, are more easily washed and undermined. The hunters have brought for the last few days, no quadruped, but deer: great quantities of young geese are seen today: one of them brought calamus, which he had gathered opposite our encampment, and a large quantity of sweetflag.

Source: Meriwether Lewis, *The Expedition of Lewis and Clark*, vol. I (Ann Arbor: Michigan University Microfilms, Inc., 1966), 28–29.

5. Zebulon Pike on the Dangers of the Early West (1806)

Lieutenant Zebulon Pike is best known today for the mountain that bears his name, Pikes Peak in Colorado, but his explorations into the southern portion of the Louisiana Purchase territory were as important as the explorations of Lewis and Clark. In the early summer of 1806 Pike was given orders to discover the origins of the Mississippi and Arkansas rivers. The terrible conditions faced by Pike and his party of twenty-four men on December 25, 1806, are presented here to show the incredible courage and suffering of the early explorers as they surveyed the new territory of a growing nation.

25th December, Thursday.—It being stormy weather and having meat to dry; I concluded to lie by this day. Here I must take the liberty of observing that in this situation, the hardships and privations we underwent, were on this day brought more fully to our mind. Having been accustomed to some degree of relaxation, and extra enjoyments, but here, 800 miles from the frontiers of our country, in the most inclement season of the year; not one person clothed for the winter, many without blankets, (having been obliged to cut them up for socks, &c.) and now laying down at night on the snow or wet ground; one side burning whilst the other was pierced with the cold wind: this was in part the situation of the party whilst some were endeavoring to make a miserable substitute of raw buffalo hide for shoes &c. I will not speak of diet, as I believe that to be beneath the serious consideration of a man on a voyage of such nature. We spent the day as agreeably as expected from men in our situation. Caught a bird of a new species, having made a trap for him.

26th December, Friday.—Marched at two o'clock and made 7½ miles to the entrance of the mountains. On this piece of prairie the river spread considerably, and formed several small Islands, a large stream enters from the south. As my boy and some others were sick, I omitted pitching our tent in order that they might have it; in consequence of which we were completely covered with snow on top, as well as that part on which we lay.

Source: Zebulon Montgomery Pike, *The Expeditions of Zebulon Montgomery Pike*, vol. 2 (New York: Francis P. Harper, 1895), 473–74.

6. John C. Frémont on the Discoveries of the West (1843)

John C. Frémont is one of the most intriguing figures of the nineteenth century. Known as "The Great Pathfinder," as a lieutenant of topographical engineers Frémont was responsible for exploring and mapping the Oregon Trail and also into the Sierra Nevada. On his expeditions he, like other government-sponsored explorers, recorded temperatures, longitude, and latitude of the areas he encountered and studied the indigenous plant life of the region, sending samples and descriptions to Washington for study. In 1856 he became the first candidate for president of the Republican Party. He served as a general during the Civil War and governor of the Arizona territory from 1878 to 1881. Despite his successes, he died in poverty in 1890, but his legacy as an explorer lives on in his writings. The following excerpt from his report of his expedition along the Oregon Trail in July 1843 gives an idea of the detailed observations Frémont made during his expeditions—typical of such reports of the era.

July 19.—A beautiful and clear morning, with a slight breeze from the northwest; the temperature of air at sunrise being 57.5°. At this time the temperature of the lower spring was 57.8°, and that of the upper 54.3°.

The trees in the neighborhood were birch, willow, pine, and an oak resembling quercus alba. In the shrubbery along the river are currant bushes (*ribe,s*) of which the fruit has a singularly piney flavor; and on the mountain side, in a red gravelly soil, is a remarkable coniferous tree, (perhaps an *abies,*) having the leaves singularly long, broad, and scattered, with bushes of *spiraea ariefolia*. By our observations, this place is 6,350 feet above the sea, in latitude 38° 52′ 10″, and longitude 105° 22′ 45″.

Resuming our journey on this morning, we descended the river, in order to reach the mouth of the eastern fork, which I proposed to ascend. The left bank of the river here is very much broken. There is a handsome little bottom on the right, and both banks are exceedingly picturesque—strata of red rock, in nearly perpendicular walls, crossing the valley from north to south. About three miles below the springs on the right bank of the river, is a nearly perpendicular limestone rock, presenting a uniformly unbroken surface, twenty to forty feet high, containing great numbers of a large univalve shell, which appears to belong to the genus *inoceramus*.

In contact with this, to the westward, was another stratum of limestone, containing fossil shells of a different character; and still higher up on the stream were parallel strata, consisting of a compact somewhat crystalline limestone, and argillaceous bituminous limestone in thin layers. During the morning, we travelled up the eastern fork of the *Fontaine-que-bouit* river, our road being roughened by frequent deep gullies timbered with pine, and halted at noon on a small branch of this stream, timbered principally with the narrow-leaved cottonwood (*populous angustifolia,*) called by the Canadians *liard amére*. On a hill, near by, were two remarkable columns of a grayish-white conglomerate rock, one of which was about twenty feet high, and two feet in diameter. They are surmounted by slabs of a ferrunginous conglomerate, forming black caps, and adding very much to their columnar effect at a distance. This rock is very destructible by the action of the weather, and the hill, of which they formerly constituted a part, is entirely abraded.

Source: John Charles Frémont, *Report of the Exploring Expedition to the Rocky Mountains in the Year 1842 and to Oregon and North California in the Years 1843–44* (Washington, DC: Gales and Seaton, Printers, 1845), 118 [174].

Health and Medicine

The development of medical science in the United States during the late eighteenth and the nineteenth centuries focused on the treatment of various illnesses that affected the human body. The idea that the consumption of alcohol on a daily basis could be considered a disease was seen by many to be the result of a religious zeal for the banning of alcoholic beverages. As we see, however, the study of Dr. Benjamin Rush on this topic was groundbreaking in the diagnosis of alcoholism and would lead to further study in the twentieth century. One of the deadliest diseases that beset Americans in the eighteenth and nineteenth centuries was yellow fever. The lack of knowledge about bacteria and the fact that the mosquito was responsible for spreading yellow fever led to many ideas on how to cure it, many that are seen today as merely wishful thinking. As the pamphlet by Matthew Carey points out, bloodletting was the most common treatment at the time.

The need to develop a proper system of care for the mentally ill had attracted little systematic analysis until the mid-nineteenth century. Most who were afflicted with mental illness were jailed or sent to asylums, where they were often abused and always out of the public consciousness. There was no professional care. As the nineteenth century progressed, many began to decry the fate of those incarcerated in these institutions and called for better care and conditions for the mentally ill. Dorothea Dix, who later became known for care of the wounded in the hospitals during the American Civil War, was a crusader for the rights of the mentally ill, as demonstrated in her letter to the Massachusetts legislature on the subject. She also was an example of women entering public life as reformers, especially in areas such as education and health, which seemed extensions of the "home" and so suitable fields for their interest and advocacy.

7. Matthew Carey on the Scourge of Yellow Fever (1794)

Matthew Carey was born in Ireland, where he became a well-known journalist, but his writings led to his fleeing Ireland for France. There he met Benjamin Franklin and worked in his printing office. Carey returned to Ireland, but emigrated for America when his criticism of the government there led to threats of imprisonment. Carey wrote on political economy and other topics, but early in his stay in America he took on the subject of yellow fever. His criticism of blacks' role in treating many people during the great yellow fever epidemic in Philadelphia in 1793, accusing them of taking advantage of the many people they nursed and buried, led to sharp rebuttals by black leaders in a series of famous pamphlets. In this excerpt from one of Carey's writings, he gives an account of the yellow fever epidemic.

THE symptoms which characterised the first stage of the fever, were, in the greatest number of cases, after a chilly fit of some duration, a quick, tense pulse—hot skin—pain in the head, back and limbs—flushed countenance—inflamed eye—moist tongue—oppression and sense of soreness at the stomach, especially upon pressure—frequent sick qualms, and retchings to vomit, without discharging any thing, except the contents last taken into the stomach—costiveness, etc. And when stools were procured, the first generally showed a defect of bile, or an obstruction to its entrance into the intestines. But brisk purges generally altered this appearance.

These symptoms generally continued with more or less violence from one to three, four, or even five days; and then gradually abating, left the patient free from every complaint, except general debility. On the febrile symptoms suddenly subsiding, they were immediately succeeded by a yellow tinge in the opaque cornea, or whites of the eyes—and increased oppression at the præcordia—a constant puking of every thing taken into the stomach, with much straining, accompanied with a hoarse, hollow noise.

If these symptoms were not soon relieved, a vomiting of matter, resembling coffee grounds in color and consistence, commonly called the black vomit, sometimes accompanied with, or succeeded by haemorrhages from the nose, sauces, gums, and other parts of the body—a yellowish purple colour, and putrescent appearance of the whole body, hiccup, agitations, deep and distressed sighing, comatose delirium, and finally, death. When the disease proved fatal, it was generally between the sixth and eighth days. This was the most usual progress of this formidable disease, through its several stages. There were, however, very considerable variations in the symptoms, as well as in the duration of its different stages, according to the constitution and temperament of the patient, the state of the weather, the manner of treatment, etc.

In some cases, signs of putriscency appeared at the beginning, or before the end of the third day. In these, the black vomiting, which was generally a mortal symptom, and universal yellowness, appeared early. In these cases, also, a low delirium, and great prostration of strength, was constant symptoms, and coma came on very speedily.

In some, the symptoms inclined more to the nervous than the inflammatory type. In these, the jaundice colour of the eye and skin, and the black vomiting, were more rare. But in the majority of cases, particularly after the nights became sensibly cooler, all the symptoms indicated violent irritation and inflammatory diathesis. In these cases, the skin was always dry, and the remissions very obscure.

The febrile symptoms, however, as has been already observed, either gave way on the third, fourth, or sixth day, and then the patient recovered; or they were soon after succeeded by a different, but much more dangerous train of symptoms, by debility, low pulse, cold skin, (which assumed a tawny colour, mixed with purple) black vomiting, haemorrhages, hiccup, anxiety, restlessness, coma, etc. Many, who survived the eighth day, though apparently out of danger, died suddenly in consequence of an haemorrhage.

This disorder having been new to nearly all our physicians, it is not surprising, although it has been exceedingly fatal, that there arose such a discordance of sentiment on the proper mode of treatment, and even with respect to its name. Dr. Rush has acknowledged, with a candour that does him honour, that in the commencement, he so far mistook the nature of the disorder, that in his early essays, having depended on gentle purges of salts to purify the bowels of his patients, they all died. He then tried the mode of treatment adopted in the West Indies, viz. bark, wine, laudanum, and the cold bath, and sailed in three cases out of four. After wards he had recourse to strong purges of calomel and jalap, and to bleeding, which he found attended with singular success.

The honour of the first essay of mercury in this disorder, is by many ascribed to Dr. Hodge and Dr. Carson, who are said to have employed it a week before Dr. Rush. On this point, I cannot pretend to decide. But whoever was the first to introduce it, one thing is certain, that its efficacy was great, and rescued many from death. I have known, however, some persons, who, I have every reason to believe, fell sacrifices to the great reputation this medicine acquired; for in several cases it was administered to persons of a previous lax habit, and brought on a speedy dissolution.

I am credibly informed that the demand for purges of calomel and jalap, was so great, that some of the apothecaries could not mix up every dose in detail; but mixed a large quantity of each, in the ordered proportions; and afterwards divided it into doses; by which means, it often happened that one patient had a much larger portion of calomel, and another of jalap, than was intended by the doctors. The fatal consequences of this may be easily conceived.

An intelligent citizen, who has highly distinguished himself by his attention to the sick, says, that he found the disorder generally come on with costiveness; and unless that was removed within the first twelve hours, he hardly knew any person to recover; on the contrary, he says, as few died, on whom the cathartics operated within that time.

The efficacy of bleeding, in all cases not attended with putridity, was great. The quantity of blood taken was in many cases astonishing. Dr. Griffits was bled seven times in five days, and appears to ascribe his recovery principally to that operation. Dr. Mease, in five days, lost seventy-two ounces of blood, by which he was recovered when at the lowest stage of the disorder. Many others were bled still more, and are now as well as ever they were.

Dr. Rush and Dr. Wistar have spoken very favorably of the salutary effects of cold air, and cool drinks, in this disorder. The latter says, that he found more benefit from cold air, than from any other remedy. He lay delirious, and in severe pain, between a window and door, the former of which was open. The wind suddenly changed, and blew full upon him, cold and raw. Its effects were so grateful, that he soon recovered from his delirium—his pain left him—in an hour he became perfectly reasonable—and his fever abated.

Source: Matthew Carey, *A Short Account of the Malignant Fever Lately Present in Philadelphia: With a Statement of the Proceedings That Took Place on the Subject, in Different Parts of the United States—to Which Are Added,*

Accounts of the Plague in London and Marseilles; and a List of the Dead, From August 1, to the middle of December 1793, 4th ed., improved (Philadelphia: Printed by the Author, January 15, 1794), 13–16.

8. Benjamin Rush on the Effects of Alcoholism (1805)

Benjamin Rush was the best-known physician of the Revolutionary period and one of America's Founding Fathers. He also was a humanitarian, educator, and writer, as well as the founder of Dickinson College in Carlisle, Pennsylvania. In 1805 he published a pamphlet on how alcohol had an effect on the physical and mental health of people. He was the first to diagnose what we now know as the disease of alcoholism. He was also considered to be the father of the American temperance movement.

The effects of ardent sprits divide themselves into such as are of a prompt, such as of are of a chronic nature. The former discover themselves in drunkenness; the latter in a numerous train of diseases and vices of the body and mind.

I. I shall begin by briefly describing their prompt, or immediate effects, in a fit of drunkenness.

This odious disease (for by that name it should be called) appears with more or less of the following symptoms, and most commonly in the order in which I shall enumerate them.

1. Unusual garrulity.
2. Unusual silence.
3. Captiousness, and a disposition to quarrel.
4. Uncommon good humour, and an insipid simpering, or laugh.
5. Profane swearing, and cursing.
6. A disclosure of their own, or other people's secrets.
7. A rude disposition to tell those persons in company whom they know, their faults.
8. Certain immodest actions. I am sorry to say, this sign of the first stage of drunkenness, sometimes appears in women, who, when sober, are uniformly remarkable for chaste and decent manners.
9. A clipping of words.
10. Fighting; a black eye, or a swelled nose, often mark this grade of drunkenness.
11. Certain extravagant acts which indicate a temporary fit of madness. These are singing, hallooing, roaring, imitating the noises of brute animals, jumping, tearing off clothes, dancing naked, breaking glasses and china, and dashing other articles of household furniture upon the ground, or floor. After a while the paroxysm of drunkenness is completely formed. The face now becomes flushed, the eyes project and are somewhat watery, winking is less frequent than is natural; the upper lip is protruded;—the head inclines a little to one shoulder;—the jaw falls;—belchings, and hiccup take place;—the limbs totter;—the whole body staggers;—The unfortunate subject of this history next falls on his seat,—he looks around him with a vacant countenance, and mutters inarticulate sounds to himself;—he attempts to rise and walk. In this attempt he falls upon his side, from which he gradually turns upon his back. He now closes his eyes, and falls into a profound sleep, frequently attended by snoring, and profuse sweats, and

sometimes with such a relaxation of the muscles which confine the bladder and the lower bowels, as to produce a symptom which delicacy forbids me to mention. In this condition, he often lies from ten, twelve, and twenty-four hours, to two, three, or four, and five days, an object of pity and disgust to his family and friends. . . .

II. Let us next attend to the chronic effects of ardent spirits upon the body and mind. In the body, they dispose to every form of acute disease; they moreover *excite* fevers in persons predisposed to them, from other causes. This has been remarked in all the yellow fevers which have visited the cities of the United States. Hard drinkers seldom escape, and rarely recover from them. The following diseases are the usual consequences of the habitual use of ardent spirits, viz.

1. A decay of appetite, sickness at stomach, and a puking of bile or a discharge of a frothy and viscid phlegm by hawking, in the morning.
2. Obstructions of the liver . . .
3. Jaundice and dropsy of the belly and limbs, and finally of every cavity of the body . . .
4. Hoarseness, and a husky cough . . .
5. Diabetes . . .
6. Redness, and eruptions on various parts of the body . . .
7. A fetid breath, composed of every thing, that is offensive in putrid animal manner.
8. Frequent and disgusting belching. Dr. Haller relates the case of a notorious drunkard having been suddenly destroyed in consequence of the vapour discharged from his stomach by belching, accidentally taking fire by coming in contact with the flame of a candle.
9. Epilepsy.
10. Gout, in all its various forms of swelled limbs, colic, palsy, and apoplexy.
11. Lastly, Madness.

Source: Benjamin Rush, *An Inquiry into the Effects of Ardent Spirits Upon the Human Body and Mind* (Philadelphia: Archibald Bartram, 1805).

9. Dorothea Dix, A Call to Help the Mentally Ill (1843)

Dorothea Dix was a schoolteacher at a Boston girls school when she accidentally stumbled upon the conditions that the mentally ill lived under in Boston in 1841. For the next two years she carried out an investigation of the conditions of the jails and insane asylums in Massachusetts. In 1843 she sent a description of these to the legislature and lobbied for improvements. Her efforts led Massachusetts to enact laws to end the horrid conditions suffered by the mentally ill. Dix spent the next fifty years fighting for better conditions in hospitals and jails not only in the United States, but in Western Europe as well.

Gentlemen,—I respectfully ask to present this Memorial, believing that the cause, which actuates to and sanctions so unusual a movement, presents no equivocal claim to public consideration and sympathy. . . .

About two years since leisure afforded opportunity and duty prompted me to visit several prisons and almshouses in the vicinity of this metropolis. I found, near Boston, in the jails and asylums for the poor, a numerous class brought into unsuitable connection with criminals and the general mass of paupers. I refer to idiots and insane persons, dwelling in circumstances not only adverse to their own physical and moral improvement, but productive of extreme disadvantages to all other persons brought into association with them. I applied myself diligently to trace the causes of these evils, and sought to supply remedies. As one obstacle was surmounted, fresh difficulties appeared. Every new investigation has given depth to the conviction that it is only by decided, prompt, and vigorous legislation the evils to which I refer, and which I shall proceed more fully to illustrate, can be remedied. I shall be obliged to speak with great plainness, and to reveal many things revolting to the taste, and from which my woman's nature shrinks with peculiar sensitiveness. But truth is the highest consideration. I tell what I have seen—painful and shocking as the details often are—that from them you may feel more deeply the imperative obligation which lies upon you to prevent the possibility of a repetition or continuance of such outrages upon humanity. . . .

I come to present the strong claims of suffering humanity. I come to place before the Legislature of Massachusetts the condition of the miserable, the desolate, the outcast. I come as the advocate of helpless, forgotten, insane, and idiotic men and women; of beings sunk to a condition from which the most unconcerned would start with real horror; of beings wretched in our prisons, and more wretched in our almshouses. . . .

I must confine myself to few examples, but am ready to furnish other and more complete details, if required.

If my pictures are displeasing, coarse, and severe, my subjects, it must be recollected, offer no tranquil, refined, or composing features. The condition of human beings, reduced to the extremest states of degradation and misery cannot be exhibited in softened language, or adorn a polished page.

I proceed, gentlemen, briefly to call your attention to the present state of insane persons confined within this Commonwealth, in cages, closets, cellars, stalls, pens! Chained, naked, beaten with rods, and lashed into obedience. . . .

It is the Commonwealth, not its integral parts, that is accountable for most of the abuses which have lately and do still exist. I repeat it, it is defective legislation which perpetuates and multiplies these abuses. In illustration of my subject, I offer the following extracts from my Note-book and Journal:—

Springfield. In the jail, one lunatic woman, furiously mad, a State pauper, improperly situated, both in regard to the prisoners, the keepers, and herself. It is a case of extreme self-forgetfulness and oblivion to all the decencies of life, to describe which would be to repeat only the grossest scenes. She is much worse since leaving Worcester. In the almshouse of the same town is a woman apparently only needing judicious care, and some well-chosen employment, to make it unnecessary to confine her in solitude, in a dreary unfurnished room. Her appeals for employment and companionship are most touching, but the mistress replied she had no time to attend to her. . . .

Lincoln. A woman in a cage. Medford. One idiotic subject chained, and one in a close stall for seventeen years.

Pepperell. One often doubly chained, hand and foot; another violent; several peaceable now.

Brookfield. One man caged, comfortable.

Granville. One often closely confined; now losing the use of his limbs from want of exercise.

Charlemont. One man caged.

Savoy. One man caged.

Lenox. Two in the jail, against whose unfit condition there the jailer protests.

Dedham. The insane disadvantageously placed in the jail. In the almshouse, two females in stalls, situated in the main building; lie in wooden bunks filled with straw; always shut up. One of these subjects is supposed curable. The overseers of the poor have declined giving her a trial at the hospital, as I was informed, on account of expense. . . .

Besides the above, I have seen many who, part of the year, are chained or caged. The use of cages all but universal. Hardly a town but can refer to some not distant period of using them; chains are less common; negligences frequent; wilful abuse less frequent than sufferings proceeding from ignorance, or want of consideration. I encountered during the last three months many poor creatures wandering reckless and unprotected through the country. . . . But I cannot particularize. In traversing the State, I have found hundreds of insane persons in every variety of circumstance and condition, many whose situation could not and need not be improved; a less number, but that very large, whose lives are the saddest pictures of human suffering and degradation.

I give a few illustrations; but description fades before reality.

Danvers. November. Visited the almshouse. A large building, much out of repair. Understand a new one is in contemplation. Here are from fifty-six to sixty inmates, one idiotic, three insane; one of the latter in close confinement at all times.

Long before reaching the house, wild shouts, snatches of rude songs, imprecations and obscene language, fell upon the ear, proceeding from the occupant of a low building, rather remote from the principal building to which my course was directed. Found the mistress, and was conducted to the place which was called the home of the forlorn maniac, a young woman, exhibiting a condition of neglect and misery blotting out the faintest idea of comfort, and outraging every sentiment of decency. She had been, I learnt, a respectable person, industrious and worthy. Disappointments and trials shook her mind, and, finally, laid prostrate reason and self-control. She became a maniac for life. She had been at Worcester Hospital for a considerable time, and had been returned as incurable. The mistress told me she understood that, while there, she was comfortable and decent. Alas, what a change was here exhibited! She had passed from one degree of violence to another, in swift progress. There she stood, clinging to or beating upon the bars of her caged apartment, the contracted size of which afforded space only for increasing accumulations of filth, a foul spectacle.

There she stood with naked arms and dishevelled hair, the unwashed frame invested with fragments of unclean garments, the air so extremely offensive, though ventilation was afforded on all sides save one, that it was not possible to remain beyond a few moments without retreating for recovery to the outward air. Irritation of body, produced by utter filth and exposure, incited her to the horrid process of tearing off her skin by inches. Her face, neck, and person were thus disfigured to hideousness. She held up a fragment just rent off. To my exclamation of horror, the mistress replied: Oh, we can't help it. Half the skin is off sometimes. We can do nothing with her; and it makes no difference what she eats, for she consumes her own filth as readily as the food which is brought her.

Men of Massachusetts, I beg, I implore, I demand pity and protection for these of my suffering, outraged sex. Fathers, husbands, brothers, I would supplicate you for this boon; but what do I say? I dishonor you, divest you at once of Christianity and humanity, does this appeal imply distrust. If it comes burdened with a doubt of your righteousness in this legislation, then blot it out; while I declare confidence in your honor, not less than your humanity. Here you will put away the cold, calculating spirit of selfishness and self-seeking; lay off the armor of local strife and political opposition; here and now, for once, forgetful of the earthly and perishable, come up to these halls and consecrate them with one heart and one mind to works of righteousness and just judgment.

Become the benefactors of your race, the just guardians of the solemn rights you hold in trust. Raise up the fallen, succor the desolate, restore the outcast, defend the helpless, and for your eternal and great reward receive the benediction, Well done, good and faithful servants, become rulers over many things!

Injustice is also done to the convicts: it is certainly very wrong that they should be doomed day after day and night after night to listen to the ravings of madmen and madwomen. This is a kind of punishment that is not recognized by our statutes, and is what the criminal ought not to be called upon to undergo. The confinement of the criminal and of the insane in the same building is subversive of that good order and discipline which should be observed in every well-regulated prison. I do most sincerely hope that more permanent provision will be made for the pauper insane by the State, either to restore Worcester Insane Asylum to what it was originally designed to be or else make some just appropriation for the benefit of this very unfortunate class of our fellow-beings.

Gentlemen, I commit to you this sacred cause. Your action upon this subject will affect the present and future condition of hundreds and of thousands. In this legislation, as in all things, may you exercise that wisdom which is the breath of the power of God.

Respectfully Submitted, D. L. Dix

Source: Dorothea Dix, "Memorial on the Condition of the Insane in Massachusetts, 1843," in *Old South Leaflets*, no. 148 (Boston, n.d.).

Language and Literature

The language of Americans reflected its predominantly English roots. The literature that was consumed by Americans in much of the eighteenth century was a mix of classics and more popular English fare, from political tracts to satires and even the new literary form, the novel. Religious literature remained the dominant form. By the mid-nineteenth century Americans began to develop their own literary voice, which marked a break with the past. Local color stories, "tall tales," and stories and novels exploring American themes, settings, and people gained currency. That this would happen was foreseen by the Frenchman Alexis de Tocqueville during his tour of the United States in 1831 and 1832; in the first document below he writes of how Americans had not developed their own style of literature, but that the nature of democracy would eventually lead them in that direction. That this style began to emerge in the decade after de Tocqueville's visit is seen in the three works that follow. The first appeared in the second issue of *The American Whig Review* in 1845 and was written under the pseudonym Quarles, known to all Americans as Edgar Allan Poe. The second work is an excerpt from Harriet Beecher Stowe's *Uncle Tom's Cabin*, which details the experiences of plantation life. The third example is an excerpt from Henry David Thoreau's *Walden*, which has become a clarion call to those who look to escape the frenetic pace of everyday life.

10. *Alexis de Tocqueville on Literary Characteristics of Democratic Ages (1841)*

Alexis de Tocqueville was a French nobleman who was fascinated with democracy. In his position as a magistrate, he made a trip to America for the ostensible purpose of studying the prison system in the United States. On his return to France, he did publish a report on the prisons in America, but he also published a four-volume work on American democracy. In the following section he discusses the eventual emergence of a distinctly American literary style.

When a traveller goes into a bookseller's shop in the United States, and examines the American books upon the shelves, the number of works appears extremely great; whilst that of known authors appears, on the contrary, to be extremely small. He will first meet with a number of elementary treatises, destined to teach the rudiments of human knowledge. Most of these books are written in Europe; the Americans reprint them, adapting them to their own country. Next comes an enormous quantity of religious works, Bibles, sermons, edifying anecdotes, controversial divinity, and reports of charitable societies; lastly, appears the long catalogue of political pamphlets. In America, parties do not write books to combat each others' opinions, but pamphlets which are circulated for a day with incredible rapidity, and then expire. In the midst of all these obscure productions of the human brain are to be found the more remarkable works of that small number of authors, whose names are, or ought to be, known to Europeans.

Although America is perhaps in our days the civilized country in which literature is least attended to, a large number of persons are nevertheless to be found there who take an interest in the productions of the mind, and who make them, if not the study of their lives, at least the charm of their leisure hours. But England supplies these readers with the larger portion of the books which they require. Almost all important English books are republished in the United States. The literary genius of Great Britain still darts its rays into the recesses of the forests of the New World. There is hardly a pioneer's hut which does not contain a few odd volumes of Shakespeare. I remember that I read the feudal play of Henry V for the first time in a loghouse.

Not only do the Americans constantly draw upon the treasures of English literature, but it may be said with truth that they find the literature of England growing on their own soil. The larger part of that small number of men in the United States who are engaged in the composition of literary works are English in substance, and still more so in form. Thus they transport into the midst of democracy the ideas and literary fashions which are current amongst the aristocratic nation they have taken for their model. They paint with colors borrowed from foreign manners; and as they hardly ever represent the country they were born in as it really is, they are seldom popular there. The citizens of the United States are themselves so convinced that it is not for them that books are published, that before they can make up their minds upon the merit of one of their authors, they generally wait till his fame has been ratified in England, just as in pictures the author of an original is held to be entitled to judge of the merit of a copy. The inhabitants of the United States have then at present, properly speaking, no literature. The only authors whom I acknowledge as American are the journalists. They indeed are not great writers, but they speak the language of their countrymen, and make themselves heard by them. Other authors are aliens; they are to the Americans what the imitators of the Greeks and Romans were to us at the revival of learning—an object of curiosity, not of general sympathy. They amuse the mind, but they do not act upon the manners of the people.

I have already said that this state of things is very far from originating in democracy alone, and that the causes of it must be sought for in several peculiar circumstances independent of the democratic principle. If the Americans, retaining the same laws and social condition, had had a different origin, and had been transported into another country, I do not question that they would have had a literature. Even as they now are, I am convinced that they will ultimately have one; but its character will be different from that which marks the American literary productions of our time, and that character will be peculiarly its own. Nor is it impossible to trace this character beforehand.

I suppose an aristocratic people amongst whom letters are cultivated; the labors of the mind, as well as the affairs of state, are conducted by a ruling class in society. The literary as well as the political career is almost entirely confined to this class, or to those nearest to it in rank. These premises suffice to give me a key to all the rest. When a small number of the same men are engaged at the same time upon the same objects, they easily concert with one another, and agree upon certain leading rules which are to govern them each and all. If the object which attracts the attention of these men is literature, the productions of the mind will soon be subjected by them to precise canons, from which it will no longer be allowable to depart. If these men occupy a hereditary position in the country, they will be naturally inclined, not only to adopt a certain number of fixed rules for themselves, but to follow those which their forefathers laid down for their own guidance; their code will be at once strict and traditional. As they are not necessarily engrossed by the cares of daily life—as they have never been so, any more than their fathers were before them—they have learned to take an interest, for several generations back, in the labors of the mind. They have learned to understand literature as an art, to love it in the end for its own sake, and to feel a scholar-like satisfaction in seeing men conform to its rules. Nor is this all: the men of whom I speak began and will end their lives in easy or in affluent circumstances; hence they have naturally conceived a taste for choice gratifications, and a love of refined and delicate pleasures. Nay more, a kind of indolence of mind and heart, which they frequently contract in the midst of this long and peaceful enjoyment of so much welfare, leads them to put aside, even from their pleasures, whatever might be too startling or too acute. They had rather be amused than intensely excited; they wish to be interested, but not to be carried away.

Now let us fancy a great number of literary performances executed by the men, or for the men, whom I have just described, and we shall readily conceive a style of literature in which everything will be regular and prearranged. The slightest work will be carefully touched in its least details; art and labor will be conspicuous in everything; each kind of writing will have rules of its own, from which it will not be allowed to swerve, and which distinguish it from all others. Style will be thought of almost as much importance as thought; and the form will be no less considered than the matter: the diction will be polished, measured, and uniform. The tone of the mind will be always dignified, seldom very animated; and writers will care more to perfect what they produce than to multiply their productions. It will sometimes happen that the members of the literary class, always living amongst themselves and writing for themselves alone, will lose sight of the rest of the world, which will infect them with a false and labored style; they will lay down minute literary rules for their exclusive use, which will insensibly lead them to deviate from common-sense, and finally to transgress the bounds of nature. By dint of striving after a mode of parlance different from the vulgar, they will arrive at a sort of aristocratic jargon, which is hardly less remote from pure language than is the coarse dialect of the people. Such are the natural perils of literature amongst aristocracies. Every aristocracy which keeps itself entirely aloof from the people becomes impotent—a fact which is as true in literature as it is in politics.

Let us now turn the picture and consider the other side of it; let us transport ourselves into the midst of a democracy, not unprepared by ancient traditions and present culture to partake in the pleasures of the mind. Ranks are there intermingled and confounded; knowledge and power are both infinitely subdivided, and, if I may use the expression, scattered on every side. Here then is a motley multitude, whose intellectual wants are to be supplied. These new votaries of the pleasures of the mind have not all received the same education; they do not possess the same degree of culture as their fathers, nor any resemblance to them—nay, they perpetually differ from themselves, for they live in a state of incessant change of place, feelings, and fortunes. The mind of each member of the community is therefore unattached to that of his fellow-citizens by tradition or by common habits; and they have never had the power, the inclination, nor the time to concert together. It is, however, from the bosom of this heterogeneous and agitated mass that authors spring; and from the same source their profits and their fame are distributed. I can without difficulty understand that, under these circumstances, I must expect to meet in the literature of such a people with but few of those strict conventional rules which are admitted by readers and by writers in aristocratic ages. If it should happen that the men of some one period were agreed upon any such rules, that would prove nothing for the following period; for amongst democratic nations each new generation is a new people. Amongst such nations, then, literature will not easily be subjected to strict rules, and it is impossible that any such rules should ever be permanent.

In democracies it is by no means the case that all the men who cultivate literature have received a literary education; and most of those who have some tinge of belles-lettres are either engaged in politics, or in a profession which only allows them to taste occasionally and by stealth the pleasures of the mind. These pleasures, therefore, do not constitute the principal charm of their lives; but they are considered as a transient and necessary recreation amidst the serious labors of life. Such man [sic] can never acquire a sufficiently intimate knowledge of the art of literature to appreciate its more delicate beauties; and the minor shades of expression must escape them. As the time they can devote to letters is very short, they seek to make the best use of the whole of it. They prefer books which may be easily procured, quickly read, and which require no learned researches to be understood. They ask for beauties, self-proffered and easily enjoyed; above all, they must have what is unexpected and new. Accustomed to the struggle, the crosses, and the monotony of practical life, they require rapid emotions, startling passages—truths or errors brilliant enough to rouse them up, and to plunge them at once, as if by violence, into the midst of a subject.

Why should I say more? or who does not understand what is about to follow, before I have expressed it? Taken as a whole, literature in democratic ages can never present, as it does in the periods of aristocracy, an aspect of order, regularity, science, and art; its form will, on the contrary, ordinarily be slighted, sometimes despised. Style will frequently be fantastic, incorrect, overburdened, and loose—almost always vehement and bold. Authors will aim at rapidity of execution, more than at perfection of detail. Small productions will be more common than bulky books; there will be more wit than erudition, more imagination than profundity; and literary performances will bear marks of an untutored and rude vigor of thought—frequently of great variety and singular fecundity. The object of authors will be to astonish rather than to please, and to stir the passions more than to charm the taste. Here and there, indeed, writers will doubtless occur who will choose a different track, and who will, if they are gifted with superior abilities, succeed in finding readers, in spite of their defects or their better qualities; but these exceptions will be rare, and even the authors who shall so depart from the received practice in the main subject of their works, will always relapse into it in some lesser details.

I have just depicted two extreme conditions: the transition by which a nation passes from the former to the latter is not sudden but gradual, and marked with shades of very various intensity. In the passage which conducts a lettered people from the one to the other, there is almost always a moment at which the literary genius of democratic nations has its confluence with that of aristocracies, and both seek to establish their joint sway over the human mind. Such epochs are transient, but very brilliant: they are fertile without exuberance, and animated without confusion. The French literature of the eighteenth century may serve as an example.

I should say more than I mean if I were to assert that the literature of a nation is always subordinate to its social condition and its political constitution. I am aware that, independently of these causes, there are several others which confer certain characteristics on literary productions; but these appear to me to be the chief. The relations which exist between the social and political condition of a people and the genius of its authors are always very numerous: whoever knows the one is never completely ignorant of the other.

Source: Alexis de Tocqueville, *Democracy in America*, vol. 2, trans. Henry Reeve (New York: J. and H. G. Langley, 1841).

11. *Edgar Allan Poe, "The Raven" (1845)*

This poem is one of the most famous in American history. Written by Edgar Allan Poe under the pseudonym Quarles, it was bought for $9 by The American Whig Review. *It became a sensation and led to Poe's success as a writer, although it did not translate into monetary success.*

The following lines from a correspondent besides the deep quaint strain of the sentiment, and the curious introduction of some ludicrous touches amidst the serious and impressive, as was doubtless intended by the author appear to us one of the most felicitous specimens of unique rhyming which has for some time met our eye. The resources of English rhythm for varieties of melody, measure, and sound, producing corresponding diversities of effect, have been thoroughly studied, much more perceived, by very few poets in the language. While the classic tongues, especially the Greek, possess, by power of accent, several advantages for versification over our own, chiefly through greater abundance of spondaic feet, we have other and very great advantages of sound by the modern usage of rhyme. Alliteration is nearly the only effect of that kind which the ancients had in common with us. It will be seen that much of the melody of The Raven arises from alliteration, and the studious use of similar sounds in unusual places. In regard to its measure, it may be noted that if all the verses were like the second, they might properly be placed merely in short lines, producing a not uncommon form; but the presence in all the others of one line mostly the second in the verse which flows continuously, with only an aspirate pause in the middle, like that before the short line in the Sapphic Adonic, while the fifth has at the middle pause no similarity of sound with any part beside, gives the versification an entirely different effect. We could wish the capacities of our noble language, in prosody, were better understood—ED. AM. Ray.

Once upon a midnight dreary, while I pondered, weak and weary,
Over many a quaint and curious volume of forgotten lore,
While 1 nodded, nearly napping, suddenly there came a tapping,
As of some one gently rapping, rapping at my chamber door.
'Tis some visitor, I muttered, tapping at my chamber door
Only this, and nothing more.

Ah, distinctly I remember it was in the bleak December,
And each separate dying ember wrought its ghost upon the floor.
Eagerly I wished the morrow; vainly I had tried to borrow
From my books surcease of sorrow—sorrow for the lost Lenore
For the rare and radiant maiden whom the angels name Lenore
Nameless here for evermore.

And the silken sad uncertain rustling of each purple curtain
Thrilled me filled me with fantastic terrors never felt before;
So that now, to still the beating of my heart, I stood repeating
'Tis some visitor entreating entrance at my chamber door
Some late visitor entreating entrance at my chamber door;
This it is, and nothing more.

Presently my soul grew stronger; hesitating then no longer,
Sir, said I, or Madam, truly your forgiveness I implore;

But the fact is I was napping, and so gently you came rapping,
And so faintly you came tapping, tapping at my chamber door,
That I scarce was sure I heard you here I opened wide the door
Darkness there, and nothing more.

Deep into that darkness peering, long I stood there wondering, fearing,
Doubting, dreaming dreams no mortal ever dared to dream before;
But the silence was unbroken, and the darkness gave no token,
And the only word there spoken was the whispered word, Lenore!
This I whispered, and an echo murmured back the word, Lenore!
Merely this, and nothing more.

Then into the chamber turning, all my soul within me burning,
Soon I heard again a tapping somewhat louder than before.
Surely, said I, surely that is something at my window lattice;
Let me see, then, what thereat is, and this mystery explore
Let my heart be still a moment and this mystery explore;
'Tis the wind, and nothing more!

Open here I flung the shutter, when, with many a flirt and flutter,
In there stepped a stately raven of the saintly days of yore;
Not the least obeisance made he; not an instant stopped or stayed he;
But, with mien of lord or lady, perched above my chamber door
Perched upon a bust of Pallas just above my chamber door
Perched, and sat, and nothing more.

Then this ebony bird beguiling my sad fancy into smiling,
By the grave and stern decorum of the countenance it wore,
Though thy crest be shorn and shaven, thou, I said, art sure no craven,
Ghastly grim and ancient raven wandering from the Nightly shore
Tell me what thy lordly name is on the Night's Plutonian shore
Quoth the raven, Nevermore.

Much I marvelled this ungainly fowl to hear discourse so plainly,
Though its answer little meaning little relevancy bore;
For we cannot help agreeing that no sublunary being
Ever yet was blessed with seeing bird above his chamber door
Bird or beast upon the sculptured bust above his chamber door,
With such name as Nevermore.

But the raven, sitting lonely on the placid but, spoke only
That one word, as if his soul in that one word he did outpour.
Nothing farther then he uttered not a feather then he fluttered
Till I scarcely more than muttered, Other friends have flown before
On the morrow he will leave me, as my hopes have flown before.
Quoth the raven, Nevermore.

Wondering at the stillness broken by reply so aptly spoken,
Doubtless, said I, what it utters is its only stock and store,
Caught from some unhappy master whom unmerciful Disaster
Followed fast and followed fasterso, when Hope he would adjure,
Stern Despair returned, instead of the sweet Hope he dared adjure
That sad answer, Nevermore!

But the raven still beguiling all my sad soul into smiling,
Straight I wheeled a cushioned seat in front of bird, and bust, and door;
Then upon the velvet sinking, I betook myself to linking
Fancy unto fancy, thinking what this ominous bird of yore
What this grim, ungainly, ghastly, gaunt, and ominous bird of yore
Meant in croaking Nevermore.

This I sat engaged in guessing, but no syllable expressing
To the fowl whose fiery eyes now burned into my bosoms core;
This and more I sat divining, with my head at ease reclining
On the cushions velvet lining that the lamplight gloated oer,
But whose velvet violet lining with the lamplight gloating oer,
She shall press, ah, nevermore!

Then, me thought, the air grew denser, perfumed from an unseen censer
Swung by angels whose faint foot-falls tinkled on the tufted floor.
Wretch, I cried, thy God hath lent thereby these angels he hath sent thee
Respite respite and Nepenthe from thy memories of Lenore!
Let me quaff this kind Nepenthe and forget this lost Lenore!
Quoth the raven, Nevermore.

Prophet! said I, thing of evil! prophet still, if bird or devil
Whether Tempter sent, or whether tempest tossed thee here ashore,
Desolate, yet all undaunted, on this desert land enchanted
On this home by Horror haunted tell me truly, I implore
Is there is there balm in Gilead? tell me tell me, I implore!
Quoth the raven, Nevermore.

Prophet! said I, thing—of evil!—prophet still, if bird or devil!
By that Heaven that bends above us by that God we both adore
Tell this soul with sorrow laden if, within the distant Aidenn,
It shall clasp a sainted maiden whom the angels name Lenore
Clasp a rare and radiant maiden whom the angels name Lenore.
Quoth the raven, Nevermore.

Be that word our sign of parting, bird or fiend! I shrieked, up starting
Get thee back into the tempest and the Nights Plutonian shore!
Leave no black plume as a token of that lie thy soul hath spoken!
Leave my loneliness unbroken! quit the bust above my door!
Take thy beak from out my heart, and take thy form from off my door!
Quoth the raven, Nevermore.

And the raven, never flitting, still is sitting, still is sitting
On the pallid bust of Pallas just above my chamber door;
And his eyes have all the seeming of a demon that is dreaming,
And the lamp-light o'er him streaming throws his shadow on the floor;
And my soul from out that shadow that lies floating on the floor
Shall be lifted nevermore!

Source: "The Raven," *The American Whig Review* 1, no. 2 (February 1845): 143–46.

12. *Harriet Beecher Stowe,* Uncle Tom's Cabin *(1852)*

The first book by an American author to have as its hero an African American, Uncle Tom's Cabin *was published serially in the* National Era, *an antislavery paper in Washington, D.C., in 1851 and 1852 and in book form later in 1852. By turns sentimental and realistic, the novel appealed strongly to nineteenth-century readers. Because the book presented the horrors of slavery in vivid human terms, it had a powerful impact. It demanded that readers consider the sin of slavery and make moral choices about their own complicity in it. While fueling antislavery sentiment in the North,* Uncle Tom's Cabin *infuriated Southerners, who charged that author Harriet Beecher Stowe knew nothing about plantation life and grossly misrepresented it. In response to her critics, Stowe published* A Key to Uncle Tom *(1853), a nonfiction work containing documentary evidence that supported her indictment of slavery in the novel. Though no one expected* Uncle Tom's Cabin *to be popular or successful, more than 300,000 copies were sold within the first year. The book was several times adapted for the stage and was ultimately translated into fifty-five languages.*

"And now," said Legree, "come here, you Tom. You see, I telled ye I didn't buy ye jest for the common work. I mean to promote ye, and make a driver of ye; and tonight ye may jest as well begin to get ye hand in. Now, ye jest take this yer gal and flog her; ye've seen enough on't to know how." "I beg Mas'r' pardon," said Tom; "hopes Mas'r won't set me at that. It's what I an't used to—never did—and can't do, no way possible."

"Ye'll larn a pretty smart chance of things ye never did know, before I've done with ye!" said Legree, taking up a cowhide and striking Tom a heavy blow across the cheek, and following up the infliction by a shower of blows.

"There!" he said, as he stopped to rest; "now, will ye tell me ye can't do it?"

"Yes, Mas'r," said Tom, putting up his hand, to wipe the blood that trickled down his face. "I'm willin' to work, night and day, and work while there's life and breath in me. But this yer thing I can't feel it right to do; and, Mas'r, I never shall do it—never!"

Tom had a remarkably smooth, soft voice, and a habitually respectful manner that had given Legree an idea that he would be cowardly and easily subdued. When he spoke these last words, a thrill of amazement went through everyone. The poor woman clasped her hands and said, "O Lord!" and everyone involuntarily looked at each other and drew in their breath, as if to prepare for the storm that was about to burst.

Legree looked stupefied and confounded; but at last burst forth: "What! Ye blasted black beast! Tell me ye don't think it right to do what I tell ye! What have any of you cussed cattle to do with thinking what's right? I'll put a stop to it! Why, what do ye think ye are? May be ye think ye're a gentleman, master Tom, to be a telling your master what's right, and what an't! So you pretend it's wrong to flog the gal!"

"I think so, Mas'r," said Tom; "the poor crittur's sick and feeble; 'twould be downright cruel, and it's what I never will do, nor begin to. Mas'r, if you mean to kill me, kill me; but, as to my raising my hand again any one here, I never shall—I'll die first!"

Tom spoke in a mild voice, but with a decision that could not be mistaken. Legree shook with anger; his greenish eyes glared fiercely, and his very whiskers seemed to curl with passion. But, like some ferocious beast, that plays with its victim before he devours it, he kept back his strong impulse to proceed to immediate violence, and broke out into bitterly raillery.

"Well, here's a pious dog, at last, let down among us sinners—a saint, a gentleman, and no less, to talk to us sinners about our sins! Powerful holy crittur, he must be! Here, you rascal, you make believe to be so pious—didn't you never hear, out of yer Bible, 'Servants, obey yer masters'? An't I yer master? Didn't I pay down twelve hundred dollars, cash, for all there is inside yer old cussed black shell? An't yer mine, now, body and soul?" he said, giving Tom a violent kick with his heavy boot; "tell me!"

In the very depth of physical suffering, bowed by brutal oppression, this question shot a gleam of joy and triumph through Tom's soul. He suddenly stretched himself up, and, looking earnestly to heaven, while the tears and blood that flowed down his face mingled, he exclaimed, "No! no! no! my soul an't yours, Mas'r! You haven't bought it—ye can't buy it! It's been bought and paid for by One that is able to keep it. No matter, no matter, you can't harm me!"

"I can't!" said Legree, with a sneer; "we'll see—we'll see! Here Sambo, Quimbo, give this dog such a breakin' in as he won't get over this month!"

The two gigantic Negroes that now laid hold of Tom, with fiendish exultation in their faces, might have formed no unapt personification of powers of darkness. The poor woman screamed with apprehension, and all rose, as by a general impulse, while they dragged him unresisting from the place.

Source: Harriet Beecher Stowe, *Uncle Tom's Cabin; Or, Life among the Lowly* (Boston: John P. Jewett & Company, 1852), 61–64.

13. *Henry David Thoreau,* Walden *(1854)*

Walden *was written by Henry David Thoreau while he was spending time in a cabin he had built on the land of his friend Ralph Waldo Emerson near Concord, Massachusetts. He saw his time there as an experiment in simple living and thus finding life; it was an opportunity to escape the mad race of modern living for the sublime of nature. After two years Thoreau emerged and began to work on a novel about his experience. After ten years of working and reworking his work, he published* Walden *in 1854, to favorable reviews but almost no sales. Future readers discovered it, and a century after its publication it became an American classic, especially for those wanting to find solitude and meaning in and with nature.*

The mass of men lead lives of quiet desperation. What is called resignation is confirmed desperation. From the desperate city you go into the desperate country, and have to console yourself with the bravery of minks and muskrats. A stereotyped but unconscious despair is concealed even under what are called the games and amusements of mankind. There is no play in them, for this comes after work. But it is a characteristic of wisdom not to do desperate things.

The greater part of what my neighbors call good I believe in my soul to be bad, and if I repent of anything, it is very likely to be my good behavior. What demon possessed me that I behaved so well? You may say the wisest thing you can, old man—you who have lived seventy years, not without honor of a kind—I hear an irresistible voice which invites me away from all that. One generation abandons the enterprises of another like stranded vessels.

I think that we may safely trust a good deal more than we do. We may waive just so much care of ourselves as we honestly bestow elsewhere. Nature is as well adapted to our weakness as to our strength. . . . Let us consider for a moment what most of the trouble and anxiety which I have referred to is about, and how much it is necessary that we be troubled, or at least careful. It would be some advantage to live a primitive and frontier life, though in the midst of an outward civilization, if only to learn what are the gross necessaries of life and what methods have been taken to obtain them; or even to look over the old day-books of the merchants, to see what it was that men most commonly bought at the stores, what they stored, that is, what are the grossest groceries. For the improvements of ages have had but little influence on the essential laws of man's existence: as our skeletons, probably, are not to be distinguished from those of our ancestors.

By the words, necessary of life, I mean whatever, of all that man obtains by his own exertions, has been from the first, or from long use has become, so important to human life that few, if any, whether from savageness, or poverty, or philosophy, ever attempt to do without it. . . .

Most of the luxuries, and many of the so-called comforts of life, are not only not indispensable, but positive hindrances to the elevation of mankind. With respect to luxuries and comforts, the wisest have ever lived a more simple and meagre life than the poor. The ancient philosophers, Chinese, Hindoo, Persian, and Greek, were a class than which none has been poorer in outward riches, none so rich in inward . . . .

* * *

I went to the woods because I wished to live deliberately, to front only the essential facts of life, and see if I could not learn what it had to teach, and not, when I came to die, discover that I had not lived. I did not wish to live what was not life, living is so dear; nor did I wish to practise resignation, unless it was quite necessary. I wanted to live deep and suck out all the marrow of life, to live so sturdily and Spartan-like as to put to rout all that was not life, to cut a broad swath and shave close, to drive life into a corner, and reduce it to its lowest terms, and, if it proved to be mean, why then to get the whole and genuine meanness of it, and publish its meanness to the world; or if it were sublime, to know it by experience, and be able to give a true account of it in my next excursion. For most men, it appears to me, are in a strange uncertainty about it, whether it is of the devil or of God, and have somewhat hastily concluded that it is the chief end of man here to "glorify God and enjoy him forever."

Still we live meanly, like ants; though the fable tells us that we were long ago changed into men; like pygmies we fight with cranes; it is error upon error, and clout upon clout, and our best virtue has for its occasion a superfluous and evitable wretchedness. Our life is frittered away by detail. An honest man has hardly need to count more than his ten fingers, or in extreme cases he may add his ten toes, and lump the rest. Simplicity, simplicity, simplicity! I say, let your affairs be as two or three, and not a hundred or a thousand; instead of a million count half a dozen, and keep your accounts on your thumb-nail. In the midst of this chopping sea of civilized life, such are the clouds and storms and quicksands and thousand-and-one items to be allowed for, that a man has to live, if he would not founder and go to the bottom and not make his port at all, by dead reckoning, and he must be a great calculator indeed who succeeds. Simplify, simplify. Instead of three meals a day, if it be necessary eat but one; instead of a hundred dishes, five; and reduce other things in proportion.

The nation itself, with all its so-called internal improvements, which, by the way are all external and superficial, is just such an unwieldy and overgrown establishment, cluttered with furniture and tripped up by its own traps, ruined by luxury and heedless expense, by want of calculation and a worthy aim, as the million households in the land; and the only cure for it, as for them, is in a rigid economy, a stern and more than Spartan simplicity of life and elevation of purpose. It lives too fast. Men think that it is essential that the Nation have commerce, and export ice, and talk through a telegraph, and ride thirty miles an hour, without a doubt, whether they do or not; but whether we should live like baboons or like men, is a little uncertain.

If we do not get out sleepers, and forge rails, and devote days and nights to the work, but go to tinkering upon our lives to improve them, who will build railroads? And if railroads are not built, how shall we get to heaven in season? But if we stay at home and mind our business, who will want railroads? We do not ride on the railroad; it rides upon us. Did you ever think what those sleepers are that underlie the railroad? Each one is a man, an Irishman, or a Yankee man. The rails are laid on them, and they are covered with sand, and the cars run smoothly over them. They are sound sleepers, I assure you. And every few years a new lot is laid down and run over; so that, if some have the pleasure of riding on a rail, others have the misfortune to be ridden upon.

Why should we live with such hurry and waste of life? We are determined to be starved before we are hungry. Men say that a stitch in time saves nine, and so they take a thousand stitches today to save nine tomorrow.

Source: Henry David Thoreau, *Walden* (Boston, 1854), 10–17.

Part V

MATERIAL LIFE

Material life encompasses many things in everyday life: the food we eat, the houses we live in, the clothes we wear, and the technology we use to carry out our everyday tasks. During the late eighteenth and early nineteenth centuries Americans saw much variety in their material lives. Although many of the foods and foodways of that era were different than the kinds of foods and ways Americans use today, the food and drink of the period from the American Revolution to the beginning of the Civil War include some recipes that are familiar to us. The first document below is a recipe that comes down from the period of the Puritans and was a very popular staple of every Thanksgiving Day feast, cranberry tarts. The second document is a recipe for fried chicken, which has become an American classic and is synonymous with America. The recipe for rice cakes in the third document comes from Emily Dickinson. The article from *The Atlantic Monthly* discusses the need for Americans to take better care when cooking their food and to eat a better balanced diet.

We also get a glimpse of how people furnished their dwellings during this period, as well as their social status. The homes of wealthy people in the cities were a great contrast to those of the working class, just as the homes of the planters of the rural South differed from those of a yeoman farmer who owned no slaves. The clothing and appearance of Americans changed as a result of the development of manufacturing, making some articles of clothing cheaper and more readily available. Other products were still made by hand. The machine age had not yet conquered all in terms of household goods. Fashion was discussed in letters and magazines, and people wanted to be "in style."

The technology developed in the United States changed the nation. Goods and people could now be moved over great distances in less time. By the outbreak of the Civil War, steamboats and railroads were moving people and goods that sustained the growth of the nation. Manufacturing practices in the United States during this period also set the standard for the remainder of the nineteenth century, as machines took over many of the tasks of skilled laborers, and the development of interchangeable parts made it easier to repair weapons and machinery. The telegraph and the photograph literally were reorienting how people understood time and reality.

Food and Drink

Food in America is a mixture of the various cultures that have come to our shores. It not only fulfills the basic needs of human beings for sustenance, but also plays an important part in holidays, religious ceremonies, and special occasions. The recipe for cranberry tarts comes down from the days of the Puritans and became a staple of Thanksgiving dinners. Fried chicken has become a staple at picnics, Sunday lunches after services, and barbeques all across America. Rice cakes have become synonymous with healthy food, but here we see a tempting recipe for a spiced rice cake. Americans are known for cooking a great deal of food and piling it on the table, and while that demonstrates the bounty of food that Americans have, it has also demonstrated a lack of preparation of the food and an ignorance of what makes up a balanced, healthy table.

1. Cranberry Tarts (1670s)

Here's a Thanksgiving food that actually was eaten by Puritans, as recorded in Maine by John Josselyn in the 1670s: "The Indians and English use them much, boyling them with Sugar for Sauce to eat with their Meat; and it is a delicate Sauce, especially for roasted Mutton: Some make Tarts with them, as with Goose Berries." Americans have kept the cranberry sauce, but have largely forgotten the tarts. This recipe was printed in an appendix of twenty-nine American recipes to the 1803 New York edition of an English cookbook, The Frugal Housewife, *and in 1805 was attached to another cookbook,* The Art of Cookery Made Plain and Easy, *published in Virginia. Food historian Karen Hess has speculated that this appendix may have originally appeared in an almanac. The recipe makes four pies, which reminds us that early Americans used pies over several days between weekly bakings and ate pie at all three meals. There would have been several bakings in the days before Thanksgiving to have many pies of several kinds.*

To one pound of flour three quarters of a pound of butter, then stew your cranberry's to a jelly, putting good brown sugar in to sweeten them, strain the cranberry's and then put them in your patty pans for baking in a moderate oven for half an hour.

Source: Susannah Carter, *The Frugal Housewife, or Complete Woman Cook; . . . Also the Making of English Wines* (New York: G. & R. Waite, no. 64, Maiden-Lane, 1803).

2. Fried Chicken (1828)

This is the first written recipe for fried chicken as we know it today, from Mary Randolph's The Virginia Housewife, *third edition. Although sixteenth- and seventeenth-century English cooking included fritters and some pan-fried foods, this kind of deep-fat frying was more characteristic of the Mediterranean and had already been brought to West Africa by Arab traders, and then by Spanish and Portuguese slavers and colonists. (Early fried-fish recipes in English cookbooks are generally attributed to Jewish people, who were coming from Spain.) Thus deep-fried food has generally followed the African American population, although fried chicken only became strongly identified with the African American community toward the end of the nineteenth century.*

Mrs. Randolph's recipe also includes fried mush, the first documented hush puppies, and fried whole parsley—a fancy touch.

Cut them up as for fricassee, dredge them well with flour, sprinkle them with salt, put them into a good quantity of boiling lard, and fry them a light brown, fry small pieces of mush and a quantity of parsley nicely picked to be served in the dish with the chickens, take a half a pint of rich milk, add to it a small bit of butter with pepper, salt, and chopped parsley, stew it a little, and pour it over the chickens, and garnish with the fried parsley.

To make mush: Put a lump of butter the size of an egg into a quart of water, make it sufficiently thick with corn meal and a little salt; it must be mixed perfectly smooth, stir it constantly till done enough.

Source: Mary Randolph, *The Virginia Housewife, or Methodical Cook* (Washington, DC: Way and Gideon, 1828).

3. Emily Dickinson's Recipe for Rice Cakes (1851)

Emily Dickinson's fame is unusual in that her poems were published only after her death in 1886, and much of her celebrity continues to rest on the contrast between her daring poems and allegedly reclusive lifestyle. This recipe was one of two published by her first cousin, Helen Bullard Wyman, in "Emily Dickinson as Cook and Poetess" in The Boston Cooking-School Magazine *for June–July 1906. Some details are based on the edited version of the recipe in the 1976 pamphlet, "Emily Dickinson: Profile of the Poet as Cook," by guides at the Dickinson household in Amherst, Massachusetts. The pamphlet quotes a Dickinson letter showing that she was baking the rice cakes as early as 1851, when she was twenty. In later years, when Emily was ill and really did stay in the house, she would lower a basket of ginger cookies from her window to her niece and her playmates. Maybe she included a few rice cakes.*

One cup of ground rice.
One cup of powdered sugar.
Two eggs.
One-half a cup of butter.
One spoonful of milk with a very little [baking] soda.
Flavor to suit.

Cousin Emily

Source: "Emily Dickinson as Cook and Poetess," *The Boston Cooking-School Magazine* (June–July 1906).

4. Cookery (1864)

This article from The Atlantic Monthly *of December 1864 discusses how in many ways the American table is inferior to a European table. It notes the abundance of food available to Americans on many tables at restaurants and at home and discusses how the preparation of food is very important, and expected by visitors in America. Concerns about proper preparation of food became more common as Americans moved to towns and away from their own planting, growing, raising, and processing of food.*

WE in America have the raw material of provision in greater abundance than any other nation. There is no country where an ample, well-furnished table is more easily spread, and for that reason, perhaps, none where the bounties of Providence are more generally neglected. I do not mean to say that the traveller through the length and breadth of our land could not, on the whole, find an average of comfortable subsistence; yet, considering that our resources are greater than those of any other civilized people, our results are comparatively poorer.

It is said, that, a list of the summer vegetables which are exhibited on New-York hotel tables being shown to a French artiste, he declared that to serve such a dinner properly would take till midnight. I recollect how I was once struck with our national plenteousness, on returning from a Continental tour, and going directly from the ship to a New-York hotel, in the bounteous season of autumn. For months I had been habituated to my neat little bits of chop or poultry garnished with the inevitable cauliflower or potato, which seemed to be the sole possibility after the reign of green-peas was over; now I sat down all at once to a carnival of vegetables: ripe, juicy tomatoes, raw or cooked; cucumbers in brittle slices; rich, yellow sweet-potatoes; broad Lima-beans, and beans of other and various names; tempting ears of Indian-corn steaming in enormous piles, and great smoking tureens of the savory succotash, an Indian gift to the table for which civilization need not blush; sliced egg-plant in delicate fritters; and marrow-squashes, of creamy pulp and sweetness: a rich variety, embarrassing to the appetite, and perplexing to the choice. Verily, the thought has often impressed itself on my mind that the vegetarian doctrine preached in America left a man quite as much as he had capacity to eat or enjoy, and that in the midst of such tantalizing abundance he really lost the apology which elsewhere bears him out in preying upon his less gifted and accomplished animal neighbors.

But with all this, the American table, taken as a whole, is inferior to that of England or France. It presents a fine abundance of material, carelessly and poorly treated. The management of food is nowhere in the world, perhaps more slovenly and wasteful. Everything betokens that want of care that waits on abundance; there are great capabilities and poor execution. A tourist through England can seldom fail, at the quietest country-inn, of finding himself served with the essentials of English table—comfort, his mutton—chop done to a turn, his steaming little private apparatus for concocting his own tea, his choice pot of marmalade or slice of cold ham, and his delicate rolls and creamy butter, all served with care and neatness. In France, one never asks in vain for delicious cafe-au-lait, good bread and butter, a nice omelet, or some savory little portion of meat with a French name. But to a tourist taking like chance in American country-fare what is the prospect? What is the coffee? what the tea? and the meat? and above all, the butter?

In lecturing on cookery, as on house-building, I divide the subject into not four, but five grand elements: first, Bread; second, Butter; third, Meat; fourth, Vegetables; and fifth, Tea, by which I mean, generically, all sorts of warm, comfortable drinks served out in teacups, whether they be called tea, coffee, chocolate, broma, or what not. I affirm, that, if these five departments are all perfect, the great ends of domestic cookery are answered, so far as the comfort and well-being of life are concerned. I am aware that there exists another department, which is often regarded by culinary amateurs and young aspirants as the higher branch and very collegiate course of practical cookery, to wit, Confectionery, by which I mean to designate all pleasing and complicated compounds of sweets and spices, devised not for health or nourishment, and strongly suspected of interfering with both, mere tolerated gratifications of the palate, which we eat, not with the expectation of being benefited, but only with the hope of not being injured by them. In this large department rank all sorts of cakes, pies, preserves, ices, etc. I shall have a word or two to say under this head before I have done. I only remark now, that in my tours about the country I have often had a virulent ill-will excited towards these works of culinary supererogation, because I thought their excellence was attained by treading under foot and disregarding the five grand essentials. I have sat at many a table garnished with three or four kinds of well-made cake, compounded with citron and spices and all imaginable good things, where the meat was tough and greasy, the bread some hot preparation of flour, lard, saleratus [leavening], and acid, and the butter unutterably detestable. At such tables I have thought, that, if the mistress of the feast had given the care, time, and labor to preparing the simple items of bread, butter, and meat that she evidently had given to the preparation of these extras, the lot of a traveller might be much more comfortable. Evidently, she never had thought of these common articles as constituting a good table. So long as she had puff pastry, rich black cake, clear jelly, and preserves, she seemed to consider that such unimportant matters as bread, butter, and meat could take care of themselves. It is the same inattention to common things as that which leads people to build houses with stone fronts and window-caps and expensive front-door trimmings, without bathing-rooms or fireplaces or ventilators.

Those who go into the country looking for summer board in farmhouses know perfectly well that a table where the butter is always fresh, the tea and coffee of the best kinds and well made, and the meats properly kept, dressed, and served, is the one table of a hundred, the fabulous enchanted island. It seems impossible to get the idea into the minds of people that what is called common food, carefully prepared, becomes, in virtue of that very care and attention, a delicacy, superseding the necessity of artificially compounded dainties.

To begin, then, with the very foundation of a good table, Bread: What you thought it to be? It should be light, sweet, and tender. This matter of lightness is the distinctive line between savage and civilized bread. The savage mixes simple flour and water into balls of paste, which he throws into boiling water, and which come out solid, glutinous masses, of which his common saying is, Man eat dis, he no die, which a facetious traveller who was obliged to subsist on it interpreted to mean, Dis no kill you, nothing will. In short, it requires the stomach of a wild animal or of a savage to digest this primitive form of bread, and of course more or less attention in all civilized modes of bread-making is given to producing lightness. By lightness is meant simply that the particles are to be separated from each other by little holes or air-cells, and all the different methods of making light bread are neither more nor less than the formation in bread of these air-cells.

So far as we know, there are four practicable methods of airating bread, namely by fermentation, by effervescence of an acid and an alkali, by airated egg, or egg which has been filled with air by the process of beating, and lastly, by pressure of some gaseous substance into the paste, by a process much resembling the impregnation of water in a soda-fountain.

All these have one and the same object, to give us the cooked particles of our flour separated by such permanent air-cells as will enable the stomach more readily to digest them.

A very common mode of airating bread, in America, is by the effervescence of an acid and an alkali in the flour. The carbonic acid gas thus formed produces minute air-cells in the bread, or, as the cook says, makes it light. When this process is performed with exact attention to chemical laws, so that the acid and alkali completely neutralize each other, leaving no overplus of either, the result is often very palatable. The difficulty is, that this is a happy conjunction of circumstances which seldom occurs. The acid most commonly employed is that of sour milk, and, as milk has many degrees of sourness, the rule of a certain quantity of alkali to the pint must necessarily produce very different results at different times. As an actual fact, where this mode of making bread prevails, as we lament to say it does to a great extent in this country, one finds five cases of failure to one of success. It is a woful thing that the daughters of New England have abandoned the old respectable mode of yeast-brewing and bread-raising for this specious substitute, so easily made, and so seldom well made. The green, clammy, acrid substance, called biscuit, which many of our worthy republicans are obliged to eat in these days, is wholly unworthy of the men and women of the Republic. Good patriots ought not to be put off in that way, they deserve better fare.

Source: "Cookery," *The Atlantic Monthly* 14, no. 86 (December 1864).

Houses and Furniture

Homes in America reflected the status of their owners. In America the houses of those in the city differed from their rural counterparts'. The houses and their furnishings marked the daily lives of those who lived in them. In the first document below we see the homes of different classes in a large American city from the viewpoint of a foreigner who has become a citizen and teacher. We then see the home of a southern planter and contrast that with a yeoman farmer's, and see that the stereotype of the wealthy plantations of the South as the common lot of southerners was more myth than reality. The home as a comfortable, peaceful dwelling for those who live in it is described by a woman visiting the United States, who is surprised to see the same serenity that European homes have in an American home.

5. *Francis J. Grund on American Homes (1837)*

Originally from Bohemia, Francis J. Grund was educated in Vienna and taught mathematics at a military school in Rio de Janeiro, Brazil, before settling in Philadelphia, Pennsylvania, in 1826. He published many essays and addresses, as well as books of his observations of American society. This excerpt from The Americans in Their Moral, Social, and Political Relations *discusses the homes of families of different classes in the United States around 1837.*

The houses of the wealthier classes resemble those of the gentry in England, and are wanting in nothing which can materially contribute to comfort. Some of the higher elegancies of life, are, indeed, confined to a few imitators of European fashions; but there is a sufficiency of all that is essential and needful. No ostentatious attempt is ever made to display either fortune or riches; but, on the contrary, every thing avoided which, being contrary to republican plainness, might offend, or unnecessarily attract the attention of the people. Furniture, dress, carriages, &c., are all of the simplest construction; and the oldest and most aristocratic families set, in this respect, the example to the more recently promoted fashionables. Whatever political reason there may exist for the prevalence of this taste; it is nevertheless a good one, and being shared by the great majority of the nation, impresses a peculiar character of simplicity on the domestic life of Americans. It is impossible for an European to live for any length of time in the United States, without being constantly reminded, in town or in the country, at home or abroad, that he is living in a republic, and that the sovereign power of that republic is solely vested in the majority; for, whatever is capable of exciting envy or jealousy by too glaring a distinction from the inferior classes is condemned by public opinion, and on that account, studiously avoided by persons of all ranks of society. But then the great prosperity of the country enables even the labouring classes to enjoy comforts much beyond the reach of superior orders in Europe; and prevents the scale from becoming too low.

On entering the house of a respectable mechanic, in any of the large cities of the United States, one cannot but be astonished at the apparent neatness and comfort of the apartments, the large airy parlours, the nice carpets and mahogany furniture, and the tolerably good library, showing the inmates' acquaintance with the standard works of English literature. These are advantages which but few individuals of the same class enjoy, by way of distinction, in Europe; but which, in America, are within the reasonable hopes and expectations of almost all the inferior classes. What powerful stimulus is not this to industry? What premium on sobriety and unexceptionable conduct? A certain degree of respectability is, in all countries, attached to property, and is, perhaps, one of the principal reasons why riches are coveted. A poor man has certainly more temptations, and requires more virtue to withstand them, than one who is in tolerable circumstances. The motives of the rich are hardly ever questioned, while the poor are but too often objects of distress and suspicion. *Pauper ubique jacet.*

The labouring classes in America are really less removed from the wealthy merchants and professional men than they are in any part of Europe; and the term "mob," with which the lower classes in England are honoured, does not apply to any portion of the American community. With greater ease and comfort in his domestic arrangements, the labouring American acquires also the necessary leisure and disposition for reading; his circle of ideas becomes enlarged, and he is rendered more capable of appreciating the advantages of the political institutions of his country. Both thought and reflection may be crushed by excessive labour, and the lofty aspirings of the mind enslaved by the cravings of the body. Liberty, without promoting the material interests of man, is a thing altogether beyond the comprehension of the multitude; and there are many who, had they attained it, would, like the Israelites of old, wish themselves back to their meat-pots. I know not whether it is quest of liberty or property which causes Europeans to emigrate to America: but I am satisfied that there is an intimate connection between the two, and a constant action of one upon the other.

Source: Francis Joseph Grund, *The Americans in Their Moral, Social, and Political Relations*, 2 vols. (London: Longman, Rees, Orme, Brown, Green & Longman, 1837), I:45–49.

6. *A Southern Planter's House (1840s)*

During Emily Burke's eight-year stay in Georgia, she was able to take in the sights and lifestyles of southerners. Her observations of slavery led her to publish a scathing indictment of the "peculiar institution." In this document she describes her stay at a plantation in Georgia, and we get a sense of what a southern plantation house looked like during the antebellum period.

The house of which I promised in my last letter to give a description, according to general custom, stood upon four posts about five feet from the ground, allowing a free circulation of air beneath, as well as forming a fine covert for the hounds, goats, and all the domestic fowls.

It was only one story high, though much taller than buildings of the same description at the North. It was divided into four apartments below, and two in the roof, and furnished with two broad piazzas, one in front of the building, which there is always the gentleman's sitting room, and one on the back of the house, where the servants await their master's orders. Houses are built low on account of the high winds they are exposed to, their foundations being so frail that if high they would be easily thrown down in one of their heavy gales. The building was slightly covered with boards, arranged like clapboards to shed the rain. This was the entire thickness of the walls, there being no ceiling, lathing, or plastering within. The floors were all single and laid in so unworkmanlike manner, I could often see the ground beneath, when the carpets were not on the floor, and they are always taken up in the summer to make the apartments cooler. The roof was covered with long shingles nailed to the timbers, to save the expense of boards beneath, the ends of one tier just lapping upon the next, and this executed so shammily [shabbily] that not only the wind, but the light and rain often finds free access into the upper apartments, through ten thousand holes among the shingles. Two chimneys, one upon each end, built of turfs, sticks, blocks of wood, and occasionally a brick, plastered over with clay, ornamented the outside of the house. The windows were furnished with panes of glass, a luxury but few enjoy; after all glazed windows were used more for ornament than comfort, for in the coldest weather they were always raised, and in stormy weather the piazzas protected the inner rooms. The above is as true a description as I can give of the singular fashioned house to which I was conducted on my arrival in the country.

Source: Emily P. Burke, *Reminiscences of Georgia* (Oberlin, OH: J.M. Fitch, 1850), 102–4.

7. *Fredrika Bremer on an American Home (1849)*

Fredrika Bremer (1801–1865) was a well-known feminist novelist from Sweden. She traveled in the United States by herself in 1849 and wrote about her experiences over two years. Here she discusses the home of one of her hosts, Andrew Jackson Downing, famous for his designs of the country cottage and efforts to relieve Americans from crowded urban living.

Newburgh, on the Hudson, October 7, 1849

He built his house himself, planted all the trees and flowers around it, giving everything, it seems to me, the stamp of a refined and earnest mind. It stands in the midst of romantic scenery and shadowy pathways, with the prettiest little bits of detail and grand views. All has been done with design, nothing by guess, nothing with formality. Here a *soul* has felt, thought, arranged. A certain darkness of tone prevails within the house; all the woodwork is brown; even the daylight is somber [sic], yet clear, or, more properly speaking, pregnant with light—a sort of imprisoned sunshine, something warm and profound, appearing to me like a reflection of the man's own brown eyes. In forms, furniture, and arrangement the finest taste prevails; everything is soft and noble, and as comfortable as it is tasteful. The only brilliant things in the rooms are the pretty flowers in lovely vases and baskets. Besides, there are books, busts, and some pictures. Above small bookcases, in the form of Gothic windows, inserted like niches in the walls of the parlor, stand busts of Linné, Franklin, Newton, and many other heroes of natural science. One sees in this dwelling a decided and thorough individuality of character, which has put its stamp on all that surrounds it, and every one ought to mold himself and his own world in a similar way. One feels here Mr. Downing's motto, *Il bello è il buono*. A real luxury obtains in food, fruits, and in many small things, but it makes no outward show; it exists, as it were, concealed in the inner richness and exquisite selection of the thing itself. I did not expect to meet this type of home in the young New World.

Source: Fredrika Bremer, *America of the Fifties: Letters of Fredrika Bremer*, ed. Adolph B. Benson (London: Oxford University Press, 1924), 8–9. Renewed 1952, The American-Scandinavian Foundation.

8. Frederick Law Olmsted on a Yeoman Farmer's Home in the South (1861)

Frederick Law Olmsted is considered the father of American landscape architecture and is best known for his design of urban parks during the nineteenth century, most notably Central Park in New York. Olmsted began his career as a journalist during the 1850s and was given an assignment by The New York Daily Times *to do an extensive research journey through the American South and Texas. The record that Olmsted eventually published provided a very in-depth look at Southern society and the institution of slavery. Here Olmsted describes the home of a yeoman farmer and his family, a far cry from the plantation life that had become the stereotypical view of the South.*

The next house at which I arrived was one of the commonest sort of cabins. I had passed twenty like it during the day, and I thought I would take the opportunity to get an interior knowledge of them. The fact that a horse and a wagon were kept, and that a considerable area of land in the rear of the cabin was planted with cotton, showed that the family were by no means of the lowest class, yet, as they were not able even to hire a slave, they be considered to represent favourably, I believe, the condition of the poor whites of the plantation districts. The whites of the country, I observe, are three to one of the slaves; in the nearest adjoining county, the proportion is reversed; within a few miles the soil was richer, and large plantations occurred.

It was raining and nearly nine o'clock. The door of the cabin was open, and I rode up and conversed with the occupant as he stood within. He said he was not in the habit of taking in travellers, and his wife was about sick, but if I was a mind to put up with common fare, he didn't care. Grateful, I dismounted and took the seat he had vacated by the fire, while he led away my horse to an open shed in the rear—his own horse ranging at large, when not in use, during the summer.

The house was all comprised in a single room, twenty-eight by twenty-five feet in area, and open to the roof above. There was a large fireplace at one end and door on each side—no windows at all. Two bedsteads, a spinning wheel, a packing case, which served as a bureau, a cupboard, made of rough hewn slabs, two or three deerskin seated chairs, a Connecticut clock, and a large poster of Jayne's patent medicines, constituted all the visible furniture, either useful or ornamental in purpose. A little girl, without having had any directions to do so, got a frying pan and chunk of bacon from the cupboard, and cutting slices from the latter, set it frying for my supper. The woman of the house sat sulkily in a chair tilted back and leaning against the logs, spitting occasionally at the fire, but took no notice of me, barely nodding when I saluted her. A baby lay crying on the floor, I quieted it and amused it with my watch until the little girl, having made "coffee" and put a piece of corn-bread on the table with the bacon, took charge of it.

I hoped the woman was not very ill.

"Got the headache right bad," she answered. "Have the headache a heap, I do. Knew I should have it to-night. Been cuttin' brush in the cotton this afternoon. Knew it would bring on my headache. Told him so when I begun."

As soon as I had finished my supper and fed [my horse] Jude, the little girl put the fragments and the dishes in the cupboard, and shoved the table into a corner, and dragged a quantity of quilts from one of the bedsteads, which she spread upon the floor, and presently crawled among them out of sight for the night. The woman picked up the child—which, though still a suckling, she said was twenty-two months old—and nursed it, retaking her old position. The man sat with me by the fire, his back towards her. The baby having fallen asleep was laid away somewhere, and the woman dragged off another lot of quilts from the beds, spreading them upon the floor. Then taking a deep tin pan, she filled it with alternate layers of corn-cobs and hot embers from the fire. This she placed upon a large block, which was evidently used habitually for the purpose, in the centre of the cabin. A furious smoke arose from it, and we soon began to cough. "Most *too* much smoke," observed the man. "Hope 'twill drive out the gnats, then," replied the woman. (There is a very minute flying insect here, the bite of which is excessively sharp.)

The woman suddenly dropped off her outer garment and stepped from the midst of its folds, in her petticoat; taking the baby from the place where she had deposited it, lay down and covered herself with the quilts upon the floor. The man told me I could take the bed which remained on one of the bedsteads, and kicking off his shoes only, rolled himself into a blanket by the side of his wife. I ventured to take off my cravat and stockings, as well as my boots, but almost immediately put on my stockings again, drawing their tops over my pantaloons. The advantage of this arrangement was that, although my face, eyes, ears, neck, and hands were immediately attacked, the vermin did not reach my legs for two or three hours. Just after the clock struck two, I distinctly heard the man and woman, and the girl and the dog scratching, and the horse out in the shed stomping and knowing himself. Soon afterward the man exclaimed, "Good God Almighty—mighty! mighty! mighty!" and jumping up pulled off one of his stockings, shook it, scratched his foot vehemently, put on the stocking, and lay down again with a groan. The two doors were open, and through the logs and the openings in the roof, I saw the clouds divide and the moon and the stars reveal themselves. The woman, after having been nearly smothered by the smoke from the pan which she had originally placed close to her own pillow, rose and placed it on the sill of the windward door, where it burned feebly and smoked lustily, like an altar to the Lares, all night. Fortunately the cabin was so open that it gave us little annoyance, while it seemed to answer the purpose of keeping all flying insects at a distance.

When, on rising in the morning, I said that I would like to wash my face, water was given me for the purpose in an earthen pie-dish. Just as breakfast, which was of exactly the same materials as my supper, was ready, rain began to fall, presently in such a smart shower, as to put the fire out and compel us to move the table under the least leaky part of the roof.

Source: Frederick Law Olmsted, *The Cotton Kingdom: A Traveller's Observations on Cotton and Slavery in the American Slave States* (New York: Mason Brothers, 1861), 79–82.

Clothing and Personal Appearance

The clothing and appearance of Americans changed from 1775 to 1860. Clothes made during the late eighteenth century were made by hand. Suits, gowns, and uniforms were made by hand by skilled workers, although there was a marked difference in the quality of those made for the upper class and the clothes worn by the middle and lower classes. As America entered the nineteenth century, more clothing was manufactured, and there was a great deal of importance attached to obtaining the latest styles. We first come across a description of eighteenth-century formal wear at court in England, by Abigail Adams. The problems attendant on trying to keep up with fashion and the pain it could cause are described next. Finally we have a description of bridal dresses from *Godey's Lady's Book* that details what ladies should wear when they attend weddings.

9. Abigail Adams on Court Dress (1796); The Uniforms of the Massachusetts Militia (1781): Officers and Gentlewomen in the Eighteenth Century

The following two excerpts from eighteenth-century documents offer very different descriptions of clothing. The first selection is a 1796 letter from Abigail Adams, wife of John Adams and later the second First Lady of the United States, to her niece about a ball she attended in

England while her husband served as the American ambassador to England. The second selection comprises orders standardizing the military uniforms of officers of the militia of Massachusetts during the American Revolutionary War in 1781. It also bears remembering that all the garments mentioned were made by hand; there were no machine-driven textile mills or sewing machines, although industrialization was pioneered in textile industries and the process was beginning in the eighteenth century. Although the cloth used for court dresses and officers' uniforms would be professionally made, most people could not afford such elaborate and expensive clothing, and many spun, wove, and sewed their own textiles and clothing in the home from wool, flax, cotton, or other materials.

The dresses described are typical of upper-class formal (or full dress) attire. Sack (or sacque) gowns were popular throughout the eighteenth century and had a kind of jacket with folds of fabric down the back from the neck to the floor. By Adams's time, the sacque or coat part of the gown was split in front to reveal a matching (or contrasting) stomacher and skirt or petticoat. Many of the other details are specific terms describing the types and colors of fabric, ribbons, headpieces, and other trimmings, to which Adams and other women paid great attention. Often these were more expensive than the dress itself—not even including jewelry—and an old dress might be retrimmed, or the trim might be transferred to a new dress for a different effect and a different occasion.

It is clear that Adams thinks it all just a bit above her, but she obviously enjoyed it nonetheless, spending substantial amounts of money for feathers and ribbons and jewelry. While conforming to general trends, it was also important for a fashionable woman to look different or unique, and she had to direct the tailor or seamstress according to her own plans; fashion designers or couturiers who told or advised people about what to wear were a later, nineteenth- and twentieth-century phenomenon.

Whereas Adams's letter describes an attempt to look unique, the second excerpt describes an attempt to look alike. The military uniforms for the Massachusetts officers are described in such detail so they can each have them made properly and still match each other, as was expected for military attire by the eighteenth century. Especially in the cash-strapped colonial armies, soldiers might not have had much of a uniform at all, and officers would be responsible for their own uniforms. To ensure as much uniformity as possible, specific regulations were issued. Prescribed are a long coat that buttoned closed at the top and opened halfway down, short trousers, waistcoat, neck cloth, and cock'd, or three-cornered, hat; notably no mention is made of weapons, stockings, or shoes.

Though styles have certainly changed, as well as the methods by which clothing is made, two dominant themes of these selections—individual expression and conformity to express membership in a group—are still important everyday functions of clothing and fashion today.

To amuse you, then, my dear niece, I will give you an account of the dress of the ladies at the ball of Comte d'Adhemar. There was as great a variety of pretty dresses, borrowed wholly from France, as I have ever seen; and amongst the rest, some with sapphire blue satin waists, spangled with silver, and laced down the back and seams with silver stripes; white satin petticoats trimmed with black and blue velvet ribbon; an odd kind of head-dress, which they term the "Helmet of Minerva." I did not observe the bird of wisdom, however, nor do I know whether those who wore the dress had any suitable pretensions to it. "And pray," say you, "how were my aunt and cousin dressed?" If it will gratify you to know, you shall hear. Your aunt, then, wore a full dress court cap without the lappets, in which was a wreath of white flowers, and blue sheafs, two black and blue flat feathers (which cost her half a guinea apiece, but that you need not tell of), three pearl pins, bought for Court, and a pair of pearl earrings, the cost of them—no matter what; less than diamonds, however. A sapphire blue demi-saison with a satin stripe, sack and petticoat trimmed with broad black lace; crape flounce, etc. leaves made of blue ribbon, and trimmed with white floss; wreaths of black velvet ribbon spotted with steel beads, which are much in fashion and brought to perfection as to resemble diamonds; white ribbon also in the Vandyke style, made up a trimming, which looks very elegant; and a full dress handkerchief, and a bouquet of roses. "Full gay, I think, for my aunt." That is true, Lucy, but nobody is old in Europe. I was seated next the Duchess of Bedford, who had a scarlet satin sack and coat, with a cushion full of diamonds, for hair she had none, and is but seventy-six neither. Well now for your cousin: a small white leghorn hat, bound with pink satin ribbon; a steel buckle and band which turned up at the side, and a confined large pink bow; a large bow of the same kind of ribbon behind; a wreath of full blown roses around the crown, and another of buds and roses withinside the hat, which, being placed at the back of the hair, brought the roses to the edge; you see it clearly; one red and black feather with two white ones, completed the head-dress. A gown and coat of Chamberi gauze, with a red satin stripe over a pink waist, and coat flounced with crape, trimmed with broad point and pink ribbon; wreaths of roses across the coat, gauze sleeves and ruffles.

Orders for the Massachusetts Line

January 5th, 1781.

The Committee of Officers appointed to fix upon the fashion of the Massachusetts uniform, have reported thereupon, and it is as follows:

The color of the coats, waistcoats, linings and buttons, to be agreeable to the General Orders of the 2nd of October, 1779.

The length of the coat, to the upper part of the knee-pan, and to be cut high in the neck. As 3 is to 5, so is the skirt to the waist of the coat; or divide the whole length of the coat into 8 equal parts, take 5 for the waist and 3 for the skirts.

The lappel, at the top of the breast, to be 3 inches wide, and the bottom 2 3/10 inches; the lapel to be as low as the waist, and its wing to button within an inch of the shoulder seam with a small button on the cape. The epaulette to be worn directly on the top of the shoulder joint on the same button with the wing of the lappel. A round and close cuff, three inches wide, with four close worked buttonholes. The cape to be made with a peak behind, and its width in proportion to the lappels. The pocket flaps to be scollopped, four buttonholes, the two inner close worked, the two outer open worked, and to be set on in a curved line from the bottom of the lappel to the button on the hip. The coat to be cut full behind, with a fold on each back skirt, and two close worked buttonholes on each.

Ten open worked buttonholes on the breast of each lappel, with ten large buttons, at equal distance; four large buttons on each cuff, four on each pocket flap, and four on each fold. Those on the cuffs and pocket flaps to be placed agreeable to the buttonholes; and those on the folds, one on the hip, one at the bottom, and two in the centre, at an equal distance with those on the lappel. The coat is to button or hook as low as the fourth buttonhole on the breast, and is to be flaunt at the bottom with a genteel and military air. Four hooks and eyes on the breast as low as the coat is allowed to button. The skirts hook up with a bleu heart at each corner, with such a device as the Field Officers of each Regiment shall direct. The bottoms of the coat to be cut square. The waistcoat to be single-breasted, with twelve buttons and holes on the breast, with pocket flaps, four close worked buttonholes and four buttons, which shall appear below the flaps. The breeches are to be made with a half fall; four buttons on each knee. The small buttons on the waistcoat are to be of the same kind with the large ones on the coat. The number of the Regiment is to be in the centre of the button, with such device as the Field Officers shall direct. The epaulettes to be worn agreeable to his Excellency the Commander-in-Chief's orders of June 18, 1780.

A fashionable military cock'd hat, with a silver button loop, and a small button with the number of the Regiment. To wear a black stock [neck cloth] when on duty and on the parade.

No edging, vellum lace, or indeed any other ornaments which are not mentioned, to be added to the uniform. No officer is to be permitted, at any time, to wear any other uniform than that of his Regiment.

Source: Elisabeth McClellan, "Officers and Gentlewomen in the Eighteenth Century," in *History of American Costume, 1607–1870* (New York: Tudor Publishing Co., 1937).

10. A *Difficult Pair of Boots* (1832)

One of the problems encountered when trying to keep up with current fashion was that often the clothes were not meant to be worn by certain individuals. This document from The New-England Magazine *shows the difficulty many encountered when trying to be fashionable.*

Tailors are superfluities, and should be heavily taxed; though they are permitted to lay a grievous impost on others. Dress, that was at first our shame, has become our pride; and we, therefore, glory in our shame. It was first used for covering; it is now made for display. A fashionable dress may hardly be defined as a covering, it is so scanty; and the plainest coat is half show. The sober drab of the Quaker, cut in straight lines, is yet ornamented in its own way. It is cut in a shape that gratifies the wearer, and that makes him proud of his humility.

All our fashions are fleeting, and the form of a cloud is not more liable to change. In the shoe and the boot, those minor and inferior parts of dress, what change may come ere we have shuffled off this square-toed pair! All human inventions, however, have a limit; for all combinations may be exhausted, and new fashions, like new boots, are but imitations of the old. Of shoes we remember the duck-billed, the snipe-billed, the pointed, the rounded, and the square; shoes horizontal, that exactly coincide with a flat surface, and others so much hollowed, that the heel and toe, only, leave a track in the sand. Others are turned up at an angle, equal to the eighth of a circle, and my toes are now pinched by a pair, small and square, of the exact fashion that has for centuries prevailed in China, that happy country where wise laws make the fashions unchangeable. Boots have been more mutable than shoes, but, after a course of changes, return to an old form. In the sculptures around the Parthenon, the work of Phidias himself: the equestrians have boots of as finical a fit and wrinkle as any in later times. Their form is that of the old white tops.

There are boots military, civic, and dramatic; there is the bootee, which is a sheer abridgement, and the jack-boot, that would not be filled after having swallowed them all.

The fashion at one time requires the boot to be wide and stiff in the back, and at another close and limber. Suwarrow and Wellington have a greater name among cordwainers than among soldiers. Of their victories, the remembrance will fade away, but their boots promise immortality. I remember my first pair of Suwarrow; they made a part of the great equipment, with which I came from college into the world. Four skeins of silk did I purchase of a mercer, and equal expense did I incur with the sweeper, for aid in twisting them into tassels for the boots. I would incur double the expense now to have the same feeling of dignity that I enjoyed then, when walking in those boots. I stepped long and slowly, and the iron heels, which it pleased me to set firmly on the pavement, made a greater clatter than a troop of horse shod with felt. But if I wore them with pride it was not without suffering; nor did I get myself into them without labor. Before I attempted to draw them on, I rubbed the inside with soap, and powdered my instep and heel with flour. I next drew the handle of two forks through the straps, lest they should cut into my fingers, and then commenced the tug of war. I contracted myself into the form of a chicken, trussed for the spit, and whatever patience and perseverance Providence had given me, I tested to the utmost. I cursed Suwarrow for a Scythian, and wished his boots hung in their own straps. I danced round the room upon one foot many times, and after several intervals for respiration and pious ejaculation, I succeeded in getting my toes into trouble, or, I may say, into purgatory. Corns I had as many as the most fanatic pilgrim would desire for peas in his shoes, yet I walked through the crowd (who were probably admiring their own boots too much to bestow a thought upon mine) as if I were a carpet knight polonaising upon rose leaves. I was in torment, yet there was not a cloud upon my brow,

Spem vultst simulat, premit altum corde dolorem.

I could not have suffered for principle as I suffered for those memorable boots.

The coat I wore, was such as fashion enjoined; the skirts were long and narrow, like a swallows tail, two thirds at least of the whole length. The portion above the waist composed the other third. The waist was directly beneath the shoulders; the collar was a huge roll reaching above the ears, and there were two lines of brilliant buttons in front. There were nineteen buttons in a row. The pantaloons, (over which I wore the boots) were of non-elastic corduroy. It would be unjust to the tailor to say that they were fitted like my skin; for they set a great deal closer. When I took them off, my legs were like fluted pillars, grooved with the cords of the pantaloons. The hat that surmounted this dress had three quarters of an inch rim, and a low tapering crown. It was circled by a ribbon two inches wide.

There is no modern dress that does not deform the human shape, and some national costumes render it more grotesque than any natural deformity. Dress, at present, seems as much worn to conceal the form, as language is used to hide and not to express the thoughts. In a fashionable costume, all forms are alike; there is no difference between Antinous or Aesop; Hyperion or a Satyr. D. L.

Source: *The New-England Magazine* 2, no. 6 (June 1832): 452–53.

11. *Bridal Dresses (1860)*

Fashionable dress for special occasions was very important, not only in higher social circles, but for everyday men and women. The magazines of the mid-nineteenth century tried to keep women abreast of the latest trends so that they would always be on the cutting edge of dress for any occasion. Here in an article from Godey's Lady's Book *we get a sense of the fashion that women were expected to wear for a wedding.*

As our issue has suggested bridal dresses, we give one or two other styles verbally, as being seasonable and useful hints:—

First, a robe of very rich white satin; the skirt is extremely full, and ornamented with a trimming formed of a plaiting of satin, set on so as to present the effect of a tunic. This plaiting is carried up each side of the corsage, and finishes at the shoulders. The corsage is plain and pointed in front of the waist. The sleeves are formed of two puffs at the upper part of the arm, and below the puffs there is a frill, edged with a plaiting corresponding with that on the other part of the dress. Collar and undersleeves of Honiton point; the collar fastened at the throat by a pearl brooch. The front hair is disposed in bands, which fall backwards from the face and join the knot of hair under the *cache-peigne* at the back of the head, the ends falling in ringlets at each side. The bridal wreath is composed of white hyacinth and daisies. Scarf veil of white thulle, fixed by pearl pins at the top part of the head, and flowing over the shoulders and back part of the dress, so as to descend nearly to the bottom of the skirt.

Book muslin, the favorite evening-dress of the past generation, is coming again into favor, as will be seen by the description of a wedding outfit, recently furnished by a celebrated French establishment. We quote the whole trosseau, as interesting to all young ladies, whether brides or bridesmaids:—

First, the wedding dress of book muslin and point lace with alternating flounces, the bride's veil of point lace, and handkerchief to match. Then an open dress for the day after the wedding, of white and blue striped moiré, with bows in front and rosettes at the side. A green silk dress for visiting, quite covered with flounces and accompanied by a scarf of the same, which has an elegant effect. A sky-blue moiré antique dress trimmed with Alencons, and another of pink silk trimmed with blonde.

For the same wedding Mme. Alexandrine supplied the following bonnets:—

One of white crape, with a branch of white lilac on the front, and a diadem bandeau of the same inside across the forehead. Another was a Tuscan, with a curtain arranged in somewhat irregular flutes, and, as trimming, a velvet torsade with a straw cord. This torsade comes down on the right side quite under the curtain, and ends on the left hand side about the middle, where it is fastened under a large poppy with great buds swaying on their slender stems. Inside, flame-colored ruche is terminated on the right hand by a branch of poppies just like those on the outside. A bonnet of white thulle embroidered with black has a wide border of felt-gray crape and a gray silk ribbon all round the crown. A Chantilly fall, fastened on the left edge of the front by an elongated tuft of red daisies, is passed slantwise across the bonnet and ends like a scarf on the right side, above the terry velvet curtain, which is laid in flat plaits at top, and has a bias piece in the middle. The bandeau is composed of bunches of small black fruit and tufts of red field daisies. Strings of narrow pink ribbon are sewed on over the wide ones of felt gray silk.

For the wedding-ball, which would be the prelude to several other large parties, Mme. Bonier-Cherre supplied some very beautiful articles. Her *Alma* coiffure of white lilac in very small branches, mixed with roses, and forming a bow at the side, from which escaped two unequal branches of lilac foliage; and her *Aissa* coiffure, composed of two garlands of rose-leaves, one of which lies on the forehead, the other on the back-hair, the second row ornamented at the side with a long tuft of mixed roses, and the first row—that on the forehead—having merely on the right a very small bunch of rosebuds. These two creations, quite new and exquisitely graceful, will be won by two cousins of the bride, who bear one of the great historical names of France.

Other coiffures, still more decidedly oriental, are: A gold diadem, with a large tuft of red roses and coffee-berries. A bow of flame colored velvet and caraib fruit mixed up with gold lace and velvet poppies.

The book-muslin brides of the last cycle of fashion would have been sadly at a loss as to the use of all this finery; but nowadays, in anything like fashionable city life, an equal, if not more expensive, outfit is considered necessary for the receptions, the parties, and other festivities that a bride is expected to attend. Happy they, who, in country life, can subside more noiselessly into the calm of domestic quiet. Even the bride's friends, with us, are expected to prepare for the great occasion, for a morning reception requires almost a full dress toilet, the dress itself to be rich and light, the scarf a shawl extremely elegant, and the bonnet as light and effective as possible. We give a costume which is considered suitable for such an occasion:—

Robe with double skirt, of pale mauve-colored silk, without any trimming; the corsage high to the throat. Collar and undersleeves of lace. Bonnet of white terry velvet, with a small plume of white feathers on one side; under-trimming of blonde and white roses; strings of white terry velvet ribbon. Shawl of India cashmere, with a white ground, and a border of rich arabesque pattern.

For an evening reception, a dress suitable for a young lady is composed of white and pink tarletane, worn over a slip of pink silk. The skirt of this dress consists of white tarletane, and is trimmed with nine gauffered flounces, five of white and four of pink tarletane, dispersed alternately. Another very pretty dress consists of mauve-colored tarletane over silk of the same color. There are two skirts of tarletane, the lower one trimmed with five narrow gauffered flounces. The upper skirt is open in the tunic form, and is bordered with a gauffering of mauve-color silk. A dress of light green tarletane over silk of the same tint is also extremely pretty; it has three skirts, each trimmed with a light ruche, edged in blonde.

For plainer dresses, the great novelty is the introduction of tight sleeves, as in the gored dress of October number, and demi-tight as in the fashion-plate of this. We consider the sleeve . . . one of the best of this style, which has certainly come into favor astonishingly. . . . The parement or mousquetaire cuff is almost universal, and takes away from the stiffness of the shallow drapery. When the sleeve is quite close to the arm, it often has a jockey, puff, or short flounce at the shoulder, flat bows, or macaroons, going from the wrist half way to the elbow. Demi-tight coat sleeves, with a seam on the back as well as the inside of the arm, are in very good taste. The pointed corsages are the favorites for thick stuffs, the points being very long and sharp; but many silks, especially for young ladies are also *a la vierge*, plain on the shoulder, and gathered into a rounded waistband. These are intended to be finished by a sash or belt. There is little doubt of the decadence of side stripes, double skirts, and nearly all robe patterns for skirts, and in their place flounces of every depth and style have come in, together with the spirals of lace and ribbons, and the oval ornaments of silk and lace, called macaroons, which are disposed in various ways on the skirt and sleeves. Flounces have a heading usually, a braiding of the same silk. They may be graduated regularly as to width from the hem to the waist, or set in groups, or a group of narrow ones—ruffles, they might be called—are sometimes placed as headings of a single deep fall, and the sleeves made in correspondence.

Striped silks, the stripes being from four to six inches wide, and alternating in color, style, etc., are among the richest figured materials for street-dress, as a stripe of dark green satin, with the alternate stripe of silk, figured in some pretty floral design. Alternate stripes of black silk and velvet are also very elegant. Moiré antique is worn rather more now than the past season, the favorite colors being royal purple and emerald green. The *broché* silks are in fact real brocades of our grandmothers, *broché* meaning only embroidery—a rich black or gray taffeta ground is sprinkled with small sprays or bouquets of flowers. These are much worn for evening-dress. Fawn, green, mode, ashes of roses, etc. are among the shades used as a ground, the flowers being in their natural colors. Black, deep purple, maroon, and deep blue taffetas, figured with black velvet, are, perhaps, the most expensive dresses.

Source: "Chitchat Upon New York and Philadelphia Fashions, for January," *Godey's Lady's Book* (January 1860).

Technology

The technology developed in America in the early nineteenth century became a part of the daily lives of Americans at home and work. The development of the steamboat by Robert Fulton changed not only the time needed for travel, but also the transportation of goods along the rivers in the U.S. Steamboats on western waters and sailing ships on oceans decreased the time and cost of moving goods, further driving the market revolution in America. The further refinement of steam power came in the development of the railroad locomotive, and its race with a horse-driven carriage led to its expanded use and helped spur the growth of the United States both economically and physically. We can see the effects both these machines had on travel in a description of a ride from New York to Philadelphia. That is followed by a description of the assembling of a musket and the manufacture of interchangeable parts. Interchangeable parts helped in the growth of industry in the United States during the American Civil War and also made it possible to repair manufactured items more easily.

12. Robert Fulton on the First Voyage of His Steamboat (1807)

Robert Fulton invented and built the first commercially viable steamboat. The following selection includes two of his own accounts of its first voyage up and down the Hudson River between the cities of New York and Albany in 1807. The first is a letter to the editor of a New York newspaper, The American Citizen; *the second is a letter to his friend and supporter Joel Barlow, which is excerpted from a book by Fulton's great-granddaughter. The steam-powered riverboat is just one of the applications of the steam engine, including oceangoing steamships, agricultural equipment, power for manufacturing equipment, and railroad engines, among others. While Fulton successfully applied steam power, he was not the inventor of the steam engine; various inventors and engineers had been developing and improving on steam engines throughout the eighteenth century. Steam power was reliable, efficient, flexible, and portable. It could be adapted to a variety of fuels; anything that can heat water to turn it into steam can be used. The pressure created by steam is then used to create mechanical energy. In short, the steam engine provided the power for the Industrial Revolution.*

Before the design of effective steam engines, the sources of mechanical energy available to power human civilization were limited to muscle—either human or animal—wind, and water. Efficiently harnessing wind and water is dependent on having falling water or blowing wind. Both were limited by the location and amount of wind or flowing water. Practical steam power represented a tremendous technological change. Steam provided immense, portable power. No longer did machinery or factories have to be built where there was falling water to power them. No longer did moving people or materials over long distances require waiting for winds to drive sailing ships or maintaining draft animals to pull them. Fulton's steamboat showed how transportation was being revolutionized, but it was just the beginning. Energy became cheap and abundant, and the process of moving and building the modern world with the technology of steam power was begun.

New York, August 20, [1807]

To the Editor of *The American Citizen*, Sir:

I arrived this afternoon, at four o'clock, [on] the steam boat from Albany. As the success of my experiment gives me great hopes that such boats may be rendered of great importance to my country, to prevent erroneous opinions and give some satisfaction to the friends of useful improvements, you will have the goodness to publish the following statement of facts:

I left New York on Monday at 1 o'clock, and arrived at Clermont, the seat of Chancellor Livingston, at 1 o'clock on Tuesday, time 24 hours; distance, one hundred and ten miles: On Wednesday I departed from the Chancellor's at 9 in the morning, and arrived at Albany at 5 in the afternoon, distance, 40 miles, time, 8 hours; the sum is 150 miles in 32 hours, equal near 5 miles an hour.

On Thursday, at 9 o'clock in the morning, I left Albany, and arrived at the Chancellor's at 6 in the evening; I started from thence at 7, and arrived at New York at 4 in the afternoon; time, 30 hours, space run through 150 miles, equal to 5 miles an hour. Throughout my whole way my going and returning the wind was ahead; no advantage could be derived from my sails—the whole has therefore been performed by the power of the steam engine.

I am, Sir,
Your most obedient,
Robert Fulton

[Letter to Joel Barlow]

My steamboat voyage to Albany and back has turned out rather more favorably than I had calculated. The distance from New York to Albany is one hundred and fifty miles. I ran it up in thirty-two hours, and down in thirty. I had a light breeze against me the whole way, both going and coming, and the voyage has been performed wholly by the power of the steam engine. I overtook many sloops and schooners, beating to the windward, and parted with them as if they had been at anchor. The power of propelling boats by steam is now fully proved. The morning I left New York there were not perhaps thirty persons in the city who believed that the boat would ever move one mile an hour, or be of the least utility; and while we were putting off from the wharf, which was crowded with spectators, I heard a number of sarcastic remarks. This is the way in which ignorant men compliment what they call philosophers and projectors.

Having employed much time, money, and zeal in accomplishing this work, it gives me, as it will you, great pleasure to see it fully answer my expectations. It will give a cheap and quick conveyance to the merchandise on the Mississippi, Missouri, and the great rivers, which are now laying open their treasures to the enterprise of our countrymen; and although the prospect of personal emolument has been some inducement to me, yet I feel indefinitely more pleasure in reflecting on the immense advantage my country will derive from the invention.

Source: Alice Crary Sutcliffe, *Robert Fulton and the "Clermont": The Authoritative Story of Robert Fulton's Early Experiments, Persistent Efforts, and Historic Achievements* (New York: The Century Co., 1909).

13. The Race between a Steam Engine and a Horse (1830)

One of the most exciting events that took place in America in the early nineteenth century was the race between the first American-built steam locomotive, the Tom Thumb, *and a horse-drawn car in 1830. The locomotive was winning until it slipped a belt, but the point had been made about the viability of the steam locomotive. The Baltimore and Ohio Railroad then began holding trials for a heavier engine capable of pulling freight and passenger cars. The development of railroads in the United States during the nineteenth century would change its economy, and make it possible for Americans to one day travel from coast to coast. Here, John H. Latrobe, an official with the B & O, describes the race.*

The boiler of Mr. Cooper's engine was not as large as the kitchen boiler attached to many a range in modern mansions. It was of about the same diameter, but not much more than half as high. It stood upright in the car, and was filled, above the furnace, which occupied the lower section, with vertical tubes. The cylinder was but three-and-a half inches in diameter, and speed was gotten up by gearing. No natural draught could have been sufficient to keep up steam in so small a boiler; and Mr. Cooper used therefore a blowing-apparatus, driven by a drum attached to one of the car wheels, over which passed a cord that in its turn worked a pulley on the shaft of the blower. . . .

Mr. Cooper's success was such as to induce him to try a trip to Ellicott's Mills; and an open car, the first used upon the road, already mentioned, having been attached to his engine, and filled with the directors and some friends, the speaker among the rest, the first journey by steam in America was commenced. The trip was most interesting. The curves were passed without difficulty at a speed of fifteen miles an hour; the grades were ascended with comparative ease; the day was fine, the company in the highest spirits, and some excited gentlemen of the party pulled out memorandum books, and when at the highest speed, which was eighteen miles an hour, wrote their names and some connected sentences, to prove that even at that great velocity it was possible to do so. The return trip from the Mills—a distance of thirteen miles—was made in fifty-seven minutes.

But the triumph of this Tom Thumb engine was not altogether without a drawback. The great stage proprietors of the day were Stockton & Stokes; and on this occasion a gallant gray of great beauty and power was driven by them from town, attached to another car on the second track—for the Company had begun by making two tracks to the Mills—and met the engine at the Relay House on its way back. From this point it was determined to have a race home; and, the start being even, away went horse and engine, the snort of the one and the puff of the other keeping time and tune.

At first the gray had the best of it, for *his* steam would be applied to the greatest advantage on the instant, while the engine had to wait until the rotation of the wheels set the blower to work. The horse was perhaps a quarter of a mile ahead when the safety valve of the engine lifted and the thin blue vapor issuing from it showed an excess of steam. The blower whistled, the steam blew off in vapory clouds, the pace increased, the passengers shouted, the engine gained on the horse, soon it lapped him—the silk was plied—the race was neck and neck, nose and nose—then the engine passed the horse, and a great hurrah hailed the victory.

But it was not repeated; for just at this time, when the gray's master was about giving up, the band which drove the pulley, which drove the blower, slipped from the drum, the safety valve ceased to scream, and the engine for want of breath began to wheeze and pant. In vain Mr. Cooper, who was his own engineman and fireman, lacerated his hands in attempting to replace the band upon the wheel: in vain he tried to urge the fire with light wood; the horse gained on the machine, and passed it; and although the band was presently replaced, and steam again did its best, the horse was too far ahead to be overtaken, and came in the winner of the race.

Source: John H. B. Latrobe, *The Baltimore and Ohio Railroad: Personal Recollections, a Lecture, Delivered before the Maryland Institute March 23, 1868* (Baltimore, MD: Sun Printing Establishment, 1868).

14. *Travel from New York to Philadelphia (1838)*

The development of the steamboat and the steam locomotive had a great impact on the lives of Americans in the nineteenth century. It was now possible to travel in a day distances that formerly took a week. In an account of his travel from New York to Philadelphia, Englishman Andrew Bell describes the speed that made it possible for those who had business in the two cities to travel quickly between them.

After some further stay at New York—nothing suitable in the way of business having presented itself there, and as I had contracted no great liking to that city, nor had the best opinion of its salubrity as a place to settle in permanently—I began to think of visiting other American cities. I had, even before coming to the country, a strong predilection for Philadelphia, and thither I determined to go. Its easy distance from New York, not quite 100 miles, and the rapidity and regularity with which the passage to it is made, enabled me to gratify my desire without much trouble. During eight months of the year the Philadelphia steam-boats start from New York twice every morning, one at eight and another at six. There is a double set of these employed; one set on the Hudson, the other on the Delaware. Intermediate between the water conveyances is that by land locomotives on the railroad, about sixty miles long, laid across New Jersey state to Camden, and ending at Camden. Here then are two transfers of passengers and baggage; and yet with such celerity and punctuality are things managed, that in midsummer it is possible for a merchant of one of the cities to pass to and fro in a day, and still leave an interval of nearly two hours to transact business in. The most admirable part of the whole affair is the disposal of the baggage. The porter is directed to take your baggage to the lower deck; where, on an open space, it is set down indiscriminately with the trunks, &c. of others; but no sooner is the boat under way, than half a dozen active fellows begin to stow them into small strongly-built wooden houses, equipped with what you take to be castors underneath, but which are wheels fitted to the rails of the road. They are numbered 1, 2, 3, &c., and so many of them as may be necessary are filled with the packages. It is desirable for a passenger to be present at this business, as he will then know out of which number his goods ought to come to light; for want of proper precaution in this way, I knew a Scotch emigrant, who lost all the clothes and money he brought with him from home, exceeding £100 in value, and the savings of several years. It was the beginning of a series of misfortunes, which brought on melancholy madness, and ended in his drowning himself in the Schuylkill a few weeks before I left. It is said there are often thieves on board these boats, ever ready to take advantage of the negligence of the unwary. As soon as the steam-boat arrives at the landing there, these heavy machines are rolled off the deck to the railroad; then they are joined to each other, and hooked on to the rearmost trains; when, the passengers having taken their places, the whole moves off in two or three minutes after leaving the boat.

Source: Andrew Bell, *Men and Things in America: Being the Experience of a Year's Residence in the United States; in a Series of Letters to a Friend*, by A. Thomason [pseud.] (London: W. Smith, 1838), 161–63.

15. *Assembling the Musket (1852)*

The assembling of the musket is discussed here in a visit to the Springfield Armory in Massachusetts. Not only do we see the growing use of machinery in the process of assembly, we also see the manufacture of a piece of equipment with interchangeable parts, something that would help soldiers during the American Civil War and become standard in the manufacture of other products as well.

When the several parts are all finished, the operation of putting them together so as to make up the musket from them complete is called assembling the musket. The workman who performs this function has all the various parts before him at his bench, arranged in boxes and compartments, in regular order, and taking one component from this place, and another from that, he proceeds to put the complicated piece of mechanism together. His bench is fitted up expressly for the work which he is to perform upon it, with a vice to hold without marring, and rests to support without confining, and every other convenience and facility which experience and ingenuity can suggest. With these helps, and by means of the dexterity which continued practice gives him, he performs the work in a manner so adroit and rapid, as to excite the wonder of every beholder. In fact it is always a pleasure to see anything done that is done with grace and dexterity, and this is a pleasure which the visitor to the Armory has an opportunity to enjoy at almost every turn.

The component parts of the musket are all made according to one precise pattern, and thus when taken up at random they are sure to come properly together. There is no individual fitting required in each particular case. Any barrel will fit into any stock, and a screw designed for a particular plate or band, will enter the proper hole in any plate or band of a hundred thousand. There are many advantages which result from this precise conformity to an established pattern in the components of the musket.

In the first place the work of manufacturing it is more easily performed in this way. It is always the tendency of machinery to produce similarity in its results, and thus although where only two things are to be made it is very difficult to get them alike, the case is very different where there is a call for two hundred thousand.

In this last case it is far easier and cheaper to have them alike than to have them different; for in manufacturing on such a scale a machinery is employed, which results in fashioning every one of its products on the precise model to which the inventor adapted the construction of it. Then besides, a great convenience and economy results from this identity of form in the component parts of the musket, when the arms are employed in service. Spare screws, locks, bands, springs, & c., can be furnished in quantities, and sent to any remote part of the country wherever they are required; so that when any part of a soldier's gun becomes injured or broken, its place can be immediately supplied by a new piece, which is sure to fit as perfectly into the vacancy as the original occupant. Even after a battle there is nothing to prevent the surviving soldiers from making up themselves, out of a hundred broken and dismantled muskets, fifty good ones as complete and sound as ever, by rejecting what is damaged, and assembling the uninjured parts anew.

To facilitate such operations as these the mechanism by which the various parts of the musket are attached to each other and secured in their places, is studiously contrived with a view to facilitating in the highest degree the taking of them apart, and putting them together. Each soldier to whom a musket is served is provided with a little tool, which, though very simple in its construction, consists of several parts and is adapted to the performance of several functions. With the assistance of this tool the soldier sitting on the bank by the roadside, at a pause in the middle of his march, if the regulations of the service would allow him to do so, might separate his gun into its forty-seven components, and spread the parts out upon the grass around him. Then if any part was doubtful he could examine it. If any was broken he could replace it and after having finished his inspection he could reconstruct the mechanism, and march on as before.

It results from this system that to make any change, however slight, in the pattern of the musket or in the form of any of the parts of it, is attended with great difficulty and expense. The fashion and form of every one of the component portions of the arm, are very exactly and rigidly determined by the machinery that is employed in making it, arid and any alteration, however apparently insignificant, would require a change in this machinery. It becomes necessary, therefore, that the precise pattern both of the whole musket and of all of its parts, once fixed, should remain permanently the same.

The most costly of the parts which lie before the workman in assembling the musket is the barrel. The value of it complete is three dollars. From the barrel we go down by a gradually descending seale to the piece of smallest value, which is a little wire called the ramrod spring wire the value of which is only one mill; that the workman is paid only one dollar a thousand for the manufacture of it. The time expended in assembling a musket is about ten minutes, and the price paid for the work is four cents.

Source: *Harper's New Monthly Magazine* 5, no. 26 (July 1852): 158.

Part VI
POLITICAL LIFE

The political life that Americans constructed after the American Revolution has become a model for democracy across the globe. The United States was founded on the principle that "all men are created equal" and has struggled to understand and realize that principle ever since. The governments that were created by the Founding Fathers in the states and then at the national level with the U.S. Constitution were premised on the principle that men needed a say in how their governments functioned. Americans were suspicious of government, but they also recognized the need for it to bring order, promote progress, and protect them from enemies, within and without. For much of the period after the American Revolution, Americans expected their governments to support economic growth, whether with internal improvements or by opening up land for settlement. But realizing the definition of "all men are created equal" proved more difficult. There was disagreement about what the concept meant in terms of allocating authority, political participation, and even basic civil rights. The prevailing assumptions of the day were that women were not to be entrusted with political power, despite their important roles in the American Revolution and later as social reformers, and that blacks had little or no claim to the same rights of public access and resources, much less political participation, that whites had. Slaves had no rights at all.

The structure of government and the balance between the rights of the majority and the rights of the minority were issues that came to threaten the very existence of the nation and would be debated from the formation of the Constitution to the eve of the Civil War. The development of America's legal system was unique in the world, and the lives of Americans were affected every day by the courts and the carrying out of justice, especially at the local level. The United States fought three major wars from 1775 to 1860: the first its struggle to free itself from Great Britain; the second in 1812, again with Great Britain to protect its sovereignty; and with Mexico over territorial ambitions and claims from Texas to California. The expansion of the United States was a political given, for virtually all public figures trumpeted support for it, but expansion brought the issue of slavery into politics, despite efforts of the major political parties to keep it out. The inability of the nation to deal with the slavery question ended in southern secession and then civil war. The ordeal of the slaves made the idea of freedom for all men seem an anachronism.

Social Hierarchy

The idea that "all men are created equal" was the core of the principles laid down by the Declaration of Independence, but the definition of all men didn't include all people. In this section we see first the treatment of slaves on a southern plantation and how this belied the idea of freedom for all. The nineteenth century saw differences of opinion on the role of women in American society. Some women argued that they should remain at home to create a stable environment for the children and teach the young the ideals of republicanism. Other women argued that they deserved the same rights as men and should be given the right to vote in order to have a say in how the government was run and to reform the corruption and cynicism of politics.

1. *Cruelty to Slaves on a Mississippi Plantation (1824)*

This letter by Henry Cogswell Knight from New Orleans details the brutality on a Mississippi plantation. Knight was an Englishman who traveled extensively in the southern and western states in the early nineteenth century under the pseudonym Arthur Singleton and published his letters to his brother during that time. Here he gives a vivid account of the cruelty slaves suffered at the hands of their masters and comments that their masters may experience justice from God when they are called to judgment.

Natchez is a city set on a hill, and yet hid. It stands two hundred feet above the river, on a *bluff* of almost perpendicular ascent, back of a low landing place, which intervenes; thus it cannot be viewed from the river. The few mansions are open with windows, and doors, for ventilation. Near Natchez, are some Indian tumuli, not unlike many in the west. The *levee*, or *embankment*, commences, on one side, at Natchez. What flat lands are in New-England called *intervales*, the Western planters call *bottoms*, or *prairies;* and the Southern, *natural meadows*, or *savannahs*. The intervales between pine tracts and the savannahs, are called *hammocks;* and, except that they have wood, are similar to the latter. The plantations here are generally sold in form of a parallelogram; forty *arpents* (French acres) deep from front to rear. The river alluvion is the best arable soil. The western-side plantations are the most valuable; being less frost-bitten by north-winds; as the vapours from the river are warmer than the air. The plantation mansions are commonly of one story, light and airy, with surrounding piazzas, and delightfully fragrant orangeries. You can imagine nothing more grateful, than to walk among these orange groves. Not far from the mansions, may be seen immense sugar-houses; and long rows, or squares, like a fort, of slave-quarters; with a tall belfry in the midst, to summon the slaves from their repose to their tasks at daybreak. It appears rather a paradox, that a planter, although he may buy slaves, yet has an abhorrence of a slave-dealer. I learnt many particulars about the living, and punishment, of slaves. The planters, although kind and hospitable to visitors, are, perhaps more from custom and policy, than inhumanity, cruel task-masters to their slaves; or boys and wenches, as they call them, however old. A sugar planter is discouraged, if he cannot pay for his plantation in five or six years; and thinks, if he gets ten years labour from a slave, he does well, although the slave then die. The slaves have three distinct tasks on every day; the before-sun task, the day-task, and the evening-task. A planter is not rich, unless he owns a hundred slaves; and, in the cotton season, may be seen, sometimes, four or five hundred at once in a field, in their loose gabardines, picking the bolls. Little children can do this work; and small boys go entirely nude, in some places. Under some masters, the slaves, unless they raise poultry themselves, which they are permitted to do, receive flesh only three times a year, and this on holidays. Their usual fare is, a peck of corn in the ear a week, which they must break in their hand-mills; and the *grit*, or refuse, of rice, like the western *screenings* of wheat; and, for relish, a salt herring. I regret to say, that the slaves will frequently exchange even this their scanty unsavoury meal for whiskey, which is sometimes distilled from the Carolina potatoe; any expedient to aid them to forget themselves. When they proceed in droves to their several tasks, a driver follows, with a huge long heavy stimulator. If a slave be slack in his labour, his feet are locked in the stocks, and his back answers it. A girl, for running out at nights, may wear, for a week, under her chin, an iron ruff, with a sharp-peaked border. My desire is not, that the Creator would have mercy on the masters, as they have mercy on their suffering slaves. Even female nature here sometimes loses its commiseration for the slave, as may be exemplified by the following unfeeling story. A rich planter's lady had long been in a consumption, and was now in the last stages of life; when, one day, one of her old slaves came to the gate, nearly blind, and bending down under the burthen of almost one hundred years of faithful service for herself, and her father, and her grandfather, before her. His remnants of clothing were so patched, that you could hardly tell what patch was ever of any colour, or substance. On his woolly head, all gray with age, was a cap of straw of his own twisting. He stood, weeping like a child, and said, that he had crept up once more from the cotton field, and had been three days coming, to see his sick mistress before she died. His mistress sent for him to come in, and spake kindly unto him; and when he was going to try to walk back again, he turned, and begged of his sick mistress to give him a little salt to put into his *grit*, or small hominy of rice. "Begone;" cried the almost dying mistress, flying into a deep rage; "Begone; out this instant, you old white-woolled skeleton; out, out, I say; or I'll send you to the driver." No words can add to this. It is painful to reflect, that, from the sweat of the brows of these trampled wretches, do we receive many of the comforts, and luxuries, of life.

Source: Henry Cogswell Knight, *Letters from the South and West; By Arthur Singleton, Esq.* (Boston: Richardson and Lord; J.H.A. Frost, printer, 1824), 110–12.

2. *Catharine Beecher's* A Treatise on Domestic Economy *(1841)*

In 1841 Catharine Beecher wrote a book that attempted to explain the duties that American women should perform at home. Rather than looking outside the home to contribute to American society, Beecher spelled out ways that the chores carried out by the wife at home were important in the development of America. She believed that women should be educated so that they could teach their children, were more needed at home, and the involvement of women in politics would corrupt them.

There are some reasons, why American women should feel an interest in the support of the democratic institutions of their Country, which it is important that they should consider which is the basis of all our civil and political institutions, is, that "all men are created equal," and that they are equally entitled to "life, liberty, and the pursuit of happiness."

But it can readily be seen, that this is only another mode of expressing the fundamental principle which the Great Ruler of the Universe has established, as the law of His eternal government. "Thou shalt love thy neighbor as thyself;" and "Whatsoever ye would that men should do to you, do ye even so to them," are the Scripture forms, by which the Supreme lawgiver requires that each individual of our race shall regard the happiness of others, as of the same value as his own; and which forbid any institution, in private or civil life, which secures advantages to one class, by sacrificing the interests of another.

The principles of democracy, then, are identical with the principles of Christianity.

But, in order that each individual may pursue and secure the highest degree of happiness within his reach, unimpeded by the selfish interests of others, a system of laws must be established, which sustain certain relations and dependencies in social and civil life. What these relations and their attending obligations shall be, are to be determined, not with reference to the wishes and interests of a few, but solely with reference to the general good of all; so that each individual shall have his own interest, as well as the public benefit, secured by them.

For this purposes it is needful that certain relations be sustained, which involve the duties of subordination. There must be the magistrate and the subject, one of whom is the superior, and the other the inferior. There must be the relations of husband and wife, parent and child, teacher and pupil, employer and employed, each involving the relative duties of subordination. The superior, in certain particulars, is to direct, and the inferior is to yield obedience. Society could never go forward, harmoniously, nor could any craft or profession be successfully pursued, unless these superior and subordinate relations be instituted and sustained.

But who shall take the higher, and who the subordinate, stations in social and civil life? This matter, in the ease [case] of parents and children, is decided by the Creator. He has given children to the control of parents as their superiors, and to them they remain subordinate, to a certain age, or so long as they are members of their household. And parents can delegate such a portion of their authority to teachers and employers as the interests of their children require.

In most other cases, in a truly Democratic State, each individual is allowed to choose for himself who shall take the position of his superior. No woman is forced to obey any husband but the one she chooses for herself; nor is she obliged to take a husband, if she prefers to remain single. So every domestic, and every artisan or laborer, after passing from parental control, can choose the employer to whom he is to accord obedience, or if he prefers to relinquish certain advantages, he can remain without taking a subordinate place to any employer.

Each subject, also has equal power with every other to decide who shall be his superior as a ruler. The weakest, the poorest, the most illiterate has the same opportunity to determine this question, as the richest, the most learned, and the most exalted.

And the various privileges that wealth secures, are equally open to all classes. Every man may aim at riches, unimpeded by any law or institution which secures peculiar privileges to a favored class, at the expense of another. Every law, and every institution, is tested by examining whether it secures equal advantages to all; and, if the people become convinced that any regulation sacrifices the good of the majority to the interests of the smaller number, they have power to abolish it.

The institutions of monarchical and aristocratic nations are based on precisely opposite principles. They secure, to certain small and favored classes, advantages, which can be maintained, only by sacrificing the interests of the great mass of the people. Thus, the throne and aristocracy of England are supported by laws and customs, which burden the lower classes with taxes, so enormous as to deprive then of all the luxuries, and of most of the comforts, of life. Poor dwellings, scanty food, unhealthy employments, excessive labor; and entire destitution of the means and time for education, are, appointed for the lower classes, that a few may live in palaces, and riot in every indulgence.

The tendencies of democratic institutions in reference to the rights and interests of the female sex, have been fully developed in the United States; and it is in this aspect, that the subject is one of peculiar interest to American women. In this Country, it is established, both by opinion and by practice, that woman has an equal interest in all social and civil concerns; and that no domestic, civil, or political, institution, is right, which sacrifices her interest to promote that of the other sex. But in order to secure her the more firmly in all these privileges, it is decided, that, in the domestic relation she take a subordinate station, and that, in civil and political concerns, her interests be intrusted to the other sex, without her taking any part in voting, or in making and administering laws. The result of this order of things has been fairly tested, and is thus portrayed by M. De Tocqueville, a writer, who for intelligence, fidelity, and ability, ranks second to none.

There are people in Europe, who, confounding together the different characteristics of the sexes, would make of man and woman beings not only equal, but alike. They would give to both the same functions, impose on both the same duties, and grant to both the same rights. They would mix them in all things,—their business, their occupations, their pleasures. It may readily be conceived, that, by *thus* attempting to make one sex equal to the other, both are degraded; and, from so preposterous a medley of the works of Nature, nothing could ever result, but weak men and disorderly women.

It is not thus that the Americans understand the species of democratic equality, which may be established between the sexes. They admit, that, as Nature has appointed such wide differences between the physical and moral constitutions of man and woman, her manifest design was to give a distinct employment to their various faculties; and they hold that improvement does not consist in making beings so dissimilar do pretty nearly the same things, but in getting each of them to fulfil their respective tasks in the best possible manner. The Americans have applied to the sexes the great principle of political economy, which governs the manufacturing of our age, by carefully dividing the duties of man from those of woman, in order that the great work of Society may be the better carried on.

"In no country has such constant care been taken, as in America, to trace two clearly distinct lines of action for the two sexes, and to make them keep pace one with the other, but in two pathways which are always different. American women never manage the outward concerns of the family, or conduct a business, or take a part in political life; nor are they, on the other hand, ever compelled to perform the rough labor of the fields, or to make any of those laborious exertions, which demand the exertion of physical strength. No families are so poor, as to form an exception to this rule.

"If, on the one hand, an American woman cannot escape from the quiet circle of domestic employments, on the other hand, she is never forced to go beyond it. Hence it is, that the women of America, who often exhibit a masculine strength of understanding, and a manly energy, generally preserve great delicacy of personal appearance, and always retain the manners of women, although they sometimes show that they have the hearts and minds of men.

"Nor have the Americans ever supposed, that one consequence of democratic principles, is, the subversion of marital power, or the confusion of the natural authorities in families. They hold, that every association must have a head, in order to accomplish its object; and that the natural head of the conjugal association is man. They do not, therefore, deny him the right of directing his partner; and they maintain, that, in the smaller association of husband and wife, as well as in the great social community, the object of democracy is, to regulate and legalize the powers which are necessary, not to subvert all power.

"This opinion is not peculiar to one sex, and contested by the other. I never observed, that the women of America considered conjugal authority as a fortunate usurpation of their rights, nor that they though themselves degraded by submitting to it. It appears to me, on the contrary, that they attach a sort of pride to the voluntary surrender of their own will, and make it their boast to bend themselves to the yoke, not to shake it off. Such, at least, is the feeling expressed by the most virtuous of their sex; the others are silent; and in the United States it is not the practice for a guilty wife to clamor for the rights of woman, while she is trampling on her holiest duties."

* * *

It is true, that the Americans rarely lavish upon women those eager attentions which are commonly paid them in Europe. But their conduct to women always implies, that they suppose them to be virtuous and refined; and such is the respect entertained for the moral freedom of the sex, that, in the presence of a woman, the most guarded language is used, lest her ear should be offended by an expression. In America, a young unmarried woman may, alone, and without fear, undertake a long journey.

Thus the Americans do not think that man and woman have either the duty, or the right, to perform the same offices, but they show; an equal regard for both their respective parts; and though their lot is different they consider both of them, as being of equal value. They do not give to the courage of woman the same form, or the same direction, as to that of a man; but they never doubt her courage and if they hold that man and his partner ought not always to exercise their intellect and understanding in the same manner, they at least believe the understanding of one to be as sound as that of the other, and her intellect to be as clear. Thus, then, while they have allowed the social inferiority of woman to subsist they have done all they could to raise her, morally and intellectually, to the level of man; and, in this respect, they appear to me to have excellently understood the true principle of democratic improvement.

"As for myself, I do not hesitate to avow, that, although the women of the United States are confined within the narrow circle of domestic life, and their situation is, in some respects, one of extreme dependence, I have nowhere seen women occupying a loftier position; and if I were asked, now I am drawing to the close of this work, in which I have spoken of so many important things done by the Americans, to what the singular prosperity and growing strength of that people ought mainly to be attributed, I should reply,—*to the superiority of their women.*"

* * *

It appears, then, that it is in America, alone, that women are raised to an equality with the other sex; and that, both in theory and practice, their interests are regarded as of equal value. They are made subordinate in station, only where a regard to their best interests demands it, while, as if in compensation for this, by custom and courtesy, they are always treated as superiors. Universally in this country, through every class of society, precedence is given to woman, in all the comforts, conveniences, and courtesies, of life.

In civil and political affairs, American women take no interest or concern, except so far as they sympathize with their family and personal friends; but in all cases, in which they do feel a concern, their opinions and feelings have a consideration, equal, or even superior, to that of the other sex.

In matters pertaining to the education of their children, in the selection and support of a clergyman, in all benevolent enterprises, and in all questions relating to morals or manners, they have a superior influence. In such concerns, it would be impossible to carry a point, contrary to their judgement and feelings; while an enterprise, sustained by them, will seldom fail of success.

If those who are bewailing themselves over the fancied wrongs and injuries of woman in this Nation, could only see things as they are, they would know, that, whatever remnants of a barbarous or aristocratic age may remain in our civil institutions, in reference to the interests of women, it is only because they are ignorant of them, or do not use their influence to have them rectified; for it is very certain that there is nothing reasonable, which American women would unite in asking, that would not readily be bestowed.

The preceding remarks, then, illustrate the position, that the democratic institutions of this Country are in reality no other than the principles of Christianity carried into operation, and that they tend to place woman in her true position in society, as having equal rights with the other sex; and that, in fact they have secured to American women a lofty and fortunate position, which, as yet, has been attained by the women of no other nation.

There is another topic, presented in the work of the above author, which demands the profound attention of American women.

The following is taken from that part of the Introduction to the work, illustrating the position, that, for ages, there has been a constant progress, in all civilized nations, towards the democratic equality attained in this Country.

> The various occurrences of national existence have every where turned to the advantage of democracy; all men have aided it by their exertions; those who have intentionally labored in its cause, and those who have served it unwittingly; those who have fought for it, and those who have declared themselves its opponents, have all been driven along in the same track, have al labored to one end;" "all have been blind instruments in the hands of God.
>
> The gradual developement of the equality of conditions, is, therefore, a Providential fact; and it possesses all the characteristics of a Divine decree: it is universal, it is durable, it constantly eludes all human interference, and all events, as well as all men, contribute to its progress.
>
> The whole book, which is here offered to the public, has been written under the impression of a kind of religious dread, produced in the author's mind, by the contemplation of so irresistible

a revolution, which has advanced for centuries, in spite of such amazing obstacles, and which is still proceeding in the midst of the ruins it has made.

It is not necessary that God Himself should speak, in order to disclose to us the unquestionable signs of His will. We can discern them in the habitual course of Nature, and in the invariable tendency of events.

If the men of our time were led, by attentive observation, and by sincere reflection, to acknowledge that the gradual and progressive developement of social equality is at once the past and future of their history, this solitary truth would confer the sacred character of a Divine decree upon the change. To attempt to check democracy, would be, in that case, to resist the will of God; and the nations would then be constrained to make the best of the social lot awarded to them by Providence.

* * *

But the part to be enacted by American women, in this great moral enterprise, is the point to which special attention should here be directed.

The success of democratic institutions, as is conceded by all, depends upon the intellectual and moral character of the mass of the people. If they are intelligent and virtuous, democracy is a blessing; but if they are ignorant and wicked, it is only a curse, and as much more dreadful than any other form of civil government, as a thousand tyrants are more to be dreaded than one. It is equally conceded, that the formation of the moral and intellectual character of the young is committed mainly to the female hand. The mother forms the character of the future man; the sister bends the fibres that are hereafter to be the forest tree; the wife sways the heart, whose energies may turn for good or for evil the destinies of a nation. Let the women of a country be made virtuous and intelligent, and the men will certainly be the same. The proper education of a man decides the welfare of an individual; but educate a woman, and the interests of a whole family are secured.

If this be so, as none will deny, then to American women, more than to any others on earth, is committed the exalted privilege of extending over the world those blessed influences, which are to renovate degraded man, and "clothe all climes with beauty."

No American woman, then, has any occasion for feeling that hers is; an humble or insignificant lot. The value of what an individual accomplishes, is to be estimated by the importance of the enterprise achieved, and not by the particular position of the laborer. The drops of heaven which freshen the earth, are each of equal value, whether they fall in the low-land meadow, or the princely parterre. The builders of a temple are of equal importance, whether they labor on the foundations, or toil upon the dome.

Thus, also, with those labors which are to be made effectual in the regeneration of the Earth. And it is by forming a habit of regarding the apparently insignificant efforts of each isolated laborer, in a comprehensive manner, as indispensable portions of a grand result, that the minds of all, however humble their sphere of service, can be invigorated and cheered. The woman, who is rearing a family of children; the woman, who labors in the schoolroom; the woman, who, in her retired chamber, earns, with her needle, the mite, which contributes to the intellectual and moral elevation of her Country; even the humble domestic, whose example and influence may be moulding [and] forming young minds, while her faithful services sustain a prosperous domestic state;—each and all may be animated by the consciousness that they are agents in accomplishing the greatest work that ever was committed to human responsibility. It is the building of a glorious temple whose base shall be coextensive with the bounds of the earth, whose summit shall pierce the skies, whose splendor shall beam on all lands, and those who hew the lowliest stone, as much as those who carve the highest capital, will be equally honored, when its top-stone shall be laid, with new rejoicings of the morning stars, and shoutings of the sons of God.

Source: Miss Catharine E. Beecher, *A Treatise on Domestic Economy, for the Use of Young Ladies at Home, and at School*, rev. ed. (Boston: T. H. Webb, 1842).

3. *Elizabeth Cady Stanton,* Address to the Legislature of New York, Adopted by the State Women's Rights Convention at Albany *(February 1854)*

Elizabeth Cady Stanton was a social activist and a leader of the women's movement in the United States. Her activities went far beyond voting rights for women and included abolition, women's custodial rights, birth control, divorce rights, and the economic rights of women. This address to the New York legislature, which was adopted by the Women's Rights Convention in Albany on February 14 and 15, 1854, gives a taste of the issues in the lives of women that Stanton believed needed to be addressed. Stanton's views on the role of women clearly differ from those of Catharine Beecher, as she believes women should have the right to participate in the political process in order to effect change.

To the Legislature of the State of New York:

"The thinking minds of all nations call for change. There is a deep-lying struggle in the whole fabric of society; a boundless, grinding collision of the New with the Old."

The tyrant, Custom, has been summoned before the bar of Common Sense. His Majesty no longer awes the multitude—his sceptre [sic] is broken—his crown is trampled in the dust—the sentence of death is pronounced upon him. All nations, ranks and classes have, in turn, questioned and repudiated his authority; and now, that the monster is chained and caged, timid woman, on tiptoe, comes to look him in the face, and to demand of her brave sires and sons, who have struck stout blows for liberty, if, in this change of dynasty, she, too, shall find relief.

Yes, gentlemen, in republican America, in the 19th century, we, the daughters of the revolutionary heroes of '76, demand at your hands the redness [redress] of our grievances—a revision of your state constitution—a new code of laws. Permit us then, as briefly as possible, to call your attention to the legal disabilities under which we labor.

1st, Look at the position of woman as woman. It is not enough for us that by your laws we are permitted to live and breathe, to claim the necessaries of life from our legal protectors—to pay the penalty of our crimes; we demand the full recognition of all our rights as citizens of the Empire State. We are persons; native, free-born citizens; property-holders, tax-payers; yet are we denied the exercise of our right to the elective franchise. We support ourselves, and, in part, your schools, colleges, churches, your poor-houses, jails, prisons, the army, the navy, the whole machinery of government, and yet we have no voice in your councils. We have every qualification required by the constitution, necessary to the legal voter, but the one of sex. We are moral, virtuous and intelligent, and in all respects quite equal to the proud white man himself, and yet by your laws we are classed with idiots, lunatics and negroes; and though we do not feel honored by the place assigned us, yet, in fact, our legal position is lower than that of either; for the negro can be raised to the dignity of a voter if he possess himself of $250; the lunatic can vote in his moments of sanity, and the idiot, too, if he be a male one, and not more than nine-tenths a fool; but we, who have guided great movements of charity, established missions, edited journals, published works on history, economy and statistics; who have governed nations, led armies, filled the professor's chair, taught philosophy and mathematics to the *savans* of our age, discovered planets, piloted ships across the sea, are denied the most sacred rights of citizens, because, forsooth, we came not into this republic crowned with the dignity of manhood! Woman is theoretically absolved from all allegiance to the laws of the state. Sec. 1, Bill of Rights, 2 R.S., 301, says that no authority can, on any pretence whatever, be exercised over the citizens of this state but such as is or shall be derived from, and *granted by, the people of this state*.

Source: *Address to the Legislature of New York, Adopted by the Women's Rights Convention Held at Albany, Tuesday and Wednesday, February 14 and 15, 1854* (Albany, NY: Weed, Parsons and Company, 1854).

Government

When the debates over the adoption of the Constitution were under way, one of the questions that emerged was the role that political factions would play in the making and enforcing of and the character of the government. This question was addressed by James Madison, who argued that a multiplicity of interests, formed into factions, was the best safeguard against tyranny, for there would be no permanent majority faction that might overrule all. Madison's great contribution was his understanding that self-interest was essential to republican politics, a concept that fit well with the ways Americans were coming to practice politics. By the 1830s political parties had become the principal means Americans used for political action. With all kinds of public performances—stump speeches, parades, bonfire gatherings—parties engaged people directly, and party loyalty was a badge almost as important as church membership for many men. But the two-party system Americans developed could not contain the nonnegotiable, divisive issue of slavery. White southerners especially worried that they were losing power in the nation as immigration swelled the northern population, and they moved to argue for protection of "minority rights"—by which they meant sectional rights. John C. Calhoun, a former vice president and senator from South Carolina, believed that the majority could be checked in accord with the needs of the minority. The issue of what obligations and role the federal government had in regard to permitting slavery to move into federal territories and what other protections it was required to provide for slaveholders' interests broke apart the old party system and gave rise to the Republican Party in the North, committed to no further extension of slavery in the territories. Southerners viewed this as the equivalent of antislavery and increased their demands for federal protection from what they regarded as a fanatical northern abolitionism taking over politics. The issue of slavery was argued in 1858 by Senator Stephen A. Douglas of Illinois and Abraham Lincoln in a series of debates that reflected the different positions northerners staked out regarding the federal government's proper role and responsibilities. The much-reported debates contributed to southern fears about Republican intentions.

4. James Madison, "The Utility of the Union as a Safeguard against Domestic Faction and Insurrection" (1787)

James Madison is considered the father of the Constitution. In the debates that took place over the ratification of the Constitution, Madison, along with Alexander Hamilton and John Jay, published a series of arguments that articulated the need for the United States to have a strong central government. In this essay written under the pseudonym Publius, Madison spells out how faction can be controlled under a strong federal government.

AMONG the numerous advantages promised by a well-constructed Union, none deserves to be more accurately developed than its tendency to break and control the violence of faction. The friend of popular governments never finds himself so much alarmed for their character and fate as when he contemplates their propensity to this dangerous vice. He will not fail, therefore, to set a due value on any plan which, without violating the principles to which he is attached, provides a proper cure for it. The instability, injustice, and confusion introduced into the public councils have, in truth, been the mortal diseases under which popular governments have everywhere perished, as they continue to be the favorite and fruitful topics from which the adversaries to liberty derive their most specious declamations. The valuable improvements made by the American constitutions on the popular models, both ancient and modern, cannot certainly be too much admired; but it would be an unwarrantable partiality to contend that they have as effectually obviated the danger on this side, as was wished and expected. Complaints are everywhere heard from our most considerate and virtuous citizens, equally the friends of public and private faith and of public and personal liberty, that our governments are too unstable, that the public good is disregarded in the conflicts of rival parties, and that measures are too often decided, not according to the rules of justice and the rights of the minor party, but by the superior force of an interested and overbearing majority. However anxiously we may wish that these complaints had no foundation, the evidence of known facts will not permit us to deny that they are in some degree true. It will be found, indeed, on a candid review of our situation, that some of the distresses under which we labor have been erroneously charged on the operation of our governments; but it will be found, at the same time, that other causes will not alone account for many of our heaviest misfortunes; and, particularly, for that prevailing and increasing distrust of public engagements and alarm for private rights which are echoed from one end of the continent to the other. These must be chiefly, if not wholly, effects of the unsteadiness and injustice with which a factious spirit has tainted our public administration.

By a faction I understand a number of citizens, whether amounting to a majority or minority of the whole, who are united and actuated by some common impulse of passion, or of interest, adverse to the rights of other citizens, or to the permanent and aggregate interests of the community.

There are two methods of curing the mischiefs of faction: the one, by removing its causes; the other, by controlling its effects.

There are again two methods of removing the causes of faction: the one, by destroying the liberty which is essential to its existence; the other, by giving to every citizen the same opinions, the same passions, and the same interests.

It could never be more truly said than of the first remedy that it was worse than the disease. Liberty is to faction what air is to fire, an aliment without which it instantly expires. But it could not be a less folly to abolish liberty, which is essential to political life, because it nourishes faction than it would be to wish the annihilation of air, which is essential to animal life, because it imparts to fire its destructive agency.

The second expedient is as impracticable as the first would be unwise. As long as the reason of man continues fallible, and he is at liberty to exercise it, different opinions will be formed. As long as the connection subsists between his reason and his self-love, his opinions and his passions will have a reciprocal influence on each other; and the former will be objects to which the latter will attach themselves. The diversity in the faculties of men, from which the rights of property originate, is not less an insuperable obstacle to a uniformity of interests. The protection of these faculties is the first object of government. From the protection of different and unequal faculties of acquiring property, the possession of different degrees and kinds of property immediately results; and from the influence of these on the sentiments and views of the respective proprietors ensues a division of the society into different interests and parties.

The latent causes of faction are thus sown in the nature of man; and we see them everywhere brought into different degrees of activity, according to the different circumstances of civil society. A zeal for different opinions concerning religion, concerning government, and many other points, as well of speculation as of practice; an attachment to different leaders ambitiously contending for pre-eminence and power; or to persons of other descriptions whose fortunes have been interesting to the human passions, have, in turn, divided mankind into parties, inflamed them with mutual animosity, and rendered them much more disposed to vex and oppress each other than to co-operate for their common good. So strong is this propensity of mankind to fall into mutual animosities that where no substantial occasion presents itself the most frivolous and fanciful distinctions have been sufficient to kindle their unfriendly passions and excite their most violent conflicts. But the most common and durable source of factions has been the various and unequal distribution of property. Those who hold and those who are without property have ever formed distinct interests in society. Those who are creditors, and those who are debtors, fall under a like discrimination. A landed interest, a manufacturing interest, a mercantile interest, a moneyed interest, with many lesser interests, grow up of necessity in civilized nations, and divide them into different classes, actuated by different sentiments and views. The regulation of these various and interfering interests forms the principal task of modern legislation and involves the spirit of party and faction in the necessary and ordinary operations of government.

No man is allowed to be a judge in his own cause, because his interest would certainly bias his judgment, and, not improbably, corrupt his integrity. With equal, nay with greater reason, a body of men are unfit to be both judges and parties at the same time; yet what are many of the most important acts of legislation but so many judicial determinations, not indeed concerning the rights of single persons, but concerning the rights of large bodies of citizens? And what are the different classes of legislators but advocates and parties to the causes which they determine? Is a law proposed concerning private debts? It is a question to which the creditors are parties on one side and the debtors on the other. Justice ought to hold the balance between them. Yet the parties are, and must be, themselves the judges; and the most numerous party, or in other words, the most powerful faction must be expected to prevail. Shall domestic manufacturers be encouraged, and in what degree, by restrictions on foreign manufacturers? are questions which would be differently decided by the landed and the manufacturing classes, and probably by neither with a sole regard to justice and the public good. The apportionment of taxes on the various descriptions of property is an act which seems to require the most exact impartiality; yet there is, perhaps, no legislative act in which greater opportunity and temptation are given to a predominant party to trample on the rules of justice. Every shilling with which they overburden the inferior number is a shilling saved to their own pockets.

It is in vain to say that enlightened statesmen will be able to adjust these clashing interests and render them all subservient to the public good. Enlightened statesmen will not always be at the helm. Nor, in many cases, can such an adjustment be made at all without taking into view indirect and remote considerations, which will rarely prevail over the immediate interest which one party may find in disregarding the rights of another or the good of the whole.

The inference to which we are brought is that the causes of faction cannot be removed and that relief is only to be sought in the means of controlling its effects.

If a faction consists of less than a majority, relief is supplied by the republican principle, which enables the majority to defeat its sinister views by regular vote. It may clog the administration, it may convulse the society; but it will be unable to execute and mask its violence under the forms of the Constitution. When a majority is included in a faction, the form of popular government, on the other hand, enables it to sacrifice to its ruling passion or interest both the public good and the rights of other citizens. To secure the public good and private rights against the danger of such a faction, and at the same time to preserve the spirit and the form of popular government, is then the great object to which our inquiries are directed. Let me add that it is the great desideratum by which alone this form of government can be rescued from the opprobrium under which it has so long labored and be recommended to the esteem and adoption of mankind.

By what means is this object attainable? Evidently by one of two only. Either the existence of the same passion or interest in a majority at the same time must be prevented, or the majority, having such coexistent passion or interest, must be rendered, by their number and local situation, unable to concert and carry into effect schemes of oppression. If the impulse and the opportunity be suffered to coincide, we well know that neither moral nor religious motives can be relied on as an adequate control. They are not found to be such on the injustice and violence of individuals, and lose their efficacy in proportion to the number combined together, that is, in proportion as their efficacy becomes needful.

From this view of the subject it may be concluded that a pure democracy, by which I mean a society consisting of a small number of citizens, who assemble and administer the government in person, can admit of no cure for the mischiefs of faction. A common passion or interest will, in almost every case, be felt by a majority of the whole; a communication and concert results from the form of government itself; and there is nothing to check the inducements to sacrifice the weaker party or an obnoxious individual. Hence it is that such democracies have ever been spectacles of turbulence and contention; have ever been found incompatible with personal security or the rights of property; and have in general been as short in their lives as they have been violent in their deaths. Theoretic politicians, who have patronized this species of government, have erroneously supposed that by reducing mankind to a perfect equality in their political rights, they would at the same time be perfectly equalized and assimilated in their possessions, their opinions, and their passions.

A republic, by which I mean a government in which the scheme of representation takes place, opens a different prospect and promises the cure for which we are seeking. Let us examine the points in which it varies from pure democracy, and we shall comprehend both the nature of the cure and the efficacy which it must derive from the Union.

The two great points of difference between a democracy and a republic are: first, the delegation of the government, in the latter, to a small number of citizens elected by the rest; secondly, the greater number of citizens and greater sphere of country over which the latter may be extended.

The effect of the first difference is, on the one hand, to refine and enlarge the public views by passing them through the medium of a chosen body of citizens, whose wisdom may best discern the true interest of their country and whose patriotism and love of justice will be least likely to sacrifice it to temporary or partial considerations. Under such a regulation it may well happen that the public voice, pronounced by the representatives of the people, will be more consonant to the public good than if pronounced by the people themselves, convened for the purpose. On the other hand, the effect may be inverted. Men of factious tempers, of local prejudices, or of sinister designs, may, by intrigue, by corruption, or by other means, first obtain the suffrages, and then betray the interests of the people. The question resulting is, whether small or extensive republics are most favorable to the election of proper guardians of the public weal; and it is clearly decided in favor of the latter by two obvious considerations.

In the first place it is to be remarked that however small the republic may be the representatives must be raised to a certain number in order to guard against the cabals of a few; and that however large it may be they must be limited to a certain number in order to guard against the confusion of a multitude. Hence, the number of representatives in the two cases not being in proportion to that of the constituents, and being proportionally greatest in the small republic, it follows that if the proportion of fit characters be not less in the large than in the small republic, the former will present a greater option, and consequently a greater probability of a fit choice.

In the next place, as each representative will be chosen by a greater number of citizens in the large than in the small republic, it will be more difficult for unworthy candidates to practice with success the vicious arts by which elections are too often carried; and the suffrages of the people being more free, will be more likely to center on men who possess the most attractive merit and the most diffusive and established characters.

It must be confessed that in this, as in most other cases, there is a mean, on both sides of which inconveniences will be found to lie. By enlarging too much the number of electors, you render the representative too little acquainted with all their local circumstances and lesser interests; as by reducing it too much, you render him unduly attached to these, and too little fit to comprehend and pursue great and national objects. The federal Constitution forms a happy combination in this respect; the great and aggregate interests being referred to the national, the local and particular to the State legislatures.

The other point of difference is the greater number of citizens and extent of territory which may be brought within the compass of republican than of democratic government; and it is this circumstance principally which renders factious combinations less to be dreaded in the former than in the latter. The smaller the society, the fewer probably will be the distinct parties and interests composing it; the fewer the distinct parties and interests, the more frequently will a majority be found of the same party; and the smaller the number of individuals composing a majority, and the smaller the compass within which they are placed, the more easily will they concert and execute their plans of oppression. Extend the sphere and you take in a greater variety of parties and interests; you make it less probable that a majority of the whole will have a common motive to invade the rights of other citizens; or if such a common motive exists, it will be more difficult for all who feel it to discover their own strength and to act in unison with each other. Besides other impediments, it may be remarked that, where there is a consciousness of unjust or dishonorable purposes, communication is always checked by distrust in proportion to the number whose concurrence is necessary.

Hence, it clearly appears that the same advantage which a republic has over a democracy in controlling the effects of faction is enjoyed by a large over a small republic—is enjoyed by the Union over the States composing it. Does this advantage consist in the substitution of representatives whose enlightened views and virtuous sentiments render them superior to local prejudices and to schemes of injustice? It will not be denied that the representation of the Union will be most likely to possess these requisite endowments. Does it consist in the greater security afforded by a greater variety of parties, against the event of any one party being able to outnumber and oppress the rest? In an equal degree does the increased variety of parties comprised within the Union increase this security? Does it, in fine, consist in the greater obstacles opposed to the concert and accomplishment of the secret wishes of an unjust and interested majority? Here again the extent of the Union gives it the most palpable advantage.

The influence of factious leaders may kindle a flame within their particular States but will be unable to spread a general conflagration through the other States. A religious sect may degenerate into a political faction in a part of the Confederacy; but the variety of sects dispersed over the entire face of it must secure the national councils against any danger from that source. A rage for paper money, for an abolition of debts, for an equal division of property, or for any other improper or wicked project, will be less apt to pervade the whole body of the Union than a particular member of it, in the same proportion as such a malady is more likely to taint a particular county or district than an entire State.

In the extent and proper structure of the Union, therefore, we behold a republican remedy for the diseases most incident to republican government, And according to the degree of pleasure and pride we feel in being republicans ought to be our zeal in cherishing the spirit and supporting the character of federalists. PUBLIUS [Madison]

Source: James Madison, "The Utility of the Union as a Safeguard Against Domestic Faction and Insurrection (Continued)," *Daily Advertiser*, November 22, 1787.

5. John C. Calhoun, "The Concurrent Majority" (1845)

John C. Calhoun, who had once been a staunch supporter of a strong central government, had changed his mind during the Nullification Crisis of 1832. South Carolina had claimed the right to nullify any federal law that acted against its interests, in this case a tariff duty. His stance led to his alienation from President Andrew Jackson and to his staunch support for states' rights. In this essay he attempts to reconcile the need for a strong central government with allowing states to repeal laws that were not in their interest.

There are two different modes in which the sense of the community may be taken; one, simply by the right of suffrage, unaided, the other, by the right through a proper organism. Each collects the sense of the majority. But one regards numbers only, and considers the whole community as a unit, having but one common interest throughout, and collects the sense of the greater number of the whole, as that of the community. The other, on the contrary regards interests as well as numbers;—considering the community as made up of different and conflicting interests, as far as the action of the government is concerned; and takes the sense of each, through its majority or appropriate organ, and the united sense of all, as the sense of the entire community. The former of these I shall call the numerical, or absolute majority; and the latter, the concurrent, or constitutional majority. I call it the constitutional majority, because it is an essential element in every constitutional government,—be its form what it may. So great is the difference, politically speaking, between the two majorities, that they cannot be confounded, without leading to great and fatal errors; and yet the distinction between them has been so entirely overlooked, that when the term *majority* is used in political discussions, it is applied to exclusively designate the numerical,—as if there were no other. Until this distinction is recognized, the better understood, there will continue to be great liability to error in properly constructing constitutional governments, especially of the popular form, and of preserving them when properly constructed. Until then the latter will have a strong tendency to slide, first, into the government of numerical majority, and finally, into absolute government of some other form. To show that such must be the case, and at the same time to mark more strongly the difference between the two, in order to guard against the danger of overlooking it, I propose to consider the subject more at length.

The first and leading error which naturally arises from overlooking the distinction referred to, is, to confound the numerical majority with the people; as this so to regard them as identical. This is a consequence that necessarily results from considering the numerical as the only majority. All admit, that a popular government, or democracy is a government of the people; for the terms imply this. A perfect government of the kind would be one which would embrace the consent of every citizen or member of the community; but as this is impracticable, in the opinion of those who regard the numerical as the only majority, and who can perceive of no other way by which the sense of the people can be taken,—they are compelled to adopt this as the only true basis of popular government, in contradistinction to governments of the aristocratical or monarchical form. Being thus constrained, they are, in the next place, forced to regard the numerical majority, as, in effect, the entire people. . . .

The necessary consequence of taking the sense of the community by concurrent majority is, [as] has been explained, to give to each interest or portion of the community a negative on the others. It is this mutual negative among its various conflicting interests, which invests each with the power of protecting itself;—and places the rights and safety of each, where only they can be safely placed, under its own guardianship. Without this there can be no systematic, peaceful, or effective resistance to the natural tendency of each to come into conflict with the others: and without this there can be no constitution. It is this negative power,—the power of preventing or arresting the action of the government,—be it called by what term it may,—veto, interposition, nullification, check, or balance of power,—which, in fact, forms the constitution. They are all but different names for the negative power.

Source: John C. Calhoun, "The Concurrent Majority (ca. 1845): A Disquisition on Government," in *The Works of John C. Calhoun*, ed. Richard Cralle (New York: D. Appleton, 1854–1857), I:28–29.

6. *The Lincoln–Douglas Debates (1858)*

The Lincoln–Douglas debates took place in Illinois during 1858 between Abraham Lincoln, the Republican Party candidate for the U.S. Senate, and Stephen A. Douglas, the incumbent Democratic Party candidate. In the early stages of the senatorial campaign, Lincoln challenged Douglas to a series of debates, which Douglas accepted. The debates were scheduled for seven towns, with the first held in Ottawa, Illinois, on August 21 and the last in Alton, Illinois, on October 15. Because the primary topic of the debates was whether or not slavery could legally be extended into free territories, the debates received wide coverage in the national press. They attracted large crowds. Stump-speaking and campaign events such as these debates were popular "entertainment" for citizens. They also were practical lessons in democracy, which the "common people" prized.

Douglas argued for the principle of popular sovereignty, which allowed for the voters of each territory to make their own decision regarding the extension of slavery. Lincoln argued that the Supreme Court, in Dred Scott v. Sandford *(1857), had allowed all new territories to have slavery, which he strongly opposed. In addition, Lincoln further distanced himself from Douglas by speaking about the moral wrongs of slavery, which he said Douglas ignored. In the election, which was decided in the Illinois legislature, Lincoln lost to Douglas by a vote of fifty-four to forty-six, but his speeches during the debates had made him a national political figure and helped him obtain the Republican Party's nomination for the presidency in 1860. Following are excerpts from the third debate, held in Jonesboro on September 15, and the seventh debate, held in Alton on October 15.*

[The Third Joint Debate, Jonesboro, September 15, 1858.]

[Abraham Lincoln's reply to Stephen Douglas:]

. . . At Freeport I propounded four interrogatories to him, claiming it as a right that he should answer as many interrogatories for me as I did for him, and I would reserve myself for a future installment when I got them ready. The Judge, in answering me upon that occasion, put in what I suppose he intends as answers to all four of my interrogatories. The first one of these interrogatories I have before me, and it is in these words:

"*Question* 1. If the people of Kansas shall, by means entirely unobjectionable in all other respects, adopt a State constitution, and ask admission into the Union under it, *before* they have the requisite number of inhabitants according to the English bill,"—some ninety-three thousand,—"will you vote to admit them?"

As I read the Judge's answer in the newspaper, and as I remember it as pronounced at the time, he does not give any answer which is equivalent to yes or no,—I will or I won't. He answers at very considerable length, rather quarrelling with me for asking the question, and insisting that Judge Trumbull had done something that I ought to say something about, and finally getting out such statements as induce me to infer that he means to be understood as he will, in that supposed case, vote for the admission of Kansas. I only bring this forward now for the purpose of saying that if he chooses to put a different construction upon his answer, he may do it. But if he does not, I shall from this time forward assume that he will vote for the admission of Kansas in disregard for the English bill. He has the right to remove any misunderstanding I may have. I only mention it now, that I may hereafter assume this to be the true construction of his answer, if he does not now choose to correct me.

The second interrogatory that I propounded to him was this:

"*Question* 2. Can the people of a United States Territory, in any lawful way, against the wish of any citizen of the United States, exclude slavery from its limits prior to the formation of a State Constitution?"

To this Judge Douglas answered that they can lawfully exclude slavery from the Territory prior to the formation of a constitution. He goes on to tell us how it can be done. As I understand him, he holds that it can be done by the Territorial Legislature refusing to make any enactments for the protection of slavery in the Territory, and especially by adopting unfriendly legislation to it. For the sake of clearness, I state it again: that they can exclude slavery from the Territory, 1st, by withholding what he assumes to be an indispensable assistance to it in the way of legislation; and, 2d, by unfriendly legislation. If I rightly understand him, I wish to ask your attention for a while to his position.

In the first place, the Supreme Court of the United States has decided that any Congressional prohibition of slavery in the Territories is unconstitutional; that they have reached this proposition as a conclusion from their former proposition, that the Constitution of the United States expressly recognizes property in slaves, and from that other Constitutional provision, that no person shall be deprived of property without due process of law. Hence they reach the conclusion that as the Constitution of the United States expressly recognizes property in slaves, and prohibits any person from being deprived of property without due process of law, to pass an Act of Congress by which a man who owned a slave on one side of a line would be deprived of him if he took him on the other side, is depriving him of that property without due process of law. That I understand to be the decision of the Supreme Court. I understand also that Judge Douglas adheres most firmly to that decision; and the difficulty is, how is it possible for any power to exclude slavery from the Territory, unless in violation of that decision? . . .

I hold that the proposition that slavery cannot enter a new country without police regulations is historically false. It is not true at all. I hold that the history of this country shows that the institution of slavery was originally planted upon this continent *without* these "police regulations" which the Judge now thinks necessary for the actual establishment of it. Not only so, but is there not another fact: how came this Dred Scott decision to be made? It was made upon the case of a negro being taken and actually held in slavery in Minnesota Territory, claiming his freedom because the Act of Congress prohibited his being so held there. *Will the Judge pretend that Dred Scott was not held there without police regulations?* There is at least one matter of record as to his having been held in slavery in the Territory, not only without police regulations, but in the teeth of Congressional legislation supposed to be valid at the time. This shows that there is vigor enough in slavery to plant itself in a new country even against unfriendly legislation. It takes not only law, but the *enforcement* of law to keep it out. That is the history of this country upon the subject.

I wish to ask one other question. It being understood that the Constitution of the United States guarantees property in slaves in the Territories, if there is any infringement of the right of that property, would not the United States courts, organized for the government of the Territory, apply such remedy as might be necessary in that case? It is a maxim held by the courts that there is no wrong without its remedy; and the courts have a remedy for whatever is acknowledged and treated as a wrong.

Again: I will ask you, my friends, if you were elected members of the Legislature, what would be the first thing you would have to do before entering upon your duties? *Swear to support the Constitution of the United States.* Suppose you believe, as Judge Douglas does, that the Constitution of the United States guarantees to your neighbors the right to hold slaves in that Territory; that they are his property: how can you clear your oaths unless you give him such legislation as is necessary to enable him to enjoy that property? What do you understand by supporting the Constitution of a State, or of the United States? Is it not to give such constitutional helps to the rights established by that Constitution as may be practically needed? Can you, if you swear to support the Constitution, and believe that the Constitution establishes a right, clear your oath, without giving it support? Do you support the Constitution if, knowing or believing there is a right established under it which needs specific legislation, you withhold that legislation? Do you not violate and disregard your oath? I can conceive of nothing plainer in the world. There can be nothing in the words "support the Constitution," if you may run counter to it by refusing support to any right established under the Constitution. And what I say here will hold with still more force against the Judge's doctrine of "unfriendly legislation." How could you having sworn to support the Constitution, and believing it guaranteed the right to hold slaves in the Territories, assist in legislation *intended to defeat that right?* That would be violating your own view of the Constitution. Not only so, but if you were to do so, how long would it take the courts to hold your votes unconstitutional and void? Not a moment.

Lastly, I would ask: Is not Congress itself under obligation to give legislative support to any right that is established under the United States Constitution? I repeat the question: Is not Congress itself bound to give legislative support to any right that is established under the United States Constitution? A member of Congress swears to support the Constitution of the United States: and if he sees a right established by that Constitution which needs specific legislative protection, can he clear his oath without giving that protection?

Let me ask you why many of us who are opposed to slavery upon principle give our acquiescence to a Fugitive Slave law? Why do we hold ourselves under obligations to pass such a law, and abide by it when it is passed? Because the Constitution makes provision that the owners of slaves shall have the right to reclaim them. It gives the right to reclaim slaves; and that right is, as Judge Douglas says, a barren right, unless there is legislation that will enforce it.

The mere declaration, "No person held to service or labor in one State under the laws thereof, escaping into another, shall in consequence of any law or regulation therein be discharged from such service or labor, but shall be delivered upon claim of the party to whom such service or labor may be due," is powerless without specific legislation to enforce it. Now, on what ground would a member of Congress, who is opposed to slavery in the abstract, vote for a Fugitive law, as I would deem it my duty to do? Because there is a constitutional right which needs legislation to enforce it. And although it is distasteful to me, I have sworn to support the Constitution; and having so sworn, I cannot conceive that I do support it if I withhold from that right any necessary legislation to make it practical. And if that is true in regard to a Fugitive Slave law, is the right to have fugitive slaves reclaimed any better fixed in the Constitution than the right to hold slaves in Territories? For this decision is a just exposition of the Constitution, as Judge Douglas thinks. Is the one right any better than the other? Is there any man who, while a member of Congress, would give support to the one any more than the other? If I wished to refuse to give legislative support to slave property in the Territories, if a member of Congress, I could not do it, holding the view that the Constitution established that right. If I did it at all, it would be because I deny that this decision properly construes the Constitution. But if I acknowledge, with Judge Douglas, that this decision properly construes the Constitution, I cannot conceive that I would be less than a perjured man if I should refuse in Congress to give such protection to that property as in its nature it needed.

[The Seventh Joint Debate, Alton, October 15, 1858.]

[Douglas' speech:]

Ladies and Gentlemen: It is now nearly four months since the canvass between Mr. Lincoln and myself commenced. On the 16th of June the Republican Convention assembled at Springfield and nominated Mr. Lincoln as their candidate for the United States Senate, and he, on that occasion, delivered a speech in which he laid down what he understood to be the Republican creed, and the platform on which he proposed to stand during the contest. The principal points in that speech of Mr. Lincoln's were: First, that the government could not endure permanently divided into free and slave States, as our fathers made it; that they must all become free or all become slave; all become one thing, or all become the other,—otherwise this Union could not continue to exist. I give you his opinions almost in the identical language he used. His second proposition was a crusade against the Supreme Court of the United States because of the Dred Scott decision, urging as an especial reason for his opposition to that decision that it deprived the negroes of the rights and benefits of the clause in the Constitution of the United States which guarantees to the citizens of each State all the rights, privileges, and immunities of the citizens of the several States. On the 10th of July I returned home, and delivered a speech to the people of Chicago, in which I announced it to be my purpose to appeal to the people of Illinois to sustain the course I had pursued in Congress. In that speech I joined issue with Mr. Lincoln on the points which he had presented. Thus there was an issue clear and distinct made up between us on these two propositions laid down in the speech of Mr. Lincoln at Springfield, and controverted by me in my reply to him at Chicago. On the next day, the 11th of July, Mr. Lincoln replied to me at Chicago, explaining at some length and reaffirming the positions which he had taken in his Springfield speech. In that Chicago speech he even went further than he had before, and uttered sentiments in regard to the negro being on an equality with the white man. He adopted in support of this position the argument which Lovejoy and Codding and other Abolition lecturers had made familiar in the northern and central portions of the State: to wit, that the Declaration of Independence having declared all men free and equal, by divine law, also that negro equality was an inalienable right, of which they could not be deprived. He insisted, in that speech, that the Declaration of Independence included the negro in the clause asserting that all men were created equal, and went so far as to say that if one man was allowed to take the position that it did not include the negro, others might take the position that it did not include other men. He said that all these distinctions between this man and that man, this race and the other race, must be discarded, and we must all stand by the Declaration of Independence, declaring that all men were created equal.

The issue thus being made up between Mr. Lincoln and myself on three points, we went before the people of the State. During the following seven weeks, between the Chicago speeches and our first meeting at Ottawa, he and I addressed large assemblages of the people in many of the central counties. In my speeches I confined myself closely to those three positions which he had taken, controverting his proposition that this Union could not exist as our fathers made it, divided into free and slave States, controverting his proposition of a crusade against the Supreme Court because of the Dred Scott decision, and controverting his proposition that the Declaration of Independence included and meant the negroes as well as the white men, when it declared all men to be created equal. . . . I took up Mr. Lincoln's three propositions in my several speeches, analyzed them, and pointed out what I believed to be the radical errors contained in them. First, in regard to his doctrine that his government was in violation of the law of God, which says that a house divided against itself cannot stand, I repudiated it as a slander upon the immortal framers of our Constitution. I then said, I have often repeated, and now again assert, that in my opinion our government can endure forever, divided into free and slave States as our fathers made it,—each State having the right to prohibit, abolish, or sustain slavery, just as it pleases. This government was made upon the great basis of the sovereignty of the States, the right of each State to regulate its own domestic institutions to suit itself; and that right was conferred with the understanding and expectation that, inasmuch as each locality had separate interest, each locality must have different and distinct local and domestic institutions, corresponding to its wants and interests. Our fathers knew when they made the government that the laws and institutions which were well adapted to the Green Mountains of Vermont were unsuited to the rice plantations of South Carolina. The [they knew] then, as well as we know now, that the laws and institutions which would be well adapted to the beautiful prairies of Illinois would not be suited to the mining regions of California. They knew that in a republic as broad as this, having such a variety of local laws,—the policy and institutions of each State adapted to its condition and wants. For this reason this Union was established on the right of each State to do as it pleased on the question of slavery, and every other question. . . .

. . . These measures [Compromise of 1850] passed on the joint action of the two parties. They rested on the great principle that the people of each State and each Territory should be left perfectly free to form and regulate their domestic institutions to suit themselves. You Whigs and we Democrats justified them in that principle. In 1854, when it became necessary to organize the Territories of Kansas and Nebraska, I brought forward the bill on the same principle. In the Kansas-Nebraska Bill you find it declared to be the true intent and meaning of the act not to legislate slavery into any State or Territory, nor to exclude it therefrom, but to leave the people thereof perfectly free to form and regulate their domestic institutions in their own way. . . . It has occurred to me that in 1854 the author of the Kansas and Nebraska Bill was considered a pretty good Democrat. It has occurred to me that in 1856, when I was exerting every nerve and every energy for James Buchanan, standing on the same platform then that I do now, that I was a pretty good Democrat. They now tell me that I am not a Democrat, because I assert that the people of a Territory, as well as those of a State, have the right to decide for themselves whether slavery can or cannot exist in such Territory. . . .

I . . . further . . . say that while, under the decision of the Supreme Court, as recorded in the opinion of Chief Justice Taney, slaves are property like all other property, and can be carried into any Territory of the United States the same as any other description of property, yet when you get them there they are subject to the local law of the Territory just like all other property. You will find in a recent speech delivered by that able and eloquent statesman Hon. Jefferson Davis, at Bangor, Maine, that he took the same view of this subject that I did in my Freeport speech. He there said:

"If the inhabitants of any Territory should refuse to enact such laws and police regulations as would give security to their property or to his, it would be rendered more or less valueless in proportion to the difficulties of holding it without such protection. In the case of property in the labor of man, or what is usually called slave property, the insecurity would be so great that the owner could not ordinarily retain it. Therefore, though the right would remain, the remedy being withheld, it would follow that the owner would be practically debarred, by the circumstances of the case, from taking slave property into a Territory where the sense of the inhabitants was opposed to its introduction. So much for the oft-repeated fallacy of forcing slavery upon any community."

You will also find that the distinguished Speaker of the present House of Representatives, Hon. Jas. L. Orr, construed the Kansas and Nebraska Bill in this same way in 1856, and also that great intellect of the South, Alex. H. Stephens, put the same construction upon it in Congress that I did in my Freeport speech. The whole South are rallying to the support of the doctrine that if the people of a Territory want slavery, they have a right to have it, and if they do not want it, that no power on earth can force it upon them. I hold that there is no principle on earth more sacred to all the friends of freedom than that which says that no institution, no law, no constitution, should be forced on an unwilling people contrary to their wishes; and I assert that the Kansas and Nebraska Bill contains that principle. It is the great principle contained in that bill. It is the principle on which James Buchanan was made President. Without that principle, he never would have been made

President of the United States. I will never violate or abandon that doctrine, if I have to stand alone. I have resisted the blandishments and threats of power on the one side, and seduction on the other, and have stood immovably for that principle, fighting for it when assailed by Northern mobs, or threatened by Southern hostility. I have defended it against the North and the South, and I will defend it against whoever assails it, and I will follow it wherever its logical conclusions lead me. I say to you that there is but one hope, one safety for this country, and that is to stand immovably by that principle which declares the right of each State and each Territory to decide these questions for themselves. . . .

[Lincoln's reply:]

. . . Now, irrespective of the moral aspect of this question as to whether there is a right or wrong in enslaving a negro, I am still in favor of our new Territories being in such a condition that white men may find a home,—may find some spot where they can better their condition; where they can settle upon new soil and better their condition in life. I am in favor of this, not merely (I must say it here as I have elsewhere) for our own people who are born amongst us, but as an outlet for *free white people everywhere*—the world over—in which Hans, and Baptiste, and Patrick, and all other men from all the world, may find new homes and better their conditions in life.

I have stated upon our former occasions, and I may as well state again, what I understand to be the real issue in this controversy between Judge Douglas and myself. . . . The real issue in this controversy—the one pressing upon every mind—is the sentiment on the part of one class that looks upon the institution of slavery *as a wrong,* and of another class that *does not* look upon it as a wrong. The sentiment that contemplates the institution of slavery in this country as a wrong is the sentiment of the Republican party. It is the sentiment around which all their actions, all their arguments, circle, from which all their propositions radiate. They look upon it as being a moral, social, and political wrong; and while they contemplate it as such, they nevertheless have due regard for its actual existence among us, and the difficulties of getting rid of it in any satisfactory way, and to all the constitutional obligations thrown about it. Yet, having a due regard for these, they desire a policy in regard to it that it should, as far as may be, *be treated* as a wrong; and one of the methods of treating it as a wrong is to *make provision that it shall grow no larger.* They also desire a policy that looks to a peaceful end of slavery at some time, as being wrong. These are the views they entertain in regard to it as I understand them: and all their sentiments, all their arguments and propositions, are brought within this range. I have said, and I repeat it here, that if there be a man amongst us who does not think that the institution of slavery is wrong in any one of the aspects of which I have spoken, he is misplaced, and ought not to be with us. And if there be a man amongst us who is so impatient of it as a wrong as to disregard its actual presence among us and the difficulty of getting rid of it suddenly in a satisfactory way, and to disregard the constitutional obligations thrown about it, that man is misplaced if he is on our platform. We disclaim sympathy with him in practical action. He is not placed properly with us.

On this subject of treating it as a wrong, and limiting its spread, let me say a word. Has anything ever threatened the existence of this Union save and except this very institution of slavery? What is it that we hold most dear amongst us? Our own liberty and prosperity. What has ever threatened our liberty and prosperity, save and except this institution of slavery? If this is true, how do you propose to improve the condition of things by enlarging slavery,—by spreading it out and making it bigger? You may have a wen or cancer upon your person, and not be able to cut it out, lest you bleed to death; but surely it is no way to cure it, to engraft it and spread it over your whole body. That is no proper way of treating what you regard as a wrong. You see this peaceful way of dealing with it as a wrong,—restricting the spread of it, and not allowing it go into new countries where it has not already existed. That is the peaceful way, the old-fashioned way, the way in which the fathers themselves set us the example.

On the other hand, I have said there is a sentiment which treats it as *not* being wrong. That is the Democratic sentiment of this day. . . .

. . . The Democratic policy in regard to that institution will not tolerate the merest breath, the slightest hint, of the least degree of wrong about it. Try it by some of Judge Douglas's arguments. He says he "don't care whether it is voted up or voted down" in the Territories. I do not care myself, in dealing with that expression, whether it is intended to be expressive of his individual sentiments on the subject, or only of the national policy he desires to have established. It is alike valuable for my purpose. Any man can say that who does not see anything wrong in slavery; but no man can logically say it who does see a wrong in it, because no man can logically say he don't care whether a wrong is voted up or voted down. He may say he don't care whether an indifferent thing is voted up or down, but he must logically have a choice between a right thing and a wrong thing. He contends that whatever community wants slaves has a right to have them. So they have, if it is not a wrong. But if it is a wrong, he cannot say people have a right to do wrong. He says that upon the score of equality slaves should be allowed to go in a new Territory, like other property. This is strictly logical if there is no difference between it and other property. If it and other property are equal, this argument is entirely logical. But if you insist that one is wrong and the other right, there is no use to institute a comparison between right and wrong. You may turn over everything in the Democratic policy from beginning to end, whether in the shape it takes on the statute book, in the shape it takes in the Dred Scott decision, in the shape it takes in conversation, or the shape it takes in short maxim-like arguments,—it everywhere carefully excludes the idea that there is anything wrong in it.

That is the real issue. That is the issue that will continue in this country when these poor tongues of Judge Douglas and myself shall be silent. It is the eternal struggle between these two principles—right and wrong—throughout the world. They are the two principles that have stood face to face from the beginning of time, and will ever continue to struggle. The one is the common right of humanity, and the other the divine right of kings. . . . And whenever we can get rid of the fog which obscures the real question, when we can get Judge Douglas and his friends to avow a policy looking to its perpetuation,—we can get out from among that class of men and bring them to the side of those who treat it as a wrong. Then there will soon be an end of it, and that end will be its "ultimate extinction." Whenever the issue can be distinctly made, and all extraneous matter thrown out so that men can fairly see the real difference between the parties, this controversy will soon be settled, and it will be done peaceably too. There will be no war, no violence. It will be placed again where the wisest and best men of the world placed it. . . .

I understand I have ten minutes yet. I will employ it in saying something about this argument Judge Douglas uses, while he sustains the Dred Scott decision, that the people of the Territories can still somehow exclude slavery. The first thing I ask attention to is the fact that Judge Douglas constantly said, before the decision, that whether they could or not, *was a question for the Supreme Court*. But after the court had made the decision he virtually says it is *not* a question for the Supreme Court, but for the people. And how is it he tells us they can exclude it? He says it needs "police regulations," and that admits of "unfriendly legislation." Although it is a right established by the Constitution of the United States to take a slave into a Territory of the United States and hold him as property, yet unless the Territorial Legislature will give friendly legislation, and more especially if they adopt unfriendly legislation, they can practically exclude him. Now, without meeting this proposition as a matter of fact, I pause to consider the real constitutional obligation. Let me take the gentleman who looks me in the face before me, and let us suppose that he is a member of the Territorial Legislature. The first thing he will do will be to swear that he will support the Constitution of the United States. His neighbor by his side in the Territory has slaves and need Territorial legislation to enable him to enjoy that constitutional right. Can he withhold the legislation which his neighbor needs for the enjoyment of a right which is fixed in his favor in the Constitution of the United States which he has sworn to support? Can he withhold it without violating his oath? And, more especially, can he pass unfriendly legislation to violate his oath? Why, this is a *monstrous* sort of talk about the Constitution of the United States! *There has never been as outlandish or lawless a doctrine from the mouth of any respectable man on earth*. I do not believe it is a constitutional right to hold slaves in a Territory of the United States. I believe the decision was improperly made and I go for reversing it. Judge Douglas is furious against those who go for reversing a decision. But he is for legislating it out of all force while the law itself stands. I repeat that there has never been so monstrous a doctrine uttered from the mouth of a respectable man. . . .

I say that no man can deny his obligations to give the necessary legislation to support slavery in a Territory, who believes it is a constitutional right to have it there. No man can, who does not give the Abolitionists an argument to deny the obligation enjoined by the Constitution to enact a Fugitive State law. Try it now. It is the strongest Abolition argument ever made. I say if that Dred Scott decision is correct, then the right to hold slaves in a Territory is equally a constitutional right with the right of a slaveholder to have his runaway returned. No one can show the distinction between them. The one is express, so that we cannot deny it. The other is construed to be in the Constitution, so that he who believes the decision to be correct believes in the right. And the man who argues that by unfriendly legislation, in spite of that constitutional right, slavery may be driven from the Territories, cannot avoid furnishing an argument by which Abolitionists may deny the obligation to return fugitives, and claim the power to pass laws unfriendly to the right of the slaveholder to reclaim his fugitive. I do not know how such an argument may strike a popular assembly like this, but I defy anybody to go before a body of men whose minds are educated to estimating evidence and reasoning, and know that there is an iota of difference between the constitutional right to reclaim a fugitive and the constitutional right to hold a slave, in a Territory, provided this Dred Scott decision is correct. I defy any man to make an argument that will justify unfriendly legislation to deprive a slaveholder of his right to hold his slave in a Territory, that will not equally, in all its length, breadth, and thickness, furnish an argument for nullifying the Fugitive Slave law. Why, there is not such an Abolitionist in the nation as Douglas, after all!

[Douglas' rejoinder:]

Mr. Lincoln tries to avoid the main issue by attacking the truth of my proposition that our fathers made this government divided into free and slave States, recognizing the right of each to decide all its local questions for itself. Did they not thus make it? It is true that they did not establish slavery in any of the States, or abolish it in any of them; but finding thirteen States, twelve of which were slave and one free, they agreed to form a government uniting them together as they stood, divided into free and slave States, and to guarantee forever to each State the right to do as it pleased on the slavery question. Having thus made the government, and conferred this right upon each State forever, I assert that this government can exist as they made it, divided into free and slave States, if any one State chooses to retain slavery. He says that he looks forward to a time when slavery shall be abolished everywhere. I look forward to a time when each State shall be allowed to do as it pleases. If it chooses to keep slavery forever, it is not my business, but its own; if it chooses to abolish slavery, it is its own business,—not mine. I care more for the great principle of self-government, the right of the people to rule, than I do for all the negroes in Christendom. I would not endanger the perpetuity of this Union, I would not blot out the great inalienable rights of the white man, for all the negroes that ever existed. Hence, I say, let us maintain this government on the principles that our fathers made it, recognizing the right of each State to keep slavery as long as its people determine, or to abolish it when they please. But Mr. Lincoln says that when our fathers made this government they did not look forward to the state of things nonexisting, and therefore he thinks the doctrine was wrong; . . . Our fathers, I say, made this government on the principle of the right of each State to do as it pleases in its own domestic affairs, subject to the Constitution, and allowed the people of each to apply to every new change of circumstances such remedy as they may see fit to improve their condition. This right they have for all time to come.

Mr. Lincoln went on to tell you that he does not at all desire to interfere with slavery in the States where it exists, nor does his party. I expected him to say that down here. Let me ask him, then, how he expects to put slavery in the course of ultimate extinction everywhere, if he does not intend to interfere with it in the States where it exists? He says that he will prohibit it in all Territories, and the inference is, then, that unless they make free States out of them he will keep them out of the Union; for, mark you, he did not say whether or not he would vote to admit Kansas with slavery or not, as her people might apply (he forgot that, as usual, etc.): he did not say whether or not he was in favor of bringing the Territories now in existence into the Union on the principle of Clay's Compromise measure on the slavery question. I told you that he would not. His idea is that he will prohibit slavery in all the Territories and thus force them all to become free States, surrounding the slave States with a cordon of free States, and hemming them in, keeping the slaves confined to their present limits whilst they go on multiplying, until the soil on which they live will no longer feed them, and he will thus be able to put slavery in a course of ultimate extinction by starvation. He will extinguish slavery in the Southern States as the French general exterminated the Algerines when he smoked them out. He is going to extinguish slavery by surrounding the Slave States, hemming in the slaves, and starving them out of existence, as you smoke a fox out of his hole. He intends to do that in the name of humanity and Christianity, in order that we may get rid of the terrible crime and sin entailed upon our fathers of holding slaves. . . .

I ask you to look into these things, and then tell me whether the Democracy or the Abolitionists are right. I hold that the people of a Territory, like those of a State . . . have the right to decide for themselves whether slavery shall or shall not exist within their limits. The point upon which Chief Justice Taney expresses his opinion is simply this, that slaves, being property, stand on an equal footing with other property, and consequently that the owner has the same right to carry that property into a Territory that he has any other, subject to the same conditions. Suppose that one of your merchants was to take fifty or one hundred thousand dollars' worth of liquors to Kansas. He has a right to go there, under that decision; but when he gets there he finds the Maine liquor law in force, and what can he do with his property after he gets it there? He cannot sell it, he cannot use it; it is subject to the local law, and that law is against him, and the best thing he can do with it is to bring it back into Missouri or Illinois and sell it. If you take negroes to Kansas, as Colonel Jefferson Davis said in his Bangor speech, from which I have quoted to-day, you must take them there subject to the local law. If the people want the institution of slavery, they will protect and encourage it; but if they do not want it, they will withhold that protection, and the absence of local legislation protecting slavery excludes it as completely as a positive prohibition. You slaveholders of Missouri might as well understand, what you know practically, that you cannot carry slavery where the people do not want it. All you have a right to ask is that the people shall do as they please: if they want slavery, let them have it; if they do not want it, allow them to refuse to encourage it.

My friends, if, as I have said before, we will only live up to this great fundamental principle, there will be peace between the North and the South. Mr. Lincoln admits that under the Constitution, on all domestic questions, except slavery, we ought not to interfere with the people of each State. What right have we to interfere with slavery any more than we have to interfere with any other question? He says that this slavery question is now the bone of contention. Why? Simply because agitators have combined in all the free States to make war upon it. Suppose the agitators in the South should combine in one half of the Union to make war upon the railroad system of the other half? They would thus be driven to the same sectional strife. Suppose one section makes war upon any other peculiar institution of the opposite section, and the same strife is produced. The only remedy and safety is that we shall stand by the Constitution as our fathers made it, obey the laws as they are passed, while they stand the proper test, and sustain the decisions of the Supreme Court and the constituted authorities.

Source: Abraham Lincoln, *Political Debates between Abraham Lincoln and Stephen A. Douglas in the Celebrated Campaign of 1858 in Illinois* (Cleveland, OH: Burrows Bros. Co., 1897).

Justice and Legal Systems

The development of the American justice system from the American Revolution to 1860 can still be felt today. It became an example of the protection of the rights of the common man, as well as an arbiter of constitutional issues that affected the whole nation. The precedents established during this period would be debated and changed to evolve with a changing nation. The following documents give us just a hint of the legal scholarship of this important time in our history. In the first document, Alexis de Tocqueville discusses the American judicial system. The everyday functioning of the courts, in this case a divorce suit, is covered in a letter by a visitor to New York. A French visitor comments on the manumission of slaves by northern states toward the end of the eighteenth century in a letter and discusses how the evil of slavery still infected America and needed to be eliminated. The Supreme Court decision that many believe set the stage for the Civil War by ruling that Congress had no authority to prevent the extension of slavery into the territories shows the power of the judiciary and how its rulings affected the everyday lives of America's citizens. In that instance, many northerners and all Republicans rejected the ruling of the Court as unconstitutional and political, which contributed to the distrust between North and South.

7. *The Manumission Laws in Various States (1788)*

By the last decade of the eighteenth century almost all northern states had changed their laws to allow for the manumission of slaves or even the outright abolition of slavery, usually with provisions for some kind of payment or service due to masters. For a brief moment some southern states also provided for an easier process of manumission—the individual freeing of slaves by masters—but a major slave rebellion conspiracy in Virginia in 1800 and the growing profitability of slavery as the cotton market spread led them to retreat on that score. The question of slavery nagged at Americans from the Revolution to the Civil War, and finding ways to deal with the moral and property issues of slavery disrupted politics. The gradual abolition of slavery in the northern states made slavery—"the peculiar institution" as some called it—a regional institution, which caused southern slaveholders to worry about protecting their interests in the nation while also expanding slavery's domain. Northerners remained invested in slavery in terms of trade, supplying credit, and working up the cotton in textile mills, but their orientation toward freedom, reflected in the ending of slavery over time in northern states, suggested they would not in all ways or forever serve or permit slavery's advance. Foreign visitors to America were very much interested in slavery as an institution and an issue and invariably reported on it in their letters home and in travel accounts of the United States. One example is the account of J. P. Brissot de Warville, a French visitor, who described the manumission laws in the late 1780s and noted each state's ability to pass these laws.

SLAVERY, my friend, has never polluted every part of the United States. There was never any law in New Hampshire, or Massachusetts, which authorised it. When, therefore, those States proscribed it, they only declared the law as it existed before. There was very little of it in Connecticut; the puritanic austerity which predominated in that colony, could scarcely reconcile itself with slavery. Agriculture was better performed there by the hands of freemen; and every thing concurred to engage the people to give liberty to the slaves:—so that almost every one has freed them; and the children, of such as are not yet free, are to have their liberty at twenty-five years of age.

The cafe of the Blacks: in New-York is nearly the same; yet the slaves there are more numerous.

It is because the basis of the population there is Dutch; that is to say, people less disposed than any other to part with their property. But liberty is assured there to all the children of the slaves, at a certain age.

The State of Rhode-Island formerly made a great business of the slave trade. It is now totally and for ever prohibited.

In New-Jersey the bulk of the population is Dutch. You find there, traces of that same Dutch spirit which I have described. Yet the Western parts of the State are disposed to free their Negroes; but the Eastern part are opposed to it.

It is probable that their obstinacy will be overcome; at least it is the opinion of the respectable Mr. Livingston, celebrated for the part he has acted in the late revolution: he has declared this opinion in a letter written to the Society at Philadelphia. He has himself freed all his slaves, which are very numerous. He is one of the most ardent apostles of humanity; and, knowing the character of his countrymen, he reasons, temporises with their interest and doubts not of being able to vanquish their prejudices. The Quakers have been more fortunate in Pennsylvania.

In the year 1758, they voted, in their general meeting, to excommunicate every member of the Society who should persist in keeping slaves. In 1780, at their request, seconded by a great number of persons from other sects, the General Assembly abolished slavery for ever, forced the owners of slaves to cause them to be enregistered, declared their children free at the age of twenty-eight years, placed them, while under that age, on a footing of hired servants, assured to them the benefit of trial by jury, &c. But this act did not provide against all abuses that avarice could afterwards invent. It was illuded in many points. A foreign commerce of slaves was carried on by speculators; and some barbarous masters sold their Blacks, to be carried into foreign countries; others sent the negro children into neighbouring States; that they might be sold, and deprived of the benefit of the law of Pennsylvania, when they should come of age; others sent their black pregnant woman into another State, that the offspring might be slaves; and other stole free negroes, and carried them to the island for sale. The Society, shocked at these abuses, applied again to the Assembly, who passed a new act in March last, effectually to prevent them. It ordained, that no black could be sent into a neighbouring state without his consent; confiscated all vessels and cargoes employed in the slave trade; condemned to the public works the stealers of negroes, &c.

Doubtless we cannot bestow too much praise on the indefatigable zeal of the Society in Pennsylvania, which solicited these laws, nor on the spirit of equity and humanity displayed by the legislature in passing them; but some regret must mingle itself with our applause. Why did not this respectable body go farther? Why did it not extend at least the hopes of freedom to those who were slaves at the time of the passing the first act? They are property, it is said; and all property is sacred. But what is a property founded on robbery and plunder? What is a property which violates laws human and divine? But let this property merit some regard. Why not limit it to a certain number of years, in order to give at least the chief consolation of hope? Why not grant to the slave, the right of purchasing his freedom? What! the child of the negro slave shall one day enjoy his liberty; and the unhappy father, though ready to leap with joy on the beholding the fortune of his son, must roll back his eyes [in] aggravated anguish on his own irrevocable bondage! The son has never felt, like him, the torture of being torn from his country, from his family, from all that is dear to man; the son has not experienced that severity of treatment . . . [so] common in this country before this revolution of sentiment; yet the son is favoured, and the father consigned to despair. But this injustice cannot long sully the law of a country where reason and humanity prevail. We may hope that a capitulation will be made with avarice; by which these slaves shall be drawn from its hands.

Again—Why, in the act of March 1780, is it declared that slave cannot be a witness against a freeman? You either suppose him less true than the freeman, or you suppose him differently organized. The last supposition is absurd; the other, if true, is against yourselves; for, why are they less conscientious, more corrupted, and more wicked?—it is because they are slaves. The crime falls on the head of the master; and the slave is thus degraded and punished for the vice of the master.

Finally, why do you ordain that the master shall be reimbursed from the public treasury, the price of the slave who may suffer death for crimes? If, as is easy to prove, the crimes of slaves are almost universally the fruit of their slavery, and are in proportion to the severity of their treatment, is it not absurd to recompense the master for his tyranny? When we recollect that these masters have hitherto been accustomed to consider their slaves as a species of cattle, and that the laws make the master responsible for the damages done by his cattle, does it not appear contradictory to reverse the law relative to there black cattle, when they do a mischief, for which society thinks it necessary to extirpate them? In this case, the real author of the crime, instead of paying damages, receives a reward.

No, my friend, we will not doubt but these stains will soon disappear from the code of Pennsylvania. Reason is too predominant to suffer them long to continue.

The little State of Delaware has followed the example of Pennsylvania. It is mostly peopled by Quakers—instances of giving freedom are therefore numerous. In this state, famous for the wisdom of its laws, for its good faith and foederal patriotism, resides that angel of peace, Warner Mislin. Like Benezet, he occupies his time in extending the opinions of his Society relative to the freedom of the Blacks, and the care of providing for their existence and their instruction. It is in part to his zeal that is owing the formation of a Society in that state, after the model of the one at Philadelphia, for the abolition of slavery.

With the State of Delaware finishes the system of protection to the blacks. Yet there are some negroes freed in Maryland, because there are some Quakers there; and you perceive it very readily, on comparing the fields of tobacco or of Indian corn belonging to there people, with those of others; you see how much superior the hand of a freeman is to that of a slave, in the operations of industry.

When you run over Maryland and Virginia, you conceive yourself in a different world; and you are convinced of it, when you converse with the inhabitants. They speak not here of projects for freeing the negroes; they praise not the societies of London and America; they read not the works of Clarkson—No, the indolent masters behold with uneasiness, the efforts that are making to render freedom universal. The Virginians are persuaded of the impossibility of cultivating tobacco without slavery; they fear, that if the Blacks become free, they will cause trouble; on rendering them free, they know not what rank to assign them in society; whether they shall establish them in a separate district, or send them out of the country. These are the objections which you will hear repeated every where against the idea of freeing them.

The strongest objection lies in the character, the manners and habits of the Virginians. They seem to enjoy the sweat of slaves. They are fond of hunting; they love the display of luxury, and disdain the idea of labour. This order of things will change when slavery shall be no more. It is not, that the work of a slave is more profitable than that of a freeman; but it is in multiplying the slaves, condemning them to a miserable nourishment, in depriving them of cloaths, and in running over a large quantity of land with a negligent culture, that they supply the necessity of honest industry.

T LETTER

Source: J. P. Brissot de Warville, *New Travels in the United States of America. Performed in 1788*, trans. from the French (Dublin: Printed by W. Corbet, for P. Byrne, A. Gueber [etc.], 1792), 274–81.

8. A *Day in Divorce Court* (1838)

The regular and ordinary operations of the court system in the United States gave law meaning in everyday life. Most Americans met the law at the local level, or perhaps the state level, over matters of property. Questions of property rights loomed ever larger with the market revolution, which pulled more people into matters of contracts and property rights. Domestic issues were also a matter of public concern, especially if they affected property and any obligations of the government to protect or care for people. Here Andrew Bell makes a visit to city hall in New York to watch a divorce trial and gives an interesting account of the workings of the justice system.

As I spent some time in New York, during which nothing eligible turned up for me, the time began to hang heavy on my hands. It was my frequent custom to step into the City Hall, and listen to the pleadings going on in the courts there. I well remember the case which interested me more than any other I heard there. It was a divorce affair. The husband was the injured party; and, as I understood at the time, had applied to the state legislature for a dissolution of the marriage tie; and that this had been granted, and a bill to that effect passed. But laws made by the state legislatures, or even by Congress itself, remain a dead letter, unless sanctioned by the decisions of the Supreme Courts. To the latter the wife had appealed, as I understood, on some legal grounds. Defective proof of her guilt it could not well be, as she had been detected *in flagrante delicto* with her paramour. But one or both of the parties were aliens, namely English; and the strongest part of the husband's case rested on the intercourse sworn to have taken place on board the packet ship from Liverpool, and therefore possibly out of the jurisdiction of the United States courts.

The evidence of the fellow passengers of the parties, and also the crew of the ship, went to prove the whole case beyond a doubt. The evidence, after the arrival of the parties on shore, where the criminal intercourse had been continued, was not so strong. The husband came to the knowledge of his wife's conduct in an odd way. He had written to her earnestly to join him in America, whither he had been sent as an agent for a mercantile house, and was settled at a town a hundred miles or more from New York. Some business delays had hitherto prevented his wife from joining him in America; he was daily expecting her arrival, and naturally anxious to hear of her safety, so that he looked into every New York paper for tidings. He knew not the name of the vessel that was to convey her; but he was aware that the New York papers always insert the names, taken from the ship's books, of every cabin passenger that arrives there. There are different reasons for this; one is, that it serves to prove the time of any one's arrival in the country, in case of his afterwards wishing to be naturalized. Not to mention too, that it is a readier way of conveying information than by letter. He was not a little delighted to see his wife's name at length in the list of the last arrived packet, and his impatience to meet and welcome her knew no bounds. Day after day passed, however, and she came not. He, at last, after waiting a reasonable time, set out half distracted for New York. He flew to interrogate the captain, the officers, the crew; for by this time the other passengers had all gone their several ways. No one would at first tell him anything. At last, remarking something mysterious in the captain's explanations, he begged, he prayed, he conjured him to say if anything, and what, were wrong. He drew from him, at last, that his lady had made herself early remarked in the voyage, which had been a long one, by the levity of her general conduct; and that it was universally believed she had been on too intimate terms with a young gentleman on board, about five years younger than herself, she being on the verge of thirty. On several occasions, too, since the ship's arrival, he was told they had been seen together in New York, and had taken their meals, if not slept together, in the same hotel. The ship's steward was now called in, and he said he could swear to having seen the parties in situations which set their guilt in the clearest point of view. The husband now hastened on shore—a mournful quest—to collect all the evidence he could as to his wife's proceedings since her arrival. But these amounted to strong probabilities only; parties applied to were either unable or unwilling to give positive testimony. It is probable that the system of publishing cabin passengers' names was unknown to the lady and her paramour: she thought probably to make her husband believe she had come by a later packet, and imagined there could be no harm to indulge, meantime, in a little *innocent* pastime, then fly to her husband's arms, and salute him with the "dutiful" kisses of impure lips. Be that as it may, during her husband's inquiries about her in New York, she left it, and when he returned home, after a week's delay, he found her installed there, just as if nothing had happened to her. His first step was to eject her thence, no doubt with utter loathing, if not with contumely. He then addressed himself to the constituted authorities to do him right, who made an award in his favour accordingly; but from that reasonable decision, probably on a writ of error, the lady now appealed. In general, the different state legislatures have the power of passing bills of divorce, on sufficient cause being shewn. There is one exception, however (if not more), to this jurisdiction; it is that of the supreme court of Massachusetts, which has original and exclusive jurisdiction in all matters of divorce and alimony. I am not sure whether a similar arrangement may not obtain in the state of New York also. Be this as it may, there could be no moral, but there was some legal, doubt of this woman's guilt. Here her advocate took his stand; and contended that if "aliens" could get that relief from American tribunals, which those of their own country (possibly for wise reasons) denied them, it would create an abuse which it would not be easy to see the end of. If it were as easy to dissolve marriages in America as to solemnise them, every packet would bring over troops of discontented or guilty couples, seeking release from relations they repented entering into. The distance presented no obstacle; for what was once a painful sea-voyage had become a pleasant summer excursion. Thus the benevolent intentions of the law, in devising an expedient for the benefit of their own citizens alone, would become a convenience for profligate foreigners, whose cases had never been so much as thought of by the law-makers.

Neither on this occasion, nor on any other, did I see any thing of the gross indecorum detailed by tourists as existing in the American courts. The appearance, manners, and language of the barristers and judges were gentlemanlike in the highest degree. True, the former had not the powdered wigs of the English judges, nor the latter the ridiculous trenchercaps or ungainly dresses of the French *avocats*; but I thought the absence of both adjuncts no loss. I have not a doubt that the lawyers number in their ranks most of the higher intellects of the *élite* of American society. The present president was a lawyer; so was the last but one, and he is even yet the foremost man of his country if not of his time—I mean John Quincy Adams. Judge Marshall, the Eldon of America, and the friend and biographer of Washington, died shortly before my arrival.

The discretionary power invested in the superior courts of this country, of nullifying the bad intentions or blunders of their legislators, must give a higher tone to the judicial mind here than elsewhere. When any case comes before them founded on a statute contrary to the Constitution, to equality, or to the common sense of mankind, they quash the proceedings at once; and this too without any further appeal. Would that such a check now and then existed with us! but that would be as bad as "reforming the reformed House of Commons."

Source: Andrew Bell, *Men and Things in America; Being the Experience of a Year's Residence in the United States, in a Series of Letters to a Friend . . .* , by A. Thomason [pseud.] (London: W. Smith, 1838), 137–42.

9. *Alexis de Tocqueville on Judicial Power in the United States (1847)*

Alexis de Tocqueville's observations on American democracy have become a source for many scholars and ordinary citizens studying how American democracy works. Here he discusses the judicial system in the United States and how it acts as a guarantor against laws that would destroy the rights of citizens and checks the power of Congress.

I have thought it essential to devote a separate chapter to the judicial authorities of the United States, lest their great political importance should be lessened in the reader's eyes by a merely incidental mention of them. Confederations have existed in other countries beside America, and republics have not been established upon the shores of the New World alone; the representative system of government has been adopted in several States of Europe, but I am not aware that any nation of the globe has hitherto organized a judicial power on the principle now adopted by the Americans. The judicial organization of the United States is the institution which a stranger has the greatest difficulty in understanding. He hears the authority of a judge invoked in the political occurrences of every day, and he naturally concludes that in the United States the judges are important political functionaries; nevertheless, when he examines the nature of the tribunals, they offer nothing which is contrary to the usual habits and privileges of those bodies, and the magistrates seem to him to interfere in public affairs of chance, but by a chance which recurs every day.

When the Parliament of Paris remonstrated, or refused to enregister an edict, or when it summoned a functionary accused of malversation to its bar, its political influence as a judicial body was clearly visible; but nothing of the kind is to be seen in the United States. The Americans have retained all the ordinary characteristics of judicial authority, and have carefully restricted its action to the ordinary circle of its functions.

The first characteristic of judicial power in all nations is the duty of arbitration. But rights must be contested in order to warrant the interference of a tribunal; and an action must be brought to obtain the decision of a judge. As long, therefore, as the law is uncontested, the judicial authority is not called upon to discuss it, and it may exist without being perceived. When a judge in a given case attacks a law relating to that case, he extends the circle of his customary duties, without however stepping beyond it; since he is in some measure obliged to decide upon the law in order to decide the case. But if he pronounces upon a law without resting upon a case, he clearly steps beyond his sphere, and invades that of the legislative authority.

The second characteristic of judicial power is that it pronounces on special cases, and not upon general principles. If a judge in deciding a particular point destroys a general principle, by passing a judgment which tends to reject all the inferences from that principle, and consequently to annul it, he remains within the ordinary limits of his functions. But if he directly attacks a general principle without having a particular case in view, he leaves the circle in which all nations have agreed to confine his authority, he assumes a more important, and perhaps a more useful, influence than that of the magistrate, but he ceases to be a representative of the judicial power.

The third characteristic of the judicial power is its inability to act unless it is appealed to, or until it has taken cognizance of an affair. This characteristic is less general than the other two; but, notwithstanding the exceptions, I think it may be regarded as essential. The judicial power is by its nature devoid of action; it must be put in motion in order to produce a result. When it is called upon to repress a crime, it punishes the criminal; when a wrong is to be redressed, it is ready to redress it; when an act requires interpretation, it is prepared to interpret it; but it does not pursue criminals, hunt out wrongs, or examine into evidence of its own accord. A judicial functionary who should open proceedings, and usurp the censorship of the laws, would in some measure do violence to the passive nature of his authority.

The Americans have retained these three distinguishing characteristics of the judicial power; an American judge can only pronounce a decision when litigation has arisen, he is only conversant with special cases, and he cannot act until the cause has been duly brought before the court. His position is therefore perfectly similar to that of the magistrate of other nations; and he is nevertheless invested with immense political power. If the sphere of his authority and his means of action are the same as those of other judges, it may be asked whence he derives a power which they do not possess. The cause of this difference lies in the simple fact that the Americans have acknowledged the right of the judges to found their decisions on the constitution rather than on the laws. In other words, they have left them at liberty not to apply such laws as may appear to them to be unconstitutional.

I am aware that a similar right has been claimed—but claimed in vain—by courts of justice in other countries; but in America it is recognized by all authorities; and not a party, nor so much as an individual, is found to contest it. This fact can only be explained by the principles of the American constitution. In France the constitution is (or at least is supposed to be) immutable; and the received theory is that no power has the right of changing any part of it. In England the Parliament has an acknowledged right to modify the constitution; as, therefore, the constitution may undergo perpetual changes, it does not in reality exist; the Parliament is at once a legislative and a constituent assembly. The political theories of America are more simple and more rational. An American constitution is not supposed to be immutable as in France, nor is it susceptible of modification by the ordinary powers of society as in England. It constitutes a detached whole, which, as it represents the determination of the whole people, is no less binding on the legislator than on the private citizen, but which may be altered by the will of the people in predetermined cases, according to established rules. In America the constitution may therefore vary, but as long as it exists it is the origin of all authority, and the sole vehicle of the predominating force.

It is easy to perceive in what manner these differences must act upon the position and the rights of the judicial bodies in the three countries I have cited. If in France the tribunals were authorized to disobey the laws on the ground of their being opposed to the constitution, the supreme power would in fact be placed in their hands, since they alone would have the right of interpreting a constitution, the clauses of which can be modified by no authority. They would therefore take the place of the nation, and exercise as absolute a sway over society as the inherent weakness of judicial power would allow them to do. Undoubtedly, as the French judges are incompetent to declare a law to be unconstitutional, the power of changing the constitution is indirectly given to the legislative body, since no legal barrier would oppose the alterations which it might prescribe. But it is better to grant the power of changing the constitution of the people to men who represent (however imperfectly) the will of the people, than to men who represent no one but themselves.

It would be still more unreasonable to invest the English judges with the right of resisting the decisions of the legislative body, since the Parliament which makes the laws also makes the constitution; and consequently a law emanating from the three powers of the State can in no case be unconstitutional. But neither of these remarks is applicable to America.

In the United States the constitution governs the legislator as much as the private citizen; as it is the first of laws it cannot be modified by a law, and it is therefore just that the tribunals should obey the constitution in preference to any law. This condition is essential to the power of the judicature, for to select that legal obligation by which he is most strictly bound is the natural right of every magistrate.

In France the constitution is also the first of laws, and the judges have the same right to take it as the ground of their decisions, but were they to exercise this right they must perforce encroach on rights more sacred than their own, namely, on those of society, in whose name they are acting. In this case the State-motive clearly prevails over the motives of an individual. In America, where the nation can always reduce its magistrates to obedience by changing its constitution, no danger of this kind is to be feared. Upon this point, therefore, the political and the logical reasons agree, and the people as well as the judges preserve their privileges.

Whenever a law which the judge holds to be unconstitutional is argued in a tribunal of the United States he may refuse to admit it as a rule; this power is the only one which is peculiar to the American magistrate, but it gives rise to immense political influence. Few laws can escape the searching analysis of the judicial power for any length of time, for there are few which are not prejudicial to some private interest or other, and none which may not be brought before a court of justice by the choice of parties, or by the necessity of the case. But from the time that a judge has refused to apply any given law in a case, that law loses a portion of its moral cogency. The persons to whose interests it is prejudicial learn that means exist of evading its authority, and similar suits are multiplied, until it becomes powerless. One of two alternatives must then be resorted to: the people must alter the constitution, or the legislature must repeal the law.

The political power which the Americans have intrusted to their courts of justice is therefore immense, but the evils of this power are considerably diminished by the obligation which has been imposed of attacking the laws through the courts of justice alone. If the judge had been empowered to contest the laws on the ground of theoretical generalities, if he had been enabled to open an attack or to pass a censure on the legislator, he would have played a prominent part in the political sphere; and as the champion or the antagonist of a party, he would have arrayed the hostile passions of the nation in the conflict. But when a judge contests a law applied to some particular case in an obscure proceeding, the importance of his attack is concealed from the public gaze, his decision bears upon the interest of an individual, and if the law is slighted it is only collaterally. Moreover, although it is censured, it is not abolished; its moral force may be diminished, but its cogency is by no means suspended, and its final destruction can only be accomplished by the reiterated attacks of judicial functionaries. It will readily be understood that by connecting the censorship of the laws with the private interests of members of the community, and by intimately uniting the prosecution of the law with the prosecution of an individual, legislation is protected from wanton assailants, and from the daily aggressions of party spirit. The errors of the legislator are exposed whenever their evil consequences are most felt, and it is always a positive and appreciable fact which serves as the basis of a prosecution.

I am inclined to believe this practice of the American courts to be at once the most favorable to liberty as well as to public order. If the judge could only attack the legislator openly and directly, he would sometimes be afraid to oppose any resistance to his will; and at other moments party spirit might encourage him to brave it at every turn. The laws would consequently be attacked when the power from which they emanate is weak, and obeyed when it is strong. That is to say, when it would be useful to respect them they would be contested, and when it would be easy to convert them into an instrument of oppression they would be respected. But the American judge is brought into the political arena independently of his own will. He only judges the law because he is obliged to judge a case. The political question which he is called upon to resolve is connected with the interest of the suitors, and he cannot refuse to decide it without abdicating the duties of his post. He performs his functions as a citizen by fulfilling the precise duties which belong to his profession as a magistrate. It is true that upon this system the judicial censorship which is exercised by the courts of justice over the legislation cannot extend to all laws indiscriminately, inasmuch as some of them can never give rise to that exact species of contestation which is termed a lawsuit; and even when such a contestation is possible, it may happen that no one cares to bring it before a court of justice. The Americans have often felt this disadvantage, but they have left the remedy incomplete, lest they should give it an efficacy which might in some cases prove dangerous. Within these limits the power vested in the American courts of justice of pronouncing a statute to be unconstitutional forms one of the most powerful barriers which has ever been devised against the tyranny of political assemblies.

Other Powers Granted to American Judges

The United States all the citizens have the right of indicting public functionaries before the ordinary tribunals—How they use this right—Art. 75 of the French Constitution of the An VIII—The Americans and the English cannot understand the purport of this clause.

It is perfectly natural that in a free country like America all the citizens should have the right of indicting public functionaries before the ordinary tribunals, and that all the judges should have the power of punishing public offences. The right granted to the courts of justice of judging the agents of the executive government, when they have violated the laws, is so natural a one that it cannot be looked upon as an extraordinary privilege. Nor do the springs of government appear to me to be weakened in the United States by the custom which renders all public officers responsible to the judges of the land. The Americans seem, on the contrary, to have increased by this means that respect which is due to the authorities, and at the same time to have rendered those who are in power more scrupulous of offending public opinion. I was struck by the small number of political trials which occur in the United States, but I had no difficulty in accounting for this circumstance. A lawsuit, of whatever nature it may be, is always a difficult and expensive undertaking. It is easy to attack a public man in a journal, but the motives which can warrant an action at law must be serious. A solid ground of complaint must therefore exist to induce an individual to prosecute a public officer, and public officers are careful not to furnish these grounds of complaint when they are afraid of being prosecuted.

This does not depend upon the republican form of American institutions, for the same facts present themselves in England. These two nations do not regard the impeachment of the principal officers of State as a sufficient guarantee of their independence. But they hold that the right of minor prosecutions, which are within the reach of the whole community, is a better pledge of freedom than those great judicial actions which are rarely employed until it is too late.

In the Middle Ages, when it was very difficult to overtake offenders, the judges inflicted the most dreadful tortures on the few who were arrested, which by no means diminished the number of crimes. It has since been discovered that when justice is more certain and more mild, it is at the same time more efficacious. The English and the Americans hold that tyranny and oppression are to be treated like any other crime, by lessening the penalty and facilitating conviction.

In the year VIII of the French Republic a constitution was drawn up in which the following clause was introduced: "Art. 75. All the agents of the government below the rank of ministers can only be prosecuted for offences relating to their several functions by virtue of a decree of the Conseil d'Etat; in which the case the prosecution takes place before the ordinary tribunals." This clause survived the "Constitution de l'An VIII," and it is still maintained in spite of the just complaints of the nation. I have always found the utmost difficulty in explaining its meaning to Englishmen or Americans. They were at once led to conclude that the Conseil d'Etat in France was a great tribunal, established in the centre of the kingdom, which exercised a preliminary and somewhat tyrannical jurisdiction in all political causes. But when I told them that the Conseil d'Etat was not a judicial body, in the common sense of the term, but an administrative council composed of men dependent on the Crown, so that the king, after having ordered one of his servants, called a Prefect, to commit an injustice, has the power of commanding another of his servants, called a Councillor of State, to prevent the former from being punished; when I demonstrated to them that the citizen who has been injured by the order of the sovereign is obliged to solicit from the sovereign permission to obtain redress, they refused to credit so flagrant an abuse, and were tempted to accuse me of falsehood or of ignorance. It frequently happened before the Revolution that a Parliament issued a warrant against a public officer who had committed an offence, and sometimes the proceedings were stopped by the authority of the Crown, which enforced compliance with its absolute and despotic will. It is painful to perceive how much lower we are sunk than our forefathers, since we allow things to pass under the color of justice and the sanction of the law which violence alone could impose upon them.

Source: Alexis de Tocqueville, *Democracy in America*, trans. Henry Reeve (New York: Edward Walker, 1847), 101–8.

10. Dred Scott v. Sandford *(1857)*

Few cases in American history have stirred more controversy than Dred Scott v. Sandford, *in which the U.S. Supreme Court ruled that Congress could not prohibit slavery from going into U.S. territories. The majority opinion, written by Chief Justice Roger B. Taney, further angered abolitionists because he averred that only white people could be citizens of the United States and that blacks had "no rights" a white person "was bound to respect." Dred Scott, a slave, had been taken by his master, an army surgeon, to a free state and a free territory and then back to Missouri, a slave state. Scott and his wife Harriet sued Sanford (incorrectly spelled by the Court reporter as Sandford), the executor of their former master's estate, for their freedom on the basis of their residence on free soil.*

MR. CHIEF JUSTICE TANEY delivered the opinion of the Court.

The question is simply this: Can a negro, whose ancestors were imported into this country, and sold as slaves, become a member of the political community formed and brought into existence by the Constitution of the United States, and as such become entitled to all the rights, and privileges, and immunities, guarantied by that instrument to the citizen? One of which rights is the privilege of suing in a court of the United States in the cases specified in the constitution. . . .

The words "people of the United States" and "citizens" are synonymous terms, and mean the same thing. They both describe the political body who, according to our republican institutions, form the sovereignty, and who hold the power and conduct the government through their representatives. They are what we familiarly call the "sovereign people," and every citizen is one of this people, and a constituent member of this sovereignty. The question before us is, whether the class of persons described in the plea in abatement compose a portion of this people, and are constituent members of this sovereignty? We think they are not, and that they are not included, and were not intended to be included, under the word "citizens" in the constitution, and can therefore claim none of the rights and privileges which that instrument provides for and secures to citizens of the United States. On the contrary, they were at that time considered as a subordinate and inferior class of beings, who had been subjugated by the dominant race, and, whether emancipated or not, yet remained subject to their authority, and had no rights or privileges but such as those who held the power and the government might choose to grant them.

It is not the province of the court to decide upon the justice or injustice, the policy or impolicy, of these laws. The decision of that question belonged to the political or law-making power; to those who formed the sovereignty and framed the constitution. The duty of the court is, to interpret the instrument they have framed, with the best lights we can obtain on the subject, and to administer it as we find it, according to its true intent and meaning when it was adopted.

In discussing this question, we must not confound the rights of citizenship which a State may confer within its own limits, and the rights of citizenship as a member of the Union. It does not by any means follow, because he has all the rights and privileges of a citizen of a State, that he must be a citizen of the United States. He may have all of the rights and privileges of the citizen of a State, and yet not be entitled to the rights and privileges of a citizen in any other State. For, previous to the adoption of the constitution of the United States, every State had the undoubted right to confer on whomsoever it pleased the character of citizen, and to endow him with all its rights. But this character of course was confirmed to the boundaries of the State, and gave him no rights or privileges in other States beyond those secured to him by the laws of nations and the comity of States. Nor have the several States surrendered the power of conferring these rights and privileges by adopting the constitution of the United States. . . .

It is very clear, therefore, that no State can, by any act or law of its own, passed since the adoption of the constitution, introduce a new member into the political community created by the constitution of the United States. It cannot make him a member of this community by making him a member of its own. And for the same reason it cannot introduce any person, or description of persons, who were not intended to be embraced in this new political family, which the constitution brought into existence, but were intended to be excluded from it.

The question then arises, whether the provisions of the constitution, in relation to the personal rights and privileges to which the citizen of a State should be entitled, embraced the negro African race, at that time in this country, or who might afterwards be imported, who had then or should afterwards be made free in any State; and to put it in the power of a single State to make him a citizen of the United States, and endue him with the full rights of citizenship in every other State without their consent? Does the constitution of the United States act upon him whenever he shall be made free under the laws of a State, and raised there to the rank of a citizen, and immediately clothe him with all the privileges of a citizen in every other State, and in its own courts?

The court think the affirmative of these propositions cannot be maintained. And if it cannot, the plaintiff in error could not be a citizen of the State of Missouri, within the meaning of the constitution of the United States, and, consequently, was not entitled to sue in its courts.

It is true, every person, and every class and description of persons, who were at the time of the adoption of the constitution recognized as citizens in the several States, became also citizens of this new political body; but none other; it was formed by them, and for them and their posterity, but for no one else. And the personal rights and privileges guaranteed to citizens of this new sovereignty were intended to embrace those only who were then members of the several State communities, or who should afterwards by birthright or otherwise become members, according to the provisions of the constitution and the principles on which it was founded. It was the union of those who were at that time members of distinct and separate political communities into one political family, whose power, for certain specified purposes, was to extend over the whole territory of the United States. And it gave to each citizen rights and privileges outside of his State which he did not before possess, and placed him in every other State upon a perfect equality with its own citizens as to rights of person and rights of property; it made him a citizen of the United States. . . .

In the opinion of the court, the legislation and histories of the times, and the language used in the declaration of independence, show, that neither the class of persons who had been imported as slaves, nor their descendants, whether they had become free or not, were then acknowledged as a part of the people, nor intended to be included in the general words used in that memorable instrument. . . .

It is too clear for dispute, that the enslaved African race were not intended to be included, and formed no part of the people who framed and adopted this declaration; for if the language, as understood in that day, would embrace them, the conduct of the distinguished men who framed the declaration of independence would have been utterly and flagrantly inconsistent with the principles they asserted; and instead of the sympathy of mankind, to which they so confidently appealed, they would have deserved and received universal rebuke and reprobation. . . .

But there are two clauses in the constitution which point directly and specifically to the negro race as a separate class of persons, and show clearly that they were not regarded as a portion of the people or citizens of the government then formed.

One of these clauses reserves to each of the thirteen States the right to import slaves until the year 1808, if it thinks proper. . . . And by the other provision the States pledge themselves to each other to maintain the right of property of the master, by delivering up to him any slave who may have escaped from his service, and be found within their respective territories. . . .

The only two provisions which point to them and include them, treat them as property, and make it the duty of the government to protect it; no other power, in relation to this race, is to be found in the constitution; and as it is a government of special, delegated powers, no authority beyond these two provisions can be constitutionally exercised. The government of the United States had no right to interfere for any other purpose but that of protecting the rights of the owner, leaving it altogether with the several States to deal with this race, whether emancipated or not, as each State may think justice, humanity, and the interests and safety of society, require. The States evidently intended to reserve this power exclusively to themselves. . . .

Upon a full and careful consideration of the subject, the court is of opinion, that, upon the facts stated . . . Dred Scott was not a citizen of Missouri within the meaning of the constitution of the United States, and not entitled as such to sue in its courts; and, consequently, that the circuit court had no jurisdiction of the case, and that the judgment on the plea in abatement is erroneous. . . .

We proceed . . . to inquire whether the facts relied on by the plaintiff entitled him to his freedom. . . .

The act of Congress, upon which the plaintiff relies, declares that slavery and involuntary servitude, except as a punishment for crime, shall be forever prohibited in all that part of the territory ceded by France, under the name of Louisiana, which lies north of thirty-six degrees thirty minutes north latitude and not included within the limits of Missouri. And the difficulty which meets us at the threshold of this part of the inquiry is whether Congress was authorized to pass this law under any of the powers granted to it by the Constitution; for, if the authority is not given by that instrument, it is the duty of this Court to declare it void and inoperative and incapable of conferring freedom upon anyone who is held as a slave under the laws of any one of the states.

The counsel for the plaintiff has laid much stress upon that article in the Constitution which confers on Congress the power "to dispose of and make all needful rules and regulations respecting the territory or other property belonging to the United States"; but, in the judgment of the Court, that provision has no bearing on the present controversy, and the power there given, whatever it may be, is confined, and was intended to be confined, to the territory which at that time belonged to, or was claimed by, the United States and was within their boundaries as settled by the treaty with Great Britain and can have no influence upon a territory afterward acquired from a foreign government. It was a special provision for a known and particular territory, and to meet a present emergency, and nothing more. . . .

We do not mean, however, to question the power of Congress in this respect. The power to expand the territory of the United States by the admission of new states is plainly given; and in the construction of this power by all the departments of the government, it has been held to authorize the acquisition of territory, not fit for admission at the time, but to be admitted as soon as its population and situation would entitle it to admission. . . .

It may be safely assumed that citizens of the United States who migrate to a territory belonging to the people of the United States cannot be ruled as mere colonists, dependent upon the will of the general government, and to be governed by any laws it may think proper to impose. The principle upon which our governments rest, and upon which alone they continue to exist, is the union of states, sovereign and independent within their own limits in their internal and domestic concerns, and bound together as one people by a general government, possessing certain enumerated and restricted powers, delegated to it by the people of the several states, and exercising supreme authority within the scope of the powers granted to it, throughout the dominion of the United States. A power, therefore, in the general government to obtain and hold colonies and dependent territories, over which they might legislate without restriction, would be inconsistent with its own existence in its present form. Whatever it acquires, it acquires for the benefit of the people of the several states who created it. It is their trustee acting for them and charged with the duty of promoting the interests of the whole people of the Union in the exercise of the powers specifically granted. . . .

But the power of Congress over the person or property of a citizen can never be a mere discretionary power under our Constitution and form of government. The powers of the government and the rights and privileges of the citizen are regulated and plainly defined by the Constitution itself. And, when the territory becomes a part of the United States, the federal government enters into possession in the character impressed upon it by those who created it. It enters upon it with its powers over the citizen strictly defined and limited by the Constitution, from which it derives its own existence, and by virtue of which alone it continues to exist and act as a government and sovereignty. It has no power of any kind beyond it; and it cannot, when it enters a territory of the United States, put off its character and assume discretionary or despotic powers which the Constitution has denied to it. It cannot create for itself a new character separated from the citizens of the United States and the duties it owes them under the provisions of the Constitution. The territory, being a part of the United States, the government and the citizen both enter it under the authority of the Constitution, with their respective rights defined and marked out; and the federal government can exercise no power over his person or property, beyond what that instrument confers, nor lawfully deny any right which it has reserved. . . .

These powers, and others, in relation to rights of person, which it is not necessary here to enumerate, are, in express and positive terms, denied to the general government; and the rights of private property have been guarded with equal care. Thus the rights of property are united with the rights of person and placed on the same ground by the Fifth Amendment to the Constitution, which provides that no person shall be deprived of life, liberty, and property without due process of law. And an act of Congress which deprives a citizen of the United States of his liberty or property, without due process of law, merely because he came himself or brought his property into a particular territory of the United States, and who had committed no offense against the laws, could hardly be dignified with the name of due process of law. . . .

It seems, however, to be supposed that there is a difference between property in a slave and other property and that different rules may be applied to it in expounding the Constitution of the United States. And the laws and usages of nations, and the writings of eminent jurists upon the relation of master and slave and their mutual rights and duties, and the powers which governments may exercise over it, have been dwelt upon in the argument.

But, in considering the question before us, it must be borne in mind that there is no law of nations standing between the people of the United States and their government and interfering with their relation to each other. The powers of the government and the rights of the citizen under it are positive and practical regulations plainly written down. The people of the United States have delegated to it certain enumerated powers and forbidden it to exercise others. It has no power over the person or property of a citizen but what the citizens of the United States have granted. And no laws or usages of other nations, or reasoning of statesmen or jurists upon the relations of master and slave, can enlarge the powers of the government or take from the citizens the rights they have reserved. And if the Constitution recognizes the right of property of the master in a slave, and makes no distinction between that description of property and other property owned by a citizen, no tribunal, acting under the authority of the United States, whether it be legislative, executive, or judicial, has a right to draw such a distinction or deny to it the benefit of the provisions and guaranties which have been provided for the protection of private property against the encroachments of the government.

Now, as we have already said in an earlier part of this opinion, upon a different point, the right of property in a slave is distinctly and expressly affirmed in the Constitution. The right to traffic in it, like an ordinary article of merchandise and property, was guaranteed to the citizens of the United States, in every state that might desire it, for twenty years. And the government in express terms is pledged to protect it in all future time if the slave escapes from his owner. That is done in plain words—too plain to be misunderstood. And no word can be found in the Constitution which gives Congress a greater power over slave property or which entitles property of that kind to less protection than property of any other description. The only power conferred is the power coupled with the duty of guarding and protecting the owner in his rights.

Upon these considerations it is the opinion of the Court that the act of Congress which prohibited a citizen from holding and owning property of this kind in the territory of the United States north of the line therein mentioned is not warranted by the Constitution and is therefore void; and that neither Dred Scott himself, nor any of his family, were made free by being carried into this territory; even if they had been carried there by the owner with the intention of becoming a permanent resident.

Source: 60 U.S. 393 (1857).

Warfare

In its wars from the American Revolution to the Civil War, the United States largely relied on citizen soldiers—volunteers and even conscripts—to carry the burden of fighting. The United States maintained only a small professional military, in part because of Americans' ideological fears of standing armies and because they did not want to bear the cost of a military establishment. Soldiers fought mostly in so-called Indians wars as part of American policy to secure as much land as possible for settlement. In the three major wars fought between 1775 and 1861, the experiences of men in arms differed. Larger contests invested the people more heavily in the outcome, by service and by support. They also required new skills and in some ways a new temperament, not only for the discipline soldiering demanded but also because of the moral questions it raised. The experience of a private soldier during the American Revolution and his thoughts about possibly taking another man's life have been a common concern of soldiers throughout all of history. Andrew Jackson's victory over the British at the Battle of New Orleans sealed America's triumph in the War of 1812, and his report details his victory. Many of the Civil War's future generals served in the Mexican War (1846–1848) as junior officers. Ulysses S. Grant was one of those officers, and his reminiscences about combat demonstrate why he was so successful during the Civil War.

11. I Hope I Didn't Kill Him (1778)

Joseph Plumb Martin enlisted in the Continental Army in June 1776 and served until the end of December 1776. He returned to the army in April 1777 and continued his service until he was discharged in 1783 as a sergeant. He began writing his memoirs in 1828, and his narrative provides a vivid description of the life of an enlisted man during the American Revolution. The following passage describes Martin's experience during the Battle of Monmouth (June 28, 1778), during which he took aim at a British soldier.

We overtook the enemy just as they were entering upon the meadow, which was rather bushy. When within about five rods of the retreating foe, I could distinguish everything about them. They were retreating in line, though in some disorder. I singled out a man and took my aim directly between his shoulders. (They were divested of their packs.) He was a good mark, being a broad-shouldered fellow. What became of him I know not, I took as deliberate aim of him as ever I did at any game in my life. But after all, I hope I did not kill him, although I intended to at the time.

Source: Joseph Plumb Martin, *Private Yankee Doodle: Being a Narrative of Some of the Adventures, Dangers and Sufferings of a Revolutionary Soldier* (Boston: Little, Brown, 1962), 130.

12. Andrew Jackson on the Battle of New Orleans (1815)

During the War of 1812 Gen. Andrew Jackson won fame for defeating the Creeks at Horseshoe Bend and the British outside New Orleans. Such victories made him a national hero, which he parlayed into winning the presidency in 1828. The Battle of New Orleans especially won accolades from citizens and military observers alike for the completeness of the Americans' defeat of the once mighty British army. Americans exalted in a sound defeat of the British by Jackson and his Tennessee "long rifles"—forgetting the role of free blacks and even some pirates in winning the day—and interpreted this as further proof that the simple yeoman American farmer, the republican ideal, could best anything the Old World had in defending liberty. In popular culture images of Jackson reinforced that idea. The document below is a letter Jackson wrote to Secretary of War James Monroe on January 9, 1815, relaying the details of the U.S. victory over the British at the Battle of New Orleans the day before.

Camp 4 miles below Orleans

9th. Jan: 1815

Sir, During the days of the 6th. & 7th. the enemy had been actively employed in making preparations for an attack on my lines. With infinite labour they had succeeded on the night of the 7th in getting their boats across from the lake to the river, by widening & deepening the canal on which they had effected their disembarkation. It had not been in my power to impede these operations by a general attack. Added to other reasons, the nature of the troops under my command, mostly militia, rendered it too hazardous to attempt extensive *offensive* movements, in an open country, against a numerous & well disciplined army. Altho my forces, as to number, had been increased by the arrival of the Kentucky division my strength had received very little addition, a small portion only of that detachment being provided with arms. Compelled thus to wait the attack of the enemy I took every measure to repell it when it should be made & to defeat the object he had in view. Genl. Morgan, with the Orleans contigent [contingent]—the Louisiana militia & a strong detachment of the Kentucky troops occupyd an entrenched Camp, on the opposite side of the river, protected by strong batteries on the bank erected & superintended by Commodore Patterson.

In *my* encampment every thing was ready for action when early on the morning of the 8th the enemy after throwing a heavy shower of bombs & congreve rockets, advanced their columns on my right & left, to storm my entrenchments. I cannot speak sufficiently in praise of the firmness & deliberation with which my whole line received their approach: *more* could not have been expected from veterans inured to war. For an hour the fire of the small arms was as incessant & severe as can be imagined. The artillery too directed by officers who displayed equal skill & courage did great execution. Yet the columns of the enemy continued to advance with a firmness which reflects upon them the greatest credit. Twice the column which approached me on my left was repulsed by the troops of Genl. Carroll—those of Genl. Coffee, & a division of the Kentucky militia, & twice they formed again & renewed the assault. At length, however, *cut* to pieces, they fled in confusion from the field leaving it covered with their dead & wounded. The loss which the enemy sustained on this occasion cannot be estimated at less than 1500 in killed wounded & prisoners—Upwards of three hundred have already been delivered over for burial; & my men are still engaged in picking them up within my lines & carrying them to the point where the enemy are to receive them. This is in addition to the dead & wounded whom the enemy have been enabled to carry from the field, during & since the action, & to those who have since died of the wounds they received. We have taken about 500 prisoners, upwards of 300 of whom are wounded, & a great part of them mortally. My loss has not exceeded, & I believe has not amounted to ten killed & as many wounded. The entire destruction of the enemy's army was now inevitable had it not been for an unfortunate occurrence which at this moment took place on the other side of the river. Simultaneously with his advance upon my lines, he had thrown over in his boats, a considerable force to the other side of the river. *Those* having landed, were hardy enough to advance against the works of Genl. Morgan; & what is strange & difficult to account for, at the very moment when their entire discomfiture was looked for with a confidence approaching to certainty, the Kentucky reinforcement in whom so much reliance had been placed, ingloriously fled—drawing after them, by their example, the remainder of the force; & thus, yeilding to the enemy, that most fortunate position. The batteries which had rendered me, for many days, the most important ser[vice] thou bravely defended, were of course, now abandoned; not however until the guns had been spiked.

This unfortunate route had totally changed the aspect of affairs. The enemy now occupied a position from which they might annoy us without hazard, & by means of which they might have been enabled to defeat, in a great measure, the effects of our success on this side of the river. It became therefore an object of the first consequence to dislodge him as soon as possible. For this object, all the means in my power, which I could with any safety use, were immediately put in preparation. Perhaps however it was owing somewhat to another cause that I succeeded even beyond my expectations. In negotiating the terms of a temporary suspension of hostilities to enable the enemy to bury their dead & provide for their wounded, I had required certain propositions to be acceded to as a basis; among which this was one—that altho' hostilities should cease on *this* side the river until 12 Ock of this day yet it was not to be understood that they should cease on the *other* side; but that no reinforcements should be sent across by *either* army until the expiration of that hour. His Excellency Major Genl. Lambert begged time to consider of those propositions until 10 Oclk of to day, & in the meantime recrossed his troops. I need not tell you with how much eagerness I immediately regained possession of the position he had thus hastily quitted.

The enemy having concentrated his forces may again attempt to drive me from my position by storm; whenever he *does*, I have no doubt my men will act with their usual firmness, & sustain a character now become dear to them. I have the honour to be with great respect yr obt st

Andrew Jackson
Major Genl comdg

Source: D. Feller, ed., *The Papers of Andrew Jackson*, vol. III (University of Tennessee Press, 1991), 239–41. Used by permission.

13. *Ulysses S. Grant on the Battle of Monterrey (1846)*

During the Mexican War Ulysses S. Grant performed bravely. Like many future officers who fought in the Civil War, he learned much about handling men and himself in combat from his experience fighting in Mexico. His coolness under fire and willingness to take the initiative marked him for advancement. During the Civil War Grant would become General in Chief of the Union Army, and in 1868 the eighteenth president of the United States. In this selection from his memoirs, Grant describes his part in the Battle of Monterrey.

Twiggs's division was at the lower end of the city, and well covered from the fire of the enemy. But the streets leading to the plaza—all Spanish or Spanish-American towns have near their centres a square called a plaza—were commanded from all directions by artillery. The houses were flat-roofed and but one or two stories high, and about the plaza the roofs were manned with infantry, the troops being protected from our fire by parapets made of sand-bags. All advances into the city were thus attended with much danger. While moving along streets which did not lead to the plaza, our men were protected from the fire, and from the view, of the enemy except at the crossings; but at these a volley of musketry and a discharge of grape-shot were invariably encountered. The 3d and 4th regiments of infantry made an advance nearly to the plaza in this way and with heavy loss. The loss of the 3d infantry in commissioned officers was especially severe. There were only five companies of the regiment and not over twelve officers present, and five of these officers were killed. When within a square of the plaza this small command, ten companies in all, was brought to a halt. Placing themselves under cover from the shots of the enemy, the men would watch to detect a head above the sand-bags on the neighboring houses. The exposure of a single head would bring a volley from our soldiers.

We had not occupied this position long when it was discovered that our ammunition was growing low. I volunteered to go back to the point we had started from, report our position to General Twiggs, and ask for ammunition to be forwarded.

We were at this time occupying ground off from the street, in rear of the houses. My ride back was an exposed one. Before starting I adjusted myself on the side of my horse furthest from the enemy, and with only one foot holding to the cantle of the saddle, and an arm over the neck of the horse exposed, I started at full run. It was only at street crossings that my horse was under fire, but these I crossed at such a flying rate that generally I was past and under cover of the next block of houses before the enemy fired. I got out safely without a scratch.

At one place on my ride, I saw a sentry walking in front of a house, and stopped to inquire what he was doing there. Finding that the house was full of wounded American officers and soldiers, I dismounted and went in. I found there Captain Williams, of the Engineer Corps, wounded in the head, probably fatally, and Lieutenant Territt, also badly wounded his bowels protruding from his wound. There were quite a number of soldiers also. Promising them to report their situation, I left, readjusted myself to my horse, recommenced the run, and was soon with the troops at the east end. Before ammunition could be collected, the two regiments I had been with were seen returning, running the same gauntlet in getting out that they had passed in going in, but with comparatively little loss. The movement was countermanded and the troops were withdrawn. The poor wounded officers and men I had found, fell into the hands of the enemy during the night, and died.

While this was going on at the east, General Worth, with a small division of troops, was advancing towards the plaza from the opposite end of the city. He resorted to a better expedient for getting to the plaza—the citadel—than we did on the east. Instead of moving by the open streets, he advanced through the houses, cutting passageways from one to another. Without much loss of life, he got so near the plaza during the night that before morning, Ampudia, the Mexican commander, made overtures for the surrender of the city and garrison. This stopped all further hostilities. The terms of surrender were soon agreed upon. The prisoners were paroled and permitted to take their horses and personal property with them.

My pity was aroused by the sight of the Mexican garrison of Monterey marching out of town as prisoners, and no doubt the same feeling was experienced by most of our army who witnessed it. Many of the prisoners were cavalry, armed with lances, and mounted on miserable little half-starved horses that did not look as if they could carry their riders out of town. The men looked in but little better condition. I thought how little interest the men before me had in the results of the war, and how little knowledge they had of "what it was all about."

Source: Ulysses S. Grant, *Personal Memoirs of U.S. Grant,* 2 vols. (New York: Charles L. Webster and Company, 1885), I: 113–18.

Slavery

In discussing the everyday lives of Americans during this period, one must always recognize that while white Americans were going about their everyday lives and experiencing the freedoms of the new republic, there were men and women living as slaves. The descriptions of their experiences that these people have left are a searing testimony to the incongruity of the principles of the American Revolution. Each of the following documents is a recounting of the life of a slave and the cruelty suffered by human beings during a time when freedom in America was limited to whites. Nat Turner left a chilling account of the hatred slaves had for their bondage. Frederick Douglass answered his critics with details of life as a slave. Josiah Henson wrote about his early days as a slave, the terrible wrenching of his family, and the cruelty of his master. And the story of Solomon Northup's kidnapping and the cruelties he suffered as a slave for twelve years is a dark testimony to the evils of slavery in America.

14. *Nat Turner,* The Confessions of Nat Turner *(1831)*

In 1831, African American Nat Turner led a slave rebellion in southern Virginia that shocked the nation. He and his supporters killed more than sixty whites in a single night but were ultimately hunted down and either killed or captured. Condemned in the Virginia courts, Turner was interviewed by lawyer Thomas Gray, who took down Turner's account and published it as The Confessions of Nat Turner. *It's not known how much of the testimony was Turner's and how much Gray's embellishments, but the account proved chilling enough to contemporaries for them to believe its essential message. Despite the ultimate failure of Nat Turner's Rebellion, the event had significant repercussions for American society. Southern states clamped down further on slavery, and abolitionists in the North had new evidence of slavery's wrongs. And the memory of "Nat" became a watchword whispered among slaves thereafter.*

To a mind like mine, restless, inquisitive and observant of every thing that was passing, it is easy to suppose that religion was the subject to which it would be directed, and although this subject principally occupied my thoughts—there was nothing that I saw or heard of to which my attention was not directed—The manner in which I learned to read and write, not only had great influence on my own mind, as I acquired it with the most perfect ease, so much so, that I have no recollection whatever of learning the alphabet—but to the astonishment of the family, one day, when a book was shewn to me to keep me from crying, I began spelling the names of different objects—this was a source of wonder to all in the neighborhood, particularly the blacks—and this learning was constantly improved at all opportunities—when I got large enough to go to work, while employed, I was reflecting on many things that would present themselves to my imagination, and whenever an opportunity occurred of looking at a book, when the school children were getting their lessons, I would find many things that the fertility of my own imagination had depicted to me before. . . .

[A]ll my time, not devoted to my master's service, was spent either in prayer, or in making experiments in casting different things in moulds made of earth, in attempting to make paper, gun-powder, and many other experiments, that although I could not perfect, yet convinced me of its practicability if I had the means.

I was not addicted to stealing in my youth, nor have ever been—Yet such was the confidence of the negroes in the neighborhood, even at this early period of my life, in my superior judgment, that they would often carry me with them when they were going on any roguery, to plan for them. Growing up among them, with this confidence in my superior judgment, and when this, in their opinions, was perfected by Divine inspiration, from the circumstances already alluded to in my infancy, and which belief was ever afterwards zealously inculcated by the austerity of my life and manners, which became the subject of remark by white and black.

Having soon discovered to be great, I must appear so, and therefore studiously avoided mixing in society, and wrapped myself in mystery, devoting my time to fasting and prayer—by this time, having arrived to man's estate, and hearing the scriptures commented on at meetings, I was struck with that particular passage which says: "Seek ye the kingdom of Heaven and all things shall be added unto you." I reflected much on this passage, and prayed daily for light on this subject—As I was praying one day at my plough, the spirit spoke to me, saying "Seek ye the kingdom of Heaven and all things shall be added unto you."

Question—what do you mean by the Spirit? Ans.—The Spirit that spoke to the prophets in former days—and I was greatly astonished, and for two years prayed continually, whenever my duty would permit—and then again I had the same revelation, which fully confirmed me in the impression that I was ordained for some great purpose in the hands of the Almighty.

Several years rolled round, in which many events occurred to strengthen me in this my belief. At this time I reverted in my mind to the remarks made of me in my childhood, and the things that had been shewn me—and as it had been said of me in my childhood by those by whom I had been taught to pray, both white and black, and in whom I had the greatest confidence, that I had too much sense to be raised, and if I was, I would never be of any use to any one as a slave. Now finding I had arrived to man's estate, and was a slave, and these revelations being made known to me, I began to direct my attention to this great object, to fulfill the purpose for which, by this time, I felt assured I was intended.

Knowing the influence I had obtained over the minds of my fellow servants (not by the means of conjuring and such like tricks—for to them I always spoke of such things with contempt) but by the communion of the Spirit whose revelations I often communicated to them, and they believed and said my wisdom came from God. I now began to prepare them for my purpose, by telling them something was about to happen that would terminate in fulfilling the great promise that had been made to me.

Source: Thomas R. Gray, *The Confessions of Nat Turner, the Leader of the Late Insurrection* (Baltimore, MD: Thomas R. Gray, 1831).

15. Frederick Douglass on the Cruelty of Slaveholders and the Suffering of Slaves (1845)

Frederick Douglass was thought by many southerners to be a fraud, as they believed that it was not possible for a former slave to be as well spoken and erudite as he was after he fled to freedom and began speaking and writing against slavery. There were many in the North who thought this as well, believing that he was an agent of the abolitionists to stir up trouble between the sections over the issue of slavery. He was an uncompromising abolitionist. Douglass answered his critics by continuing to speak and write. His memoirs especially revealed the essential truth he argued—that slavery corrupted all that it touched and that each man must will himself to freedom. The power of his words and force of his personality made him a compelling figure, and a much sought-after speaker. He traveled across the North and to Europe with his message about the absolute wrong of slavery. In this excerpt from Douglass's autobiography, he discusses the cruelty he suffered as a slave.

I have had two masters. My first master's name was Anthony. I do not remember his first name. He was generally called Captain Anthony—a title which, I presume, he acquired by sailing a craft on the Chesapeake Bay. He was not considered a rich slave-holder. He owned two or three farms, and about thirty slaves. His farms and slaves were under the care of an overseer. The overseer's name was Plummer.

Mr. Plummer was a miserable drunkard, a profane swearer, and a savage monster. He always went armed with a cowskin and a heavy cudgel. I have known him to cut and slash the women's heads so horribly, that even master would be enraged at his cruelty, and would threaten to whip him if he did not mind himself. Master, however, was not a humane slaveholder. It required extraordinary barbarity on the part of an overseer to affect him. He was a cruel man, hardened by a long life of slaveholding. He would at times seem to take great pleasure in whipping a slave. I have often been awakened at the dawn of day by the most heart-rending shrieks of an own aunt of mine, whom he used to tie up to a joist, and whip upon her naked back till she was literally covered with blood. No words, no tears, no prayers, from his gory victim, seemed to move his iron heart from its bloody purpose. The louder she screamed, the harder he whipped; and where the blood ran fastest, there he whipped longest. He would whip her to make her scream, and whip her to make her hush; and not until overcome by fatigue, would he cease to swing the blood-clotted cowskin. I remember the first time I ever witnessed this horrible exhibition. I was quite a child, but I well remember it. I never shall forget it whilst I remember any thing. It was the first of a long series of such outrages, of which I was doomed to be a witness and a participant. It struck me with awful force. It was the blood-stained gate, the entrance to the hell of slavery, through which I was about to pass. It was a most terrible spectacle. I wish I could commit to paper the feelings with which I beheld it.

This occurence [sic] took place very soon after I went to live with my old master, and under the following circumstances. Aunt Hester went out one night,—where or for what I do not know,—and happened to be absent when my master desired her presence. He had ordered her not to go out evenings, and warned her that she must never let him catch her in company with a young man, who was paying attention to her belonging to Colonel Lloyd. The young man's name was Ned Roberts, generally called Lloyd's Ned. Why master was so careful of her, may be safely left to conjecture. She was a woman of noble form, and of graceful proportions, having very few equals, and fewer superiors, in personal appearance, among the colored or white women of our neighborhood.

Aunt Hester had not only disobeyed his orders in going out, but had been found in company with Lloyd's Ned; which circumstance, I found, from what he said while whipping her was the chief offence. Had he been a man of pure morals himself, he might have been thought interested in protecting the innocence of my aunt; but those who knew him will not suspect him of any such virtue. Before he commenced whipping Aunt Hester, he took her into the kitchen, and stripped her from neck to waist, leaving her neck, shoulders, and back, entirely naked. He then told her to cross her hands, calling her at the same time a d—d b—h. After crossing her hands, he tied them with a strong rope, and led her to a stool under a large hook in the joist, put in for the purpose. He made her get upon the stool, and tied her hands to the hook. She now stood fair for his infernal purpose. Her arms were stretched up at their full length, so that she stood upon the ends of her toes. He then said to her, "Now, you d—d b—h, I'll learn you how to disobey my orders!" and after rolling up his sleeves, he commenced to lay on the heavy cowskin, and soon the warm, red blood (amid heart-rending shrieks from her, and horrid oaths from him) came dripping to the floor. I was so terrified and horror-stricken at the sight, that I hid myself in a closet, and dared not venture out till long after the bloody transaction was over. I expected it would be my turn next. It was all new to me. I had never seen any thing like it before. I had always lived with my grandmother on the outskirts of the plantation, where she was put to raise the children of the younger women. I had therefore been, until now, out of the way of the bloody scenes that often occurred on the plantation.

Source: Frederick Douglass, *Narrative of the Life of Frederick Douglass, an American Slave* (Boston: Published at the Anti-slavery Office, No.25, Cornhill, 1845), 5–8.

16. The Slave Life of Josiah Henson (1849)

Josiah Henson was born a slave in Maryland in 1789 and later escaped to Ontario, Canada, in 1829, where he set up a community known as the Dawn Settlement to support escaped slaves. There are many who believe that Henson's narrative was the inspiration for Harriet Beecher Stowe's novel Uncle Tom's Cabin, *though evidence for this is circumstantial at best. He updated his autobiography in 1858, and it was published as* Truth Stranger Than Fiction: Father Henson's Story of His Own Life. *Twenty years later another biography was published,* Uncle Tom's Story of His Life: An Autobiography of the Rev. Josiah Henson. *Henson and his family never returned to the United States, and he died in 1883 at age ninety-three. Autobiographies of life in bondage and in freedom were an important instrument of the anti-slavery movement and also of self-emancipation for the writer, who could tell his or her own story and thus "own himself." Slave narratives were popular fare in the North and in Europe, helping to give voice to those who previously had been "voiceless."*

I was born, June 15, 1789, in Charles County, Maryland, on a farm belonging to Mr. Francis N., about a mile from Port Tobacco. My mother was the property of Dr. Josiah McP., but was hired by Mr. N., to whom my father belonged. The only incident I can remember, which occurred while my mother continued on N.'s farm, was the appearance of my father one day, with his head bloody and his back lacerated. He was in a state of great excitement, and though it was all a mystery to me at the age of three or four years, it was explained at a later period, and I understood that he had been suffering the cruel penalty of the Maryland law for beating a white man. His right ear had been cut off close to his head, and he had received a hundred lashes on his back. He had beaten the overseer for a brutal assault on my mother, and this was his punishment. Furious at such treatment, my father became a different man, and was so morose, disobedient, and intractable, that Mr. N. determined to sell him. He accordingly parted with him, not long after, to his son, who lived in Alabama; and neither my mother nor I, ever heard of him again. He was naturally, as I understood afterwards from my mother and other persons, a man of amiable temper, and of considerable energy of character; but it is not strange that he should be essentially changed by such cruelty and injustice under the sanction of law.

After the sale of my father by N., and his leaving Maryland for Alabama, Dr. McP. would no longer hire out my mother to N. She returned, therefore, to the estate of the doctor, who was very much kinder to his slaves than the generality of planters, never suffering them to be struck by any one. He was, indeed, a man of good natural impulses, kind-hearted, liberal, and jovial. The latter quality was so much developed as to be his great failing; and though his convivial excesses were not thought of as a fault by the community in which he lived, and did not even prevent his having a high reputation for goodness of heart, and an almost saint-like benevolence, yet they were, nevertheless, his ruin. My mother, and her young family of three girls and three boys, of which I was the youngest, resided on this estate for two or three years, during which my only recollections are of being rather a pet of the doctor's, who thought I was a bright child, and of being much impressed with what I afterwards recognized as the deep piety and devotional feeling and habits of my mother. I do not know how, or where she acquired her knowledge of God, or her acquaintance with the Lord's prayer, which she so frequently repeated and taught me to repeat. I remember seeing her often on her knees, endeavoring to arrange her thoughts in prayers appropriate to her situation, but which amounted to little more than constant ejaculation, and the repetition of short phrases, which were within my infant comprehension, and have remained in my memory to this hour.

After this brief period of comparative comfort, however, the death of Dr. McP. brought about a revolution in our condition, which, common as such things are in slave countries, can never be imagined by those not subject to them, nor recollected by those who have been, without emotions of grief and indignation deep and ineffaceable. The doctor was riding from one of his scenes of riotous excess, when, falling from his horse, in crossing a little run, not a foot deep, he was unable to save himself from drowning.

In consequence of his decease, it became necessary to sell the estate and the slaves, in order to divide the property, among the heirs; and we were all put up at auction and sold to the highest bidder, and scattered over various parts of the country. My brothers and sisters were bid off one by one, while my mother, holding my hand, looked on in an agony of grief, the cause of which I but ill understood at first, but which dawned on my mind, with dreadful clearness, as the sale proceeded. My mother was then separated from me, and put up in her turn. She was bought by a man named Isaac R., residing in Montgomery county, and then I was offered to the assembled purchasers. My mother, half distracted with the parting forever from all her children, pushed through the crowd, while the bidding for me was going on, to the spot where R. was standing. She fell at his feet, and clung to his knees, entreating him in tones that a mother only could command, to buy her *baby* as well as herself, and spare to her one of her little ones at least. Will it, can it be believed that this man, thus appealed to, was capable not merely of turning a deaf ear to her supplication, but of disengaging himself from her with such violent blows and kicks, as to reduce her to the necessity of creeping out of his reach, and mingling the groan of bodily suffering with the sob of a breaking heart? Yet this was one of my earliest observations of men; an experience which has been common to me with thousands of my race, the bitterness of which its frequency cannot diminish to any individual who suffers it, while it is dark enough to overshadow the whole after-life with something blacker than a funeral pall.—I was bought by a stranger.—Almost immediately, however, whether my childish strength, at five or six years of age, was overmastered by such scenes and experiences, or from some accidental cause, I fell sick, and seemed to my new master so little likely to recover, that he proposed to R., the purchaser of my mother, to take me too at such a trifling rate that it could not be refused. I was thus providentially restored to my mother; and under her care, destitute as she was of the proper means of nursing me, I recovered my health, and grew up to be an uncommonly vigorous and healthy boy and man.

The character of R., the master whom I faithfully served for many years, is by no means an uncommon one in any part of the world; but it is to be regretted that a domestic institution should anywhere put it in the power of such a one to tyrannize over his fellow beings, and inflict so much needless misery as is sure to be produced by such a man in such a position. Coarse and vulgar in his habits, unprincipled and cruel in his general deportment, and especially addicted to the vice of licentiousness, his slaves had little opportunity for relaxation from wearying labor, were supplied with the scantiest means of sustaining their toil by necessary food, and had no security for personal rights. The natural tendency of slavery is to convert the master into a tyrant and the slave into the cringing, treacherous, false, and thieving victim of tyranny and his slaves were no exception to the general rule, but might be cited as apt illustrations of the nature of the case.

My earliest employments were, to carry buckets of water to the men at work, to hold a horseplough, used for weeding between the rows of corn, and as I grew older and taller, to take care of master's saddle-horse. Then a hoe was put into my hands, and I was soon required to do the day's work of a man; and it was not long before I could do it, at least as well as my associates in misery.

The every-day life of a slave on one of our southern plantations, however frequently it may have been described, is generally little known at the North and must be mentioned as a necessary illustration of the character and habits of the slave and the slave-holder, created and perpetuated by their relative position. The principal food of those upon my master's plantation consisted of corn meal, and salt herrings; to which was added in summer a little buttermilk, and the few vegetables which each might raise for himself and his family, on the little piece of ground which was assigned to him for the purpose, called a truck patch. The meals were two, daily. The first, or breakfast, was taken at 12 o'clock, after laboring from daylight; and the other when the work of the remainder of the day was over. The only dress was of tow cloth, which for the young, and often even for those who had passed the period of childhood, consisted of a single garment, something like a shirt, but longer, reaching to the ancles; and for the older, a pair of pantaloons, or a gown, according to the sex; while some kind of round jacket, or overcoat, might be added in winter, a wool hat once in two or three years, for the males, and a pair of coarse shoes once a year. Our lodging was in log huts, of a single small room, with no other floor than the trodden earth, in which ten or a dozen persons—men, women, and children—might sleep, but which could not protect them from dampness and cold, nor permit the existence of the common decencies of life. There were neither beds, nor furniture of any description—a blanket being the only addition to the dress of the day for protection from the chillness of the air or the earth. In these hovels were we penned at night, and fed by day; here were the children born, and the sick—neglected. Such were the provisions for the daily toil of the slave.

Source: Josiah Henson, *The Life of Josiah Henson, Formerly a Slave, Now an Inhabitant of Canada, as Narrated by Himself* (Boston: Arthur D. Phelps, 1849), 1–7.

17. Solomon Northup, Twelve Years a Slave *(1853)*

Solomon Northup was born a free man in Minerva, Essex County, New York, in 1808. He was a "mulatto," his mother being a quadroon. His father had been a slave who was manumitted by his master upon his death. Northup was well educated, and he married and had three children. He settled in Saratoga Springs, New York, with his wife and three children. He worked at various jobs and was hired to play his fiddle for a circus in Washington, D.C., in April 1841. However, while there he was drugged and sold into slavery. Beaten repeatedly, Northup spent the next twelve years as a slave in New Orleans until he got word to his family of his whereabouts. He was eventually freed with the help of the governor of New York and authorities in Louisiana. He published a book, Twelve Years a Slave, *and began speaking throughout the North about his experiences. He disappeared in 1863, and there has never been any conclusive evidence about the circumstances of his death.*

Next day many customers called to examine Freeman's "new lot" [of slaves]. The latter gentleman was very loquacious, dwelling at much length upon our several good points and qualities. He would make us hold up our heads, walk briskly back and forth, while customers would feel of our hands and arms and bodies, turn us about, ask us what we could do, make us open our mouths and show our teeth, precisely as a jockey examines a horse which he is about to barter for or purchase.

Sometimes a man or woman was taken back to the small house in the yard, stripped, and inspected more minutely. Scars upon a slave's back were considered evidence of a rebellious or unruly spirit, and hurt his sale.

One old gentleman, who said he wanted a coachman, appeared to take a fancy to me. From his conversation with Freeman, I learned he was a resident of the city [New Orleans]. I very much desired that he would buy me, because I conceived it would not be difficult to make my escape from New Orleans on some Northern vessel. Freeman asked him $1500 for me. The old gentleman insisted it was too much, as times were very hard. Freeman, however, declared that I was sound and healthy, of a good constitution, and intelligent. He made it a point to enlarge upon my musical attainments. The old gentleman argued quite adroitly that there was nothing extraordinary about the nigger, and finally, to my regret, went out, saying he would call again.

During the day, however, a number of sales were made. David and Caroline were purchased together by a Natchez planter. They left us, grinning broadly, and in the most happy state of mind, caused by the fact of their not being separated. Lethe was sold to a planter of Baton Rouge, her eyes flashing with anger as she was led away.

The same man also purchased Randall. The little fellow was made to jump, and run across the floor, and perform many other feats, exhibiting his activity and condition. All the time the trade was going on, Eliza [the mother] was crying aloud, and wringing her hands. She besought the man not to buy him unless he also bought herself and Emily. She promised, in that case, to be the most faithful slave that ever lived. The man answered that he could not afford it, and then Eliza burst into a paroxysm of grief, weeping plaintively.

Freeman turned round to her, savagely, with his whip in his uplifted hand, ordering her to stop her noise, or he would flog her. He would not have such work—such sniveling; and unless she ceased that minute, he would take her to the yard and give her a hundred lashes. Yes, he would take the nonsense out of her pretty quick—if he didn't, might he be d—d.

Eliza shrunk before him, and tried to wipe away her tears, but it was all in vain. She wanted to be with her children, she said, the little time she had to live. All the frowns and threats of Freeman could not wholly silence the afflicted mother. She kept on begging and beseeching them, most piteously, not to separate the three. Over and over again she told them how she loved her boy. A great many times she repeated her former promises—how very faithful and obedient she would be; how hard she would labor day and night, to the last moment of her life, if he would only buy them all together.

But it was of no avail; the man could not afford it. The bargain was agreed upon, and Randall must go alone. Then Eliza ran to him; embraced him passionately; kissed him again and again; told him to remember her—all the while her tears falling in the boy's face like rain.

Source: Solomon Northup, *Twelve Years a Slave: Narrative of Solomon Northup . . .* (Auburn, NY: Derby and Miller, 1853).

Native Americans

Even before the American Revolution, Americans had begun moving west and starting new lives. This movement had brought them into contact with Native Americans, who did not share their ideas on land ownership. The victory over the British in the American Revolution accelerated the process, and the purchase of the Louisiana Territory in 1803 led to further incursions onto Indian lands. By 1830 the government had begun a policy of relocating Indians living east of the Mississippi River farther west. Many promises were made to the Indians of a better life and noninterference from white settlers if they would give up their lands in the South and Old Northwest for ones staked out farther west by the U.S. government. What we see in the following documents are the promises made by the government to the Indians and how the Indians viewed these promises, as more often than not they were broken by the government and the whites settling on their lands; few Indian leaders believed such promises, but defeated in battles and pressured by state and federal governments, they found resistance almost impossible. Americans and Indians were told that the resettlement of the Indians farther west would be good for all parties involved, but the promises were not kept, conflict ensued, and many Indian chiefs began to talk of the lies spoken by the "Great Father."

18. *Black Hawk's Surrender Speech (1832)*

The Black Hawk War of 1832 lasted only fifteen weeks, but marked the demise of both the Sauk and Fox tribes as political and military forces in the Old Northwest. The leader and guiding spirit behind the conflict, Chief Black Hawk, delivered this address at the time of his surrender to U.S. Army troops in August 1832. Spending a year in prison after his capture, upon his release Black Hawk traveled around the country as something of a public attraction, subsequently publishing his autobiography.

Black-hawk is an Indian. He has done nothing for which an Indian ought to be ashamed. He has fought for his countrymen, the squaws and papooses, against white men, who came, year after year, to cheat them and take away their lands. You know the cause of our making war. It is known to all white men. They ought to be ashamed of it. The white men despise the Indians, and drive them from their homes. But the Indians are not deceitful. The white men speak bad of the Indian, and look at him spitefully. But the Indian does not tell lies; Indians do not steal.

An Indian, who is as bad as the white men, could not live in our nation; he would be put to death, and eat up by the wolves. The white men are bad schoolmasters; they carry false looks, and deal in false actions; they smile in the face of the poor Indian to cheat him; they shake them by the hand to gain their confidence, to make them drunk, to deceive them, and ruin our wives. We told them to let us alone, and keep away from us; but they followed on, and beset our paths, and they coiled themselves among us, like the snake. They poisoned us by their touch. We were not safe. We lived in danger. We were becoming like them, hypocrites and liars, adulterers, lazy drones, all talkers, and no workers.

We looked up to the Great Spirit. We went to our great father. We were encouraged. His great council gave us fair words and big promises; but we got no satisfaction. Things were growing worse. There were no deer in the forest. The opossum and beaver were fled; the springs were drying up, and our squaws and papooses without victuals to keep them from starving; we called a great council, and built a large fire. The spirit of our fathers arose and spoke to us to avenge our wrongs or die. We all spoke before the council fire. It was warm and pleasant. We set up the war-whoop, and dug up the tomahawk; our knives were ready, and the heart of Black-hawk swelled high in his bosom, when he led his warriors to battle. He is satisfied. He will go to the world of spirits contented. He has done his duty. His father will meet him there, and commend him.

Source: Frank E. Stevens, *The Black Hawk War* (Chicago: Frank E. Stevens, 1903), 372–73.

19. *Andrew Jackson's "Permanent Habitation for the American Indians" Speech (1835)*

President Andrew Jackson believed that the best policy for preventing conflict between whites and Indians was for the Indians to move west beyond the Mississippi, where they would be protected by the government. Jackson's policies belied this idea, as he believed in the superiority of whites and that the Indians were a nuisance that needed to be removed. Here he announces his policy of relocation, along with promises of a better life for the Indians.

The plan of removing the aboriginal people who yet remain within the settled portions of the United States to the country west of the Mississippi River approaches its consummation. It was adopted on the most mature consideration of the condition of this race, and ought to be persisted in till the object is accomplished, and prosecuted with as much vigor as a just regard to their circumstances will permit, and as fast as their consent can be obtained. All preceding experiments for the improvement of the Indians have failed. It seems now to be an established fact that they can not live in contact with a civilized community and prosper. Ages of fruitless endeavors have at length brought us to a knowledge of this principle of intercommunication with them. The past we can not recall, but the future we can provide for.

Independently of the treaty stipulations into which we have entered with the various tribes for the usufructuary rights they have ceded to us, no one can doubt the moral duty of the government of the United States to protect and if possible to preserve and perpetuate the scattered remnants of this race which are left within our borders. In the discharge of this duty an extensive region in the West has been assigned for their permanent residence. It has been divided into districts and allotted among them. Many have already removed and others are preparing to go, and with the exception of two small bands living in Ohio and Indiana not exceeding 1,500 persons, and of the Cherokees, all the tribes on the east side of the Mississippi, and extending from Lake Michigan to Florida, have entered into engagements which will lead to their transplantation.

The plan for their removal and reestablishment is founded upon the knowledge we have gained of their character and habits, and has been dictated by a spirit of enlarged liberality. A territory exceeding in extent that relinquished has been granted to each tribe. Of its climate, fertility, and capacity to support an Indian population the representatives are highly favorable. To these districts the Indians are removed at the expense of the United States, and with certain supplies of clothing, arms, ammunition, and other indispensable articles; they are also furnished gratuitously with provisions for the period of a year after their arrival at their new homes. In that time, from the nature of the country and of the products raised by them, they can subsist themselves by agricultural labor, if they choose to resort to that mode of life; if they do not they are upon the skirts of the great prairies, where countless herds of buffalo roam, and a short time suffices to adapt their own habits to the changes which a change of the animals destined for their food may require.

Ample arrangements have also been made for the support of schools; in some instances council houses and churches are to be erected, dwellings constructed for the chiefs, and mills for common use. Funds have been set apart for the maintenance of the poor; the most necessary mechanical arts have been introduced, and blacksmiths, gunsmiths, wheelwrights, millwrights, etc., are supported among them. Steel and iron, and sometimes salt, are purchased for them, and plows and other farming utensils, domestic animals, looms, spinning wheels, cards, etc., are presented to them. And besides these beneficial arrangements, annuities are in all cases paid, amounting in some instances to more than thirty dollars for each individual of the tribe, and in all cases sufficiently great, if justly divided and prudently expended, to enable them, in addition to their own exertions, to live comfortably. And as a stimulus for exertion, it is now provided by law that "in all cases of the appointment of interpreters or other persons employed for the benefit of the Indians a preference shall be given to persons of Indian descent, if such can be found who are properly qualified for the discharge of the duties."

Such are the arrangements for the physical comfort and for the moral improvement of the Indians. The necessary measures for their political advancement and for their separation from our citizens have not been neglected. The pledge of the United States has been given by Congress that the country destined for the residence of this people shall be forever "secured and guaranteed to them." A country west of Missouri and Arkansas has been assigned to them, into which the white settlements are not to be pushed. No political communities can be formed in that extensive region, except those which are established by the Indians themselves or by the United States for them and with their concurrence. A barrier has thus been raised for their protection against the encroachment of our citizens, and guarding the Indians as far as possible from those evils which have brought them to their present condition.

Summary authority has been given by law to destroy all ardent spirits found in their country, without waiting the doubtful result and slow process of a legal seizure. I consider the absolute and unconditional interdiction of this article among these people as the first and great step in their melioration. Halfway measures will answer no purpose. These can not successfully contend against the cupidity of the seller and the overpowering appetite of the buyer. And the destructive effects of the traffic are marked in every page of the history of our Indian intercourse.

Some general legislation seems necessary for the regulation of the relations which will exist in this new state of things between the government and people of the United States and these transplanted Indian tribes, and for the establishment among the latter, and with their own consent, of some principles of intercommunication which their juxtaposition will call for; that moral may be substituted for physical force, the authority of a few and simple laws for the tomahawk, and that an end may be put to those bloody wars whose prosecution seems to have made part of their social system.

After the further details of this arrangement are completed, with a very general supervision over them, they ought to be left to the progress of events. These, I indulge the hope, will secure their prosperity and improvement, and a large portion of the moral debt we owe them will then be paid.

Source: *A Compilation of the Messages and Papers of the Presidents 1789–1897*, vol. 3, ed. James D. Richardson (1920), 147–77.

20. Response of Speckled Snake (Cherokee) to Andrew Jackson's Removal Policy (1841)

With the discovery of gold on Cherokee land in Georgia, white Americans rushed onto those lands. Conflicts ensued. Such contacts, and the demands of American settlers and others for access to and even ownership of lands recognized by treaty as reserved for Indians, led Andrew

Jackson to call for the resettlement of the Cherokee west of the Mississippi River, where they would be free of white settlers and would be protected by the government. Here the Cherokee chief Speckled Snake speaks to his people about the continued westward incursions of the whites and the broken promises of the U.S. government.

Brothers! We have heard the talk of our great father; it is very kind. He says he loves his red children. Brothers! When the white man first came to these shores, the Muscogees gave him land, and kindled him a fire to make him comfortable; and when the pale faces of the south made war on him, their young men drew the tomahawk, and protected his head from the scalping knife. But when the white man had warmed himself before the Indian's fire, and filled himself with the Indian's hominy, he became very large; he stopped not for the mountain tops, and his feet covered the plains and the valleys. His hands grasped the eastern and the western sea. Then he became our great father. He loved his red children; but he said, "You must move a little farther, lest I should, by accident, tread on you." With one foot he pushed the red man over the Oconee, and with the other he trampled down the graves of his fathers. But our great father still loved his red children, and he soon made them another talk. He said much; but it all meant nothing, but "move a little farther; you are too near to me." I have heard a great many talks from our great father, and they began and ended the same. Brothers! When he made us a talk on a former occasion, he said, "Get a little farther; go beyond the Oconee and the Oakmulgee; there is pleasant country." He also said, "It shall be yours forever." Now he says, "The land you live on is not yours; go beyond the Mississippi; there is game; there you may remain while the grass grows or the water runs." Brothers! Will not our great father come there also? He loves his red children, and his tongue is not forked.

Source: Samuel G. Drake, *Biography and History of the Indians of North America*, 11th ed. (Boston, 1841), 450.

Part VII
RECREATIONAL LIFE

Americans did not spend all their time working, praying, or studying in school. Many leisure activities were enjoyed by Americans in their everyday lives. Such activities included games and sports, such as billiards and wrestling (animals or people), skating, and later baseball. Some leisure activities combined relaxation with usefulness, such as hunting and fishing, while others were principally for the pleasure alone. Americans also spent their time traveling. They did so on horseback or by stagecoach in the years during and after the Revolution, and during the nineteenth century many did so on steamboats plying rivers, or later on railroads. Better maps and guidebooks expanded the range of travel and interest. Some even went as far as California, now prepared with the information and supplies needed for a long, arduous journey. The music of the period also entertained Americans in homes, at public gatherings, in churches, and at work. Music also inspired patriotism for the country as well as giving sound and lyrics to regional cultures. People living in towns and cities had more varied entertainments than those living in rural places. Traveling troupes, exhibitions, and even museums brought wonders to urban audiences. Theater also prospered, as much through minstrel shows as renditions of Shakespeare. Much entertainment included alcohol, which fact began to worry reformers concerned about the debilitating effects of so much consumption. Interestingly, by foreign traveler's observations, Americans seemed always in a hurry in their recreational lives as in their work. Americans admired the speed of horses, boats, and men, and paid money to spur on their favorites.

Games and Sports

The recreational activities of Americans during this period changed in the various games and sports that people played. In the early colonial period hunting was important to the survival of the early settlers, and it would continue to be so for the settlers who were heading west during America's expansion after the American Revolution, right through the nineteenth century. In rural areas of the established part of the country, mainly in the southeast, hunting became less a necessity for survival and more a recreational sport enjoyed by members of the upper class, and also became a mark of distinction in an increasingly class-based society, but that didn't mean that Americans had reached the status of their European counterparts. Another example of leisure activity was the growth of fishing as a means of escaping the strains of everyday life and taking the opportunity to experience the natural beauty of the countryside and become one with nature. Americans and travelers to America noted the availability of fish in the lakes and rivers of this great country and took advantage of every opportunity to go fishing.

One of the more popular indoor games was billiards, or pool. The game was played by both the wealthy and the common worker. Those who had the means had a table set off in a separate room of their homes, thereby marking them as members of the upper class and giving them a sense of status in society. Those who could not afford their own tables and lived in homes that had no space could go play a game or two in a pool hall. In many of these pool halls men would come to spend time with friends, and many also used gambling on pool as a means to supplement their income. In some of the poorer neighborhoods, the pool hall served as a conduit for prostitution and a meeting place for neighborhood gangs. The pool hall described in the second document below may have been such a place.

Another sport that began making inroads into American culture was baseball. During the early part of the nineteenth century the game was still developing, but it became a popular recreational sport for members of the working class, and many took the opportunity to play when they had free time. By the time of the Civil War the game was attracting more attention and gaining in popularity. It became a favorite for soldiers on both sides to break up the monotony of camp life; as the century progressed it began to attract spectators of all classes and was well on its way to becoming the "great American pastime." Comparisons were made between baseball and the British game of cricket, but for reasons that are explained in the article excerpted below, cricket never gained much of a following in the United States.

1. Hunting in Virginia (1799)

At the end of the eighteenth and the beginning of the nineteenth centuries, the United States was still a vast wilderness and sparsely inhabited. Most of the population still lived within several hundred miles of the coast. In the South, hunting was a very popular sport. The southern planters who engaged in it for sport were trying to imitate the hunts of the English gentry. Here John Bernard, a British-born actor and comedian who spent many years in the United States, describes his experiences with hunting in Virginia in 1799 and notes that the experiences of hunting in America was nothing like that in England.

The last and least frequent mode of passing time that I partook of in Virginia was hunting. It was a very curious thing that, with few or none of the domestic tastes of the mother-country, the slave states alone were decidedly English in their public amusements. Whether the importation of these had been generally beneficial to so young a country is another question. The planters had wealth and leisure, two incentives to enjoyment, besides a greater than either—a warm climate. Climate, in fact, makes all the difference. It is an easy thing to be a stoic in a cold one, the absence of temptation always leading a man to flatter himself into a belief of his superior goodness. However, hunting . . . could not come under the ban of even the "Blue Laws." It was a healthy recreation and served to increase a man's knowledge of topography. . . .

But hunting in Virginia, like every other social exotic, was a far different thing from its English original. The meaning of the latter is simple and explicit. A party of horsemen meet at an appointed spot and hour, to turn up or turn out a deer or a fox, and pursue to a standstill. Here a local peculiarity—the abundance of game—upsets all systems. The practice seemed to be for the company to enter the wood, beat up the quarters of anything, from a stag to a snake, and take their chance for a chase. If the game went off well, and it was possible to follow it through the thickets and morasses, ten to one that at every hundred yards up spring so many rivals that horses and hunters were puzzled which to select, and every buck, if he chose, could have a deer to himself—an arrangement that I was told proved generally satisfactory, since it enabled the worst rider, when all was over, to talk about as many difficulties surmounted as the best. . . .

Source: John Bernard, *Retrospections of America, 1797–1811*, ed. Mrs. Bayle Bernard (New York: Harper & Brothers, 1887), 156–57.

2. A Pool Hall in Cincinnati (1828)

James Hall was born in Philadelphia in 1793 to an upper-class family. His mother taught him and his brothers a love of literature that would remain with him for the rest of his life. He began his studies in law, but joined the army for the War of 1812 and remained in the army until 1818, when he resigned to return to the study of law. By 1820 he was a practicing attorney in Illinois. He also edited and wrote for the local papers, and after his election as state treasurer in 1828 he created The Illinois Monthly Magazine, *which was the first literary review in the state, and also founded The Antiquarian and Historical Society of Illinois. He died in Cincinnati in 1868. Billiards was a popular game for men of all classes. Here Hall gives a description of the interior of a billiard parlor.*

It was a large apartment, indifferently lighted, and meanly furnished. In the centre stood the billiard table, whose allurements had enticed so many on this evening to forsake the quiet and virtuous comforts of social life, and to brave the biting blast, and not less "pitiless peltings" of parental or conjugal admonition. Its polished mahogany frame, and neatly brushed cover of green cloth, its silken pockets, and party-covered ivory balls, presented a striking contrast to the rude negligence of the rest of the furniture; while a large canopy suspended over the table, and intended to collect and refract the rays of a number of well trimmed lamps, which hung within its circumference, shed an intense brilliancy over that little spot, and threw a corresponding gloom upon the surrounding scene. Indeed, if that gay altar of dissipation had been withdrawn, the temple of pleasure would have presented rather a desolate appearance of the house of mourning.

The stained and dirty floor was strewed with fragments of segars, playbills, and nut shells; the walls blackened with smoke seem to have witnessed the orgies of many a midnight revel. A few candles, destined to illumine the distant recesses of the room, hung neglected against the walls—bowing their long wicks, and marking their stations by streams of tallow, which had been suffered to accumulate through many a long winter night. The ceiling was hung with cobwebs, curiously intermingled with dense clouds of tobacco smoke, and tinged by the straggling rays of light which occasionally shot from the sickly tapers. A set of benches attached to the walls, and raised sufficiently high to overlook the table, accommodated the loungers, who were not engaged at play, and who sat or reclined, solemnly puffing their segars, idly sipping their brandy and water, or industriously counting their chances of the game, but all observing a profound silence which would have done honor to a turbaned divan, and was well suited to the important subjects of their contemplation. Little coteries of gayer spirits laughed and chatted aside, or made their criticisms on the players in subdued accents—any remarks on that subject being forbidden to all but the parties engaged; while the marker announced the state of the game, trimmed the lamps, and supplied refreshments to the guests.

Source: James Hall, *The Western Souvenir, a Christmas and New Year's Gift for 1829* (Cincinnati, OH: N. & G. Guilford, 1828), 194–211.

3. Baseball vs. Cricket (1859)

Baseball emerged as the great American game by the end of the nineteenth century. The game evolved from several sources, including a colonial game known as rounders, and over time developed into a game with clear boundaries and rules of play. It became an organized sport, though in the antebellum period local variations were rife as men's clubs set their own rules. Baseball would gain more popularity during the Civil War as men on both sides played the game when they had free time, and its popularity continued to grow through the end of the century and beyond. Already Americans had developed their own lore about the game and its origins, insisting it was an American invention. Europeans saw the game as being closely related to English cricket. The following article from the New York Herald *in 1859 discusses the positive effect of the game on America.*

Cricket . . . has not extended much. . . . For two reasons: first; because base ball—an American national game—was in possession, and was too like cricket to be superceded by it, and secondly, in the points on which it differs from cricket it is more suited to the genius of the people. It is rapid and simple. Even if there were no base ball in existence cricket could never become a national sport in America—it is too slow, intricate and plodding a game for our go ahead people.

Base ball has been from time immemorial a favorite and popular recreation in this country; but it is only within the last fifteen years that the game has been systematized and clubs formed for the purpose of playing at stated periods and under a code of written laws. The Knickerbocker Cub, for New York, organized in 1845, was the first and since then numerous clubs have sprung up in this city, and Brooklyn, and throughout the country. But the great increase has been within the past three or four years. . . .

The good effect produced on the health and strength and morals of the young men engaged in this outdoor exercise is the theme of all who are conversant with them. It has taken them from the unhealthy haunts of dissipation indoors, and given them a taste for manly sport which cannot fail to have a beneficial effect, not only in the physical development of our citizens, but on the national character. No "refreshments" are allowed on the occasion of matches, which are visited by thousands of spectators, including a large number of ladies.

Source: *New York Herald*, October 16, 1859.

4. Line Fishing (Early 1860s)

Benedict Henry Révoil was a well-known French author who spent nine years in the United States, and much of his writing was based on his American experiences. One of his works was published in two volumes and discusses his experiences hunting and fishing in the United States. Here he discusses line fishing and the opportunity to experience the beauty of nature in a land that by this time was untouched by man.

I am convinced that the perusal of *Robinson Crusoe,* the *Swiss Robinson,* and the works of Cooper, Mayne Reid, and other authors of the same kind—of even my own, it may be—has attracted from the paternal roof many of our most celebrated sailors, and that it will continue to produce the same effect as often as occasion offers, but I am still more certain that the greater part of the anglers who line the banks of the Seine, the Marne, and the other great rivers of the world, have been inspired with the "fatal" passion by reading fishing manuals, and works which promise to teach the devotees of the gentle art how to catch large quantities of fish in a short time,—works which develope the theory without paying due attention to the practice, and which serve up their lessons with an accompaniment or sauce composed of anecdotes, stories of marvellous takes of fish, and often of exciting illustrations.

I, who wrote this, good fellow angler, read my Walton years ago—alas, how many!—with three companions of my own age; and at the conclusion of that captivating reading, we started off at once for a certain small lake not far from the paternal mansion, duly furnished with rods, lines, hooks, red worms, and morsels of cheese—like true Quixotes as we were in the art of fishing. The season was propitious. Spring was beginning to melt into summer, and a warm breeze, perfumed with sage, thyme, and lavender, freshened our foreheads and played with our curly locks. I speak of myself as from afar, and my readers will understand the pleasure I take in thinking of what I then was, as we ran on to abridge the distance between my father's house and the lake of Baux.

One of us—I see him as if it were yesterday—had accoutred himself after a fashion equally artistic and picturesque. He had dressed himself in a serge coat, which was cut in the shape of a long waistcoat, with large pockets before and behind; his legs were encased in wading boots, and he held in one hand a creel, to contain the fish he intended to catch, and in the other a fishing-rod and reel, and a landing-net. The good people whom we met on the road looked with amazement, as if they could not understand why M. Max de C. (whom they all knew well) should dress himself up like a play-actor. In their eyes, he produced just the same effect that the hero of La Mancha did upon the knights of the Sierra Morena, when he appeared before them all cased in iron, his helmet on his head, and his lance in rest.

We soon arrived at the brink of the lake, which bathed with its clear waters a tuft of green oaks, whose foliage offered us a shelter against the fervour of the southern sun. At a short distance from the spot which we had chosen for our first attempt at the gentle sport, a clear rivulet flowed into the pond from the mountains of La Yacquière, as if to warm its icy streams in the warmer waters of the lake. Often with one of my uncles had I visited this place in search of water-hens and snipe. It was, in fact, an excellent place for water-fowl, and from the occasional disturbance of the surface of the water, it was easy to see that there were fish lurking down below among the roots of the aquatic vegetation.

I had forgotten to state that, without being at the time acquainted with the sporting maxims of du Fonilleux (whose curious pages I have since read), we had brought with us a sufficient quantity of "mouth tackle," in order that we might enjoy the pleasures of a breakfast *al fresco*. Before attacking the victuals, however, it was determined upon that we should fish; so to fish we prepared forthwith.

Max was the first to cast his line into the water. Myself and the others had to put our primitive tackle in order, and awkward enough we were about it, you may be sure. All, however, was finally arranged to the satisfaction of everybody.

Max was lucky enough. He had soon captured two tench and a little carp, when Gabriel (friend number two) cast his line into a corner of the mouth of the rivulet, and drew out successively several carp, tench, and an eel. The rest of us now made haste to join in the sport, and at last I threw my bait into the water, arranged, as I thought, with admirable art. At first, fortune smiled upon my efforts, and I soon added to the basket three perch and a small pike, and then—luck turned against me.

I must confess, to my shame, that I am somewhat of a poacher, and fond as I am of net-fishing, line-fishing has but few attractions for me, principally because it is so often without result. Moreover I had not then sufficient adroitness to manage the tackle. Often I hung up my hook in the endeavour to recover it for the purpose of changing the bait. Then my line got entangled in the branches of a tree; finally, I broke the top of my rod, and grew out of patience. Disgusted with my own want of skill, I gave it up in despair, and, throwing myself on the mossy bank at the foot of the oaks, contented myself with watching my three friends.

We breakfasted at mid-day, and after a short rest the fishing re-commenced, and when evening had come the basket was so heavy, that we had to obtain the assistance of a countryman to carry it home for us.

Source: Benedict Henry Révoil, *Shooting and Fishing in the Rivers, Prairies, and Backwoods of North America*, trans. and rev. by the Chronicler, vol. 2 (London: Tinsley Brothers, 1865), 22–25.

Travel

As maps and guidebooks improved and became more widely distributed, and as transportation improvements spread during the nineteenth century, increasing numbers of Americans began to travel for pleasure, not just business. For the wealthy, this usually meant trips to the country or to other states. Much of their time was spent on the road, and finding a well-appointed inn was important. Europeans also traveled to and in America. Many wanted to see this vast new land and experience the countryside that supposedly had been untouched by man. The observations left by these travelers give us a valuable insight into the changes in travel during this period and the hazards they faced, not only bad roads and potential bandits, but also bad fare and bad company.

The English diarist Nicholas Cresswell left a fascinating account of his three-year stay in America and the problems he encountered in his travels as the American Revolution raged all around him, which gives us good insight into the hazards a noncombatant faced during the war. A ride on a steamboat along the Mississippi is the subject of the remembrance of a traveler to the South, which takes us to the period when this method of transportation made travel available to many Americans. The pioneers who crossed the American plains during the nineteenth century took many risks, and preparations for the journey were crucial in increasing the odds of successfully traversing hostile territory. Guidebooks told people what materials were necessary for such an arduous undertaking. We take a look at the preparations made for a journey across the plains and the need to know the habits of the Indians the travelers might encounter. Such travel accounts were widely read in America and served to broaden Americans' sense of their own land, though also sometimes making them resentful of European criticism of their habits, manners, and interests.

5. *Travel during the Revolution (1776)*

Nicholas Cresswell came to America to visit a friend and to explore Britain's American colonies in 1776 but found himself caught up in the American Revolution. His support of Britain made travel difficult, and at one point he was detained on suspicion of being a spy. Cresswell eventually reached New York and was able to sail back to England.

Tuesday, September 3rd, 1776. This is a large, rich, populous and regular town. The Delaware River is on the North side the town and Schuykill River on the South West. Streets run parallel with the Delaware River, others in direct lines which forms it in squares. The streets are sixty foot wide, except Market Street which is an hundred, but the Market house is set in the middle of this street which entirely spoils the beauty of it. These are paved with brick and kept very clean with walks on each side for the foot people. Well supplied with pumps, very level, and so remarkably straight there is nothing to obstruct your view from one end of the town to the other. Three English Churches, Christ Church, St. Paul's and St. Peter's, and two Dutch Lutheran Churches. Nine dissenting meeting houses, two Roman Chapels, Four Quaker meeting houses, and a Swedish Church. All neat plain buildings but none of them elegant ones. The State house is a good building but does not make a grand appearance. Here all public business is done. Now the nest of the great and mighty Sanhedrim. Near this is the New Jail, a good and large stone building now occupied with *Sgnik Sdneirf*. A Handsome brick Hospital, but not large. Here is a good building they call a Bettering House, where all strolling and disorderly people are confined to labour till they can give a sufficient account of themselves. Here is a College for the education of Youth. It makes no great appearance, and how it is endowed I cannot tell. The

Buildings are Brick, very plain, convenient and neat, no very grand edifices as the Quakers have the management of public affairs. Here is a large and plentiful Market, but chiefly supplied from the Jerseys. It is a Corporation town, governed by a Mayor and 20 Aldermen and Common Councilmen. Everything is kept in the greatest order. Here is Barracks for 7 or 8 thousand men. They build as fine Ships here as any part of the World and with as great dispatch. There are four continental Frigates built here in a few months, two of them 111 foot keel and two 96, as fine vessels as I ever saw. I suppose they will be ready for sea in a month, if they can get hands to man them. This is the most regular, neat and convenient city I ever was in and has made the most rapid progress to its present greatness. Spent the day with Mr. Buchhannan.

Wednesday, September 4th, 1776. Spent the day with Mr. Buchhannan and Mr. Thornbur. Great many ships laid up and unrigged at the wharfs. Took my passage in the Stage for New York. Left the Horse in care of Marchington to send him to Leesburg if I don't return in 6 days.

Thursday, September 5th, 1776. Set out from Philadelphia about 5 o'clock this morning in a vehicle neither coach nor waggon but between both. It holds 15 persons and is not uneasy travelling. Breakfasted at *The Wheatsheaf* 12 miles. Crossed Shammory Ferry. Stopped at Bristol, a small town opposite Burlington where we changed Horses, 20 miles from Philadelphia.

Prince-town, New Jersey—Thursday, September 5th, 1776. Crossed Delaware River at Trenton Ferry. Dined at Trenton, this is a small town and very little trade. Through a small town or rather village called Maidenhead. Lodged at Prince-town. This is a neat Little town with an Elegant College for the education of Youth. I believe there are 60 rooms in it for the students, each room has two closets and two beds, a Chapel, Library and Schoolroom. Cellars and storerooms complete. Saw the Orrery and Electrical Machine made by the famous David Written-house. Electrical machine and apparatus not complete. Doctor Witherspoon. Lodged at *The Sign of Hudibras.*

Newark, New Jersey—Friday, September 6th, 1776. Left Prince-town. Passed thro' Kingstown. Breakfasted at Brunswick. This is a small trading town, situated on Rareaton River, which is navigable to the town for small craft. Crossed Rareaton River, several pleasant seats along the Banks. Land good. Changed horses at Woodbridge and paid the other half of the fare, 11s. here and 10s. at Philadelphia. This is a small, neat town. Dined at Elizabeth town, this is a small town of some trade. Lodged at Newark. This is nothing more than a Village. Country populous in general but now in distraction. Land along the Rivers good. Hills rather poor. Believe one of the company is a Spy upon my actions.

New York, Saturday, September 7th, 1776. Left Newark. Crossed Passihack or Second River, then Hackensack River, then North River at Powlershook Ferry. River about 1½ miles wide. Landed in New York about nine o'clock, when one Collins, an Irish merchant, and myself rambled about the town till three in the afternoon before we could get anything for breakfast. At length we found a little Dutch tippling house and persuaded the old woman to get us something to eat. It was a stew of pork bones and cabbage so full of Garlic, nothing but necessity would have compelled me to eat it, my companion would not taste another mouthful. Nothing to be got here. All the inhabitants are moved out. The town full of Soldiers. Viewing the town and fortifications and contriving means to effect my escape, but despair of it, the Rivers are too well guarded.

This town is the best situated for trade of any place I ever saw. It is on a point of Land with wharfs two thirds of the way round the town and very near the Sea. The town is not so regular as Philadelphia, nor so extensive, neither has it so many good buildings, but more elegant ones both public and private. Here are three English Churches, the old Trinity Church, St. Paul's and St. George's Chapel, two Dutch Churches, four dissenting meeting houses, one Quaker Meeting, and a Jews' Synagogue and a French Church. A College and Hospital, two elegant buildings. There was a fine equestrian statute of his Majesty, but the *Sleber* has pulled it down and cast it into Bullets. The Statue of the Earl of Chatham is still standing unhurt in the attitude of an apple woman, dressed like a Roman Orator. I am not a judge, but don't think it clever. The liberty pole, as they call it, is covered with Iron bars. Streets fortified with small batteries towards the River. My fellow-traveller, Mr. Collins, and I should have lodged in the streets, had we not luckily met one Godard, Postmaster, who got us a sorry lodging at the Hull Tavern. From the top of this house have a prospect of Long Island, Staten Island, Governor's Island, Bedlow's Island and Gilbert's Island, three last small ones. All the British Fleet and part of the Army make a fine appearance, but it is utterly out of my power to get to them. I never, till now, thought of it, but honour forbids it, as I am enabled to travel by the interest of Mr. Mason. Was I to make my escape, he might be reflected on.

Newark, New Jersey—Sunday, September 8th, 1776. Left New York early this morning. Crossed the North River to Powlershook. While we waited for the Stage, viewed the *Sleber* Fortifications here. They are made of earth, but what number of Guns or what size I cannot tell. No admittance into the Fort. The Troops stationed here are Yankee men, the nastiest Devils in creation. It would be impossible for any human creature whose organs of smelling was more delicate than that of a hog to live one day under the Lee of this Camp, such a complication of stinks. Saw a Yankee put a pint of molasses into about a gallon of Mutton Broth. The Army here is numerous, but ragged, dirty, sickly, and ill-disciplined. If my countrymen are beaten by these ragamuffins I shall be much surprized. Their Fleet is large and it is said their Army is numerous. New York must fall into their hands, their batteries on Long Island command the town. Heard a smart cannonade crossing the Ferry this morning, supposed to be at Hellgate. The Fleet is within 2 miles of the town. Got to Newark to dinner. Great scarcity of provisions, the roads full of soldiers. Very uneasy. Must be obliged to go into Canada or stay in this D—d Country.

Prince-town, New Jersey—Monday, September 9th, 1776. Left Newark. Breakfasted at Elizabeth town. Dined at Brunswick. Lodged at Prince-town. Great numbers of soldiers on the road. Our company chiefly Irishmen.

Philadelphia—Tuesday, September 10th, 1776. Left Prince-town. Breakfasted at Trenton. Dined at Bristol, where we changed horses. Got to Philadelphia in the evening. Lodged at one Mrs. Stretch's in Second Street, my old lodging took up. Spent the evening with the French Officers that are prisoners here, taken at St. John's. Very polite gentlemen, but exceedingly cautious. Town full of soldiers.

Wednesday, September 11th, 1776. Dined at Mr. Brewer's. Spent the afternoon with Mr. Buchhannan. Lodged at Mrs. Stretch's. My designs are frustrated. Spend a good deal of money to no sort of purpose. I must return to Virginia and endeavour to get to Canada.

Thursday, Sept. 12th, 1776. Determined to set out to Virginia to-morrow. Dined at Mrs. Stretch's. Supped and spent the evening at *The Golden Fleece* in company with Marchington, Gresswold, Brewer and Thornbur, all *Sgnik Sdneirf*, very merry. News that General Prescott and General McDonald were exchanged for G. Sullivan and G. Sterling, *Sleber* took at Long Island.

Christiana Bridge—Friday, September 13th, 1776. Left Philadelphia in company with Messrs. Marchington & Gresswold. Crossed Schuylkill at Grey's Ferry. Through Derby, a little place. Dined at Chester, a smart little town on the Delawar River. Here Marchington and Gresswold left me and I joined an Irish Tailor metamorphised into a Captn. and an Irish Blacksmith his Lieutenant. Both going to Baltimore. Passed Brandywine Mills. Here are 8 of them in a quarter of a mile, so convenient that they can take the grain out of the Vessels into the Mills. Wilmington, a pretty town on the River, then Newport a trifling place. Lodged at Christiana Bridge, a little town situated on a Creek of the same name.

Source: *The Journal of Nicholas Cresswell, 1774–1777*, ed. Lincoln MacVeigh (New York: The Dial Press, 1924), 155–60.

6. A *Steamboat Ride on the Mississippi* (1850s)

John Benwell was an Englishman who traveled extensively throughout the United States in the 1850s and recorded his experiences with the people and places he encountered. In this excerpt, he discusses a steamboat ride along the Mississippi River, noting not only the scenery, but his fellow passengers.

The *Narraganset*, like most of the large river steamers, was constructed with three decks, and fitted up in sumptuous style. One large saloon, with a portion partitioned off for the ladies, serving as a cabin and dining apartment. There is no professed distinction of class in the passengers on board steam-boats in America. I found, however, that the higher grades, doubtless from the same causes that operate in other parts of the world, kept aloof from those beneath them.

The scene from the upper or hurricane deck (as it is called) was very attractive. Flowing, as the river Hudson does, through a fine mountainous country, the magnificent scenery on the banks strikes the observer with feelings allied to awe. The stream being broad and tortuous, beetling crags, high mountains and bluffs, and dense forests, burst suddenly and unexpectedly into view; fearful precipices abound here and there, amidst luxuriant groves and uncouth pine barrens, forming altogether a diversity that gives the whole the character of a stupendous panorama.

Before we were out of the tide, which for miles flows up the river, our vessel grounded three times, but after puffing and straining for a considerable time, she got off without damage and pursued her onward course. Most of my fellow-voyagers were disposed to be distant and taciturn, and so I enjoyed the grandeurs of the scene in solitary musings, to which the steamers, sloops under sail, and other vessels proceeding up and down the river, gave a pleasant enlivenment. The promenade deck, crowded with lady passengers and beautiful children, under a gay awning, added to the cheerfulness of the surrounding aspect, and the fineness of the weather, but for the fear of collapsing boilers, would have made the trip one of great enjoyment.

Another drawback I had nearly forgotten, and as it serves to illustrate steam-boat and indeed all other travelling [sic] inconveniences in America, I must not pass it over; I refer to the vulgarity of the men passengers, who, in default of better occupation, chew tobacco incessantly, and, to the great annoyance of those who do not practise the vandalism, eject the impregnated saliva over everything under foot. The deck of the vessel was much defaced by the noxious stains; and even in converse with ladies the unmannerly fellows expectorated without sense of decency. The ladies, however, seemed not to regard it, and one bright-eyed houri [sic] I saw looking into the face of a long sallow-visaged young man, who had the juice oozing out at each angle of his mouth with disgusting effect, so that enunciation was difficult.

Source: John Benwell, *An Englishman's Travels in America: His Observations of Manners in the Free and Slave States* (London: Ward & Lock, 1857), 35–37.

7. *Randolph Marcy,* The Prairie Traveler *(1859)*

To assist travelers moving out to the western frontier, Randolph Marcy, a captain in the U.S. Army, published The Prairie Traveler: A Handbook for Overland Expeditions *(1859). Such guidebooks were popular fare, providing useful information for travelers and prospective settlers and making the west more "accessible and knowable" and thus less daunting. In this excerpt, Marcy lists the supplies needed for the trip. Take note of his descriptions of American Indians and their keen abilities.*

Supplies for a march should be put up in the most secure, compact, and portable manner.

Bacon should be packed in strong sacks of a hundred pounds to each; or, in very hot climates, put in boxes and surrounded with bran, which in a great measure prevents the fat from melting away.

Flour should be packed in stout double canvas sacks well sewed, a hundred pounds in each sack.

Butter may be preserved, and skimming off the scum as it rises to the top until it is quite clear like oil. It is then placed in tin canisters and soldered up. This mode of preserving butter has been adopted in the hot climate of southern Texas, and it is found to keep sweet for a great length of time, and its flavor is but little impaired by the process.

Sugar may be well secured in India-rubber or gutta-purcha sacks, or so placed in the wagon as not to risk getting wet.

Desiccated or dried vegetables are almost equal to the fresh, and are put up in such a compact and portable form as easily to be transported over the plains. They have been exclusively used in the Crimean war, and by our own army in Utah, and have been very generally approved. They are prepared by cutting the fresh vegetables into thin slices and subjecting them to very powerful press, which removes the juice and leaves the solid cake, which after having been thoroughly dried in an oven, becomes almost hard as a rock. A small piece of this, about half the size of a man's hand, when boiled, swells up so as to fill a vegetable disk, and is sufficient for four men. It is believed that the antiscorbutic properties of vegetables are not impaired by desiccation, and they will keep for years if not exposed to dampness. Canned vegetables are very good for campaigning, but are not so portable as when put up in the other form. . . .

When the deer are lying down in the smooth prairie, unless the grass is tall, it is difficult to get near them, as they are generally looking around, and become alarmed at the least noise.

The Indians are in the habit of using a small instrument which imitates the bleat of the young fawn, with which they lure the doe within range of their rifles. The young fawn gives out no scent upon its track until it is sufficiently grown to make good running, and instinct teaches the mother that this wise provision of nature to preserve the helpless little quadruped from the ravages of wolves, panthers, and other carnivorous beasts, will be defeated if she remains with it, as her tracks can not be concealed. She therefore hides her fawn in the grass, where it is almost impossible to see it, even when very near it, goes off to some neighboring thicket within call, and makes her bed alone. The Indian pot-hunter, who is but little scrupulous as to the means he employs in accomplishing his ends, sounds the bleat along near the places where he thinks the game is lying, and the unsuspicious doe, who imagines that her offspring is in distress, rushes with headlong impetuosity toward the sound, and often goes within a few yards of the hunter to receive her death-wound. . . .

I once undertook to experiment with the instrument myself, and made my first essay in attempting to call up an antelope which I discovered in the distance. I succeeded admirably in luring the way [wary] victim within shooting range, had raised upon my knees, and was just in the act of pulling trigger, when a rustling in the grass to my left drew my attention in that direction, where, much to my surprise, I beheld a huge panther within about twenty yards, bounding with gigantic strides directly toward me. I turned my rifle, and in an instant, much to my relief and gratification, its contents were lodged in the heart of the beast.

Source: Randolph A. Marcy, *The Prairie Traveler: A Handbook for Overland Expeditions* (Published by Authority of the War Department, 1859).

Music and Dance

Music is another form of recreation that Americans enjoyed. Much of the music listened to was of the classical variety that came from Europe, but as the republic grew, a distinctive American style of music began to emerge. Pride in the new nation and its environs became the theme of much of the music of the period after the Revolution. The three songs that are presented in this section represent the growing confidence of the nation during this period. All are familiar to us today and were very popular then. The first song was meant to be an insult to Americans, sung by British troops with the hope that it would hurt American morale, but it was adopted as a symbol of America by the Continental soldiers and became synonymous with America. The second song was written during a key engagement of the War of 1812, the bombardment of Fort McHenry in Baltimore Harbor. The song became a symbol of American resistance and strength. Thereafter it became America's unofficial national anthem, until it was made the official anthem by President Herbert Hoover. The final song, although written by a northerner, became the unofficial anthem of the Confederacy during the Civil War. It has since become a symbol for some people of the racism and oppression of the antebellum south, while others see it as an example of a way of life that has passed from existence.

8. *"Yankee Doodle"* (1778)

Originally sung by British troops to insult the American colonists, "Yankee Doodle" became a popular song during the American Revolution. It was initially introduced in America during the French and Indian War, although it fell out of fashion in the 1760s. By the mid-1770s, however, it had reemerged, probably reintroduced by the earliest units of British troops brought over to quell the American rebellion. Although printed versions of the tune and lyrics appeared in Britain as early as 1778, the song was not printed in the United States until 1794.

Father and I went down to camp,
Along with Captain Gooding;
And there we saw the men and boys,
As thick as hasty pudding.

Yankee doodle, keep it up,
Yankee doodle dandy;
Mind the music and the step,
And with the girls be handy.

There was Captain Washington
Upon a slapping stallion,
A-giving orders to his men,
I guess there was a million.
And then the feathers on his hat,
They looked so' tarnal fin-a,
I wanted pockily to get
To give to my Jemima.
And then we saw a swamping gun,
Large as a log of maple;
Upon a deuced little cart,
A load for father's cattle.
And every time they shoot it off,
It takes a horn of powder;

It makes a noise like father's gun,
Only a nation louder.
I went as nigh to one myself,
As' Siah's underpinning;
And father went as nigh agin,
I thought the deuce was in him.
We saw a little barrel, too,
The heads were made of leather;
They knocked upon it with little clubs,
And called the folks together.
And there they'd fife away like fun,
And play on cornstalk fiddles,
And some had ribbons red as blood,
All bound around their middles.
The troopers, too, would gallop up
And fire right in our faces;
It scared me almost to death
To see them run such races.
Uncle Sam came there to change
Some pancakes and some onions,
For' lasses cake to carry home
To give his wife and young ones.
But I can't tell half I see
They kept up such a smother;
So I took my hat off, made a bow,
And scampered home to mother.
Cousin Simon grew so bold,
I thought he would have cocked it;
It scared me so I streaked it off,
And hung by father's pocket.
And there I saw a pumpkin shell,
As big as mother's basin;
And every time they touched it off,
They scampered like the nation.

Yankee doodle, keep it up,
Yankee doodle dandy;
Mind the music and the step,
And with the girls be handy.

Source: "Yankee Doodle," Library of Congress, http://www.loc.gov/teachers/lyrical/songs/yankee_doodle.html.

9. *"Star Spangled Banner" (1814)*

Now hailed as the national anthem, the "Star Spangled Banner" was written by Francis Scott Key on the night of September 13–14, 1814. The United States was in the midst of fighting the War of 1812 against the British when Key visited the British fleet in Chesapeake Bay to negotiate the release of an American prisoner. While onboard one of the British ships, Key watched the British guns shell nearby Fort McHenry. Convinced that the fort would collapse under such heavy shelling, Key was overjoyed to see the American flag remain aloft throughout the night, prompting him to write the song, which he originally composed as a poem entitled "The Defense of Fort M'Henry." The poem became widely popular throughout the United States and was ironically set to the tune of a British song, "To Anacreon in Heaven." The U.S. government officially declared it the national anthem in 1931.

O say, can you see, by the dawn's early light,
What so proudly we hail'd at the twilight's last gleaming?
Whose broad stripes and bright stars, thro' the perilous fight,
O'er the ramparts we watch'd, were so gallantly streaming?
And the rockets' red glare, the bombs bursting in air,
Gave proof thro' the night that our flag was still there.
O say, does that star-spangled banner yet wave
O'er the land of the free and the home of the brave?

On the shore dimly seen thro' the mists of the deep,
Where the foe's haughty host in dread silence reposes,
What is that which the breeze, o'er the towering steep,
As it fitfully blows, half conceals, half discloses?
Now it catches the gleam of the morning's first beam,
In full glory reflected, now shines on the stream:
'Tis the star-spangled banner: O, long may it wave
O'er the land of the free and the home of the brave!

And where is that band who so vauntingly swore
That the havoc of war and the battle's confusion,
A home and a country should leave us no more?
Their blood has wash'd out their foul footsteps' pollution.
No refuge could save the hireling and slave
From the terror of flight or the gloom of the grave:
And the star-spangled banner in triumph doth wave
O'er the land of the free and the home of the brave.

O thus be it ever when free-men shall stand
Between their lov'd home and the war's desolation;
Blest with vict'ry and peace, may the heav'n-rescued land
Praise the Pow'r that hath made and preserv'd us a nation!
Then conquer we must, when our cause it is just,
And this be our motto: "In God is our trust!"
And the star-spangled banner in triumph shall wave
O'er the land of the free and the home of the brave!

Source: Library of Congress.

10. "Dixie's Land" (1860)

Originally this song was part of blackface minstrel shows during the 1850s, and it became very popular. Using an exaggerated version of African American vernacular, it tells the story of a slave who misses the life of the plantation he worked on. It became the unofficial anthem of the

Confederacy and went through several different versions during the war. Although credited to Daniel Decatur Emmett, others have claimed credit for the song. The popularity of the song was such that on the eve of Lee's surrender in April 1865, Lincoln is said to have requested that it be played by a regimental band in front of the White House.

I wish I was in de land ob cotton
Old times dar am not forgotten
Look away! Look away!
Look away! Dixie Land.
In Dixie Land whar I was born in
Early on a frosty mornin'
Look away! Look away!
Look away! Dixie Land.

[Chorus] Den I wish I was in Dixie
Hooray! Hooray!
In Dixie Land I'll take my stand
To lib and die in Dixie,
Away, away, away down south in Dixie.
Away, away, away down south in Dixie.

Ole missus marry "Will de Weaber,"
William was a gay deceiber;
Look away! Look away!
Look away! Dixie Land.
But when he put his arm around'er,
He smiled as fierce as a forty pounder,
Look away! Look away! Look away! Dixie Land.
His face was sharp as a butcher's cleaber,
But dat did not seem to greab' er;
Look away, etc.
Ole missus acted de foolish part,
And died for a man dat broke her heart,
Look away, etc.
Now here's a health to the next old Missus,
An' all de gals dat want to kiss us;
Look away, etc.
But if you want to drive'way sorrow,
Come and hear dis song tomorrow,
Look away, etc.
Dar's buck-wheat cakes and Ingen' batter,
Makes you fat or a little fatter;
Look away, etc.
Den hoe it down an' scratch your grabble,
To Dixie's Land I'm bound to trabble,
Look away, etc.

Source: Library of Congress.

Part VIII
RELIGIOUS LIFE

Religion has always played an important role in the everyday life of Americans. For example, many of the first settlers came to America from England to escape religious persecution. Many colonies established certain rules that favored a particular Protestant denomination, but by the time of the American Revolution most colonies "tolerated" different Protestant denominations, and several even let Catholics and Jews worship in private. After the Revolution there was a belief in American society that no religion should be sponsored by the government and that religion should be kept separate from state policies and functions. Many states wrote this into their constitutions. Thomas Jefferson, George Mason, and others included separation of church and state in Virginia's constitution, and it later became part of the U.S. Constitution in the Bill of Rights.

Religion was felt in the lives of Americans in various ways during the eighty-five years between the Revolution and the eve of the Civil War. Certainly religious belief, practice, and custom informed the daily lives of people—in their prayers, in their ideas about and raising of their families, in their reading, and so much more. Protestantism ruled America, but it was splintered into different denominations, some emphasizing good works and others the miracle of saving grace. Religious revivals, which became more organized during the nineteenth century, kept the nation ablaze in religious enthusiasm. Indeed, evangelical Protestantism surged and exercised a powerful influence on public morality, education, and social issues, including slavery. The variety of religions in America before and after the Revolution led to many ideas about how to deal with the different ideologies that were entering the country. Much experimentation with religion occurred—in communitarian groups, for example—and Mormonism, a distinctly new American religion, was born in the "burned over district" of upper New York. Differences in religion often brought about conflict. Anti-Catholic violence was rife in northern cities during the antebellum period, which contributed to Catholics building their own schools, orphanages, and voluntary organizations to protect themselves from Protestant incursions and to build up their faith. Americans prided themselves on their religious diversity and tolerance, but in fact were uncomfortable with it.

The following section on religions in contact provides examples of differing views on religious freedom in America. In the section on forms of worship, the documents deal with the practices of the various religious groups in the United States during this period. In the section on systems of belief we see how visitors to America noted the differences in how American churches conducted their services, from their churches to their homes. In the section on life after death we see how death and ideas about heaven and hell were viewed in American churches.

Religions in Contact

There were many and diverse religions in America during the time of the Revolution, and that number and variety grew during the nineteenth century due to immigration; new ideas about theological and social questions; personalities; evangelism; and the spread of literacy, which allowed more religious literature, from accounts of conversion to psalmbooks, to reach across the country. The American Bible Society and the American Tract Society were organized to get a Bible and religious tracts into every home in the country, a huge mission unmatched anywhere. Protestantism remained dominant, with Presbyterians, Methodists, and Baptists counting the most members by the Civil War. Catholics and Jews, especially in urban areas, established a firmer, if contested, place. By the 1840s "freethinkers" were arriving, fleeing the failed European Revolutions of 1848 or simply wanting to find a friendlier environment to live free of established state churches. How these "outsiders" were viewed varied.

In many cases religious prejudice was present, as we see in Thomas Paine's attack on the Catholic Church and Jews, which reflects the views held by many during this period. The ideas on religion that permeated the nation during this time can also be seen in those adopted by the Indians in their struggle against the encroachment of whites and their religion. In contrast to Paine, the idea that America was open to the faiths of all is expounded in Tocqueville's essay on the Catholic Church in America and his vision of a bright future for it here. And because the churches in America were not supported by the state, the volunteer support for the great number of churches here is seen by an outsider as an example of the power of religious freedom.

1. *Thomas Paine, "The Monk and the Jew" (1775)*

Thomas Paine was an English-born intellectual, revolutionary, inventor, radical, and pamphleteer who was passionately committed to liberal values and Enlightenment ideals. Among his ideas were a progressive income tax, abolition of slavery, guaranteed minimum incomes, and many other ideas radical for his era, and even ours. After immigrating to America in 1774, he began promoting American independence. He is perhaps best known today for his 1776 pamphlet Common Sense, *which dramatically solidified support in America for declaring independence from Britain. As a deist who believed in an unknowable and noninterfering God, he despised revealed, organized religion as dangerous superstition and an impediment to social progress and liberty, claiming, "My own mind is my own Church." In this he was hardly alone: widespread sectarianism, anti-Semitism, and anticlericalism (especially in the French- and English-speaking world) were facts of life in the late eighteenth century. His poem "The Monk and the Jew" both displays the clever satirical wit valued among Enlightenment thinkers and attacks some of their favorite targets: social and religious attitudes formed outside of enlightened reason. Paine evidences a sharply prejudiced attitude toward Christianity in general and the Roman Catholic Church in particular, as well as an anti-Semitism that marred some of the most open minds of the age, including those of Voltaire and Immanuel Kant. Though the*

Monk comes across as a heartless and doctrinaire hypocrite who refuses to help his neighbor as Christ commanded, the Jew is an ugly caricature of speech and personality, willing to lie, cheat, and deceive to get what he wants. While Paine makes a valid point about Christian anti-Semitism and religious intolerance, one can only conclude that Paine himself was little more tolerant of others' beliefs than those he satirized.

An unbelieving Jew one day
Was skating o'er the icy way,
Which being brittle let him in,
Just deep enough to catch his chin;
And in that woeful plight he hung,
With only power to move his tongue.
A brother skater near at hand,
A Papist born in foreign land,

With hasty strokes directly flew
To save poor Mordecai the Jew—
"But first," quoth he, "I must enjoin
That you renounce your faith for mine;
There's no entreaties else will do,
'Tis heresy to help a Jew—"

"Forswear mine fait! No! Cot forbid!
Dat would be very base indeed,
Come never mind such tings as deeze,
Tink, tink, how fery hard it freeze.
More coot you do, more coot you be,
Vat signifies your faith to me?
Come tink agen, how cold and vet,
And help me out von little bit."

"By holy mass, 'tis hard, I own,
To see a man both Hang and drown,
And can't relieve him from his plight
Because he is an Israelite;
The Church refuses all assistance,
Beyond a certain pale and distance;
And all the service I can lend
Is praying for your soul, my friend."

"Pray for my soul, ha! Ha! You make me laugh.
You petter help me out py half:
Mine soul I farrant vill take care,
To pray for her own self, my tear:
So tink a little now for me,
'Tis I am in the hole not she."

"The Church forbids it, friend, and saith
That all shall die who had no faith."
"Vell, if I must pelieve, I must,
But help me out von little first."

"No, not an inch without Amen
That seals the whole"—
"Vell, hear me den,
I here renounce for coot and all
De race of Jews both great and small;
'Tis de verst trade peneath the sun,
Or vurst religion; dat's all von.
Dey cheat, and get deir living py't,
Amd lie, and swear the lie is right.
I'll co to mass as soon as ever
I get to toder side the river.
So help me out, dow Christian friend,
Dat I may do as I *intend*."

"Perhaps you do intend to cheat,
If once you get upon your feet."
"No, no, I do intend to be
A *Christian*, such as one as *dee*."
For, thought the Jew, he is as much
A Christian man as I am such.
The bigot Papist joyful hearted
To hear the heretic converted,
Replied to the *designing* Jew,

"This was a happy fall for you:
You'd better die a Christian now,
For if you live you'll break your vow."
Then said no more, but in a trice
Popp'd Mordecai beneath the ice.

Source: Thomas Paine, *The Life and Writings of Thomas Paine*, vol. 10, ed. Daniel Edwin Wheeler (New York: Vincent Parke and Co., 1908).

2. Tenkswataya, Speech on a System of Religion (1808)

Tenkswataya, a Shawnee Indian popularly known as the Prophet, hoped to forge a massive Native American alliance in the Old Northwest with the help of his brother Tecumseh in the early 1800s. The Prophet was the spiritual leader behind the movement and preached a gospel of pan-Indian religion that emphasized the need to purge oneself of the dependence and corruption of European goods and ways and gain a spiritual rebirth. The Prophet and his brother intended to unite all the tribes into a single, powerful unit, capable of standing up to and bargaining with the Americans. The Prophet delivered this speech to the governor of Indiana, William Henry Harrison, in August 1808.

Father, It is three years since I first began with that system of religion which I now practice. The white people and some of the Indians were against me; but I had no other intention but to introduce among the Indians, those good principles of religion which the white people profess. I was spoken badly of by the white people, who reproached me with misleading the Indians; but I defy them to say that I did anything amiss.

Father, I was told that you intended to hang me. When I heard this, I intended to remember it, and tell my father, when I went to see him, and relate to him the truth.

I heard, when I settled on the Wabash, that my father, the governor, had declared that all the land between Vicennes and fort Wayne, was the property of the Seventeen Fires. I also heard that you wanted to know, my father, whether I was God or man; and that you said if I was the former, I should not steal horses. I heard this from Mr. Wells, but I believed it originated with himself.

The Great Spirit told me to tell the Indians that he had made them, and made the world—that he had placed them on it to do good, not evil.

I told all the red skins, that the way they were in was not good, and that they ought to abandon it.

That we ought to consider ourselves as one man; but we ought to live agreeably to our several customs, the red people after their mode, and the white people after theirs; particularly, that they should not drink whiskey; that it was not made for them, but the white people, who alone knew how to use it; and that it is the cause of all the mischief which the Indians suffer; and that they must always follow the directions of the Great Spirit, and we must listen to him, as it was he that made us: determine to listen to nothing that is bad: do not take up the tomahawk, should it be offered by the British, or by the long knives: do not meddle with any thing that does not belong to you, but mind your own business, and cultivate the ground, that your women and your children may have enough to live on.

I now inform you, that it is our intention to live in peace with our father and his people forever.

My father, I have informed you what we mean to do, and I call the Great Spirit to witness the truth of my declaration. The religion which I have established for the last three years, has been attended to by the different tribes of Indians in this part of the world. Those Indians were once different people; they are now but one: they are all determined to practice what I have communicated to them, that has come immediately from the Great Spirit through me.

Brother, I speak to you as a warrior. You are one. But let us lay aside this character, and attend to the care of our children, that they may live in comfort and peace. We desire that you will join us for the preservation of both red and white people. Formerly, when we lived in ignorance, we were foolish; but now, since we listen to the voice of the Great Spirit, we are happy.

I have listened to what you have said to us. You have promised to assist us: I now request you, in behalf of all the red people, to use your exertions to prevent the sale of liquor to us. We are all well pleased to hear you say that you will endeavor to promote our happiness. We give you every assurance that we will follow the dictates of the Great Spirit.

We are all well pleased with the attention that you have showed us; also with the good intentions of our father, the President. If you give us a few articles, such as needles, flints, hoes, powder, &c., we will take the animals that afford us meat, with powder and ball.

Source: Benjamin Drake, *Life of Tecumseh, and of His Brother, the Prophet* (New York, 1841), 107–9.

3. *Alexis de Tocqueville on the Progress of Roman Catholicism in the United States (1847)*

Alexis de Tocqueville, perhaps the most astute foreign observer and commentator on antebellum America, noted the importance of religion in shaping the American character. He was impressed that in a nation with no official state church, religion counted for so much in people's lives and in public life. He also noted that despite the fact that the Protestant denominations dominated the United States, American principles and habits of democracy would allow the Roman Catholic Church to flourish. The Church did flourish in time, despite prejudices and violence directed at it in the 1840s and 1850s.

America is the most democratic country in the world, and it is at the same time (according to reports worthy of belief) the country in which the Roman Catholic religion makes most progress. At first sight this is surprising. Two things must here be accurately distinguished: equality inclines men to wish to form their own opinions; but, on the other hand, it imbues them with the taste and the idea of unity, simplicity, and impartiality in the power which governs society. Men living in democratic ages are therefore very prone to shake off all religious authority; but if they consent to subject themselves to any authority of this kind, they choose at least that it should be single and uniform. Religious powers not radiating from a common centre are naturally repugnant to their minds; and they almost as readily conceive that there should be no religion, as that there should be several. At the present time, more than in any preceding one, Roman Catholics are seen to lapse into infidelity, and Protestants to be converted to Roman Catholicism. If the Roman Catholic faith be considered within the pale of the church, it would seem to be losing ground; without that pale, to be gaining it. Nor is this circumstance difficult of explanation. The men of our days are naturally disposed to believe; but, as soon as they have any religion, they immediately find in themselves a latent propensity which urges them unconsciously towards Catholicism. Many of the doctrines and the practices of the Romish Church astonish them; but they feel a secret admiration for its discipline, and its great unity attracts them. If Catholicism could at length withdraw itself from the political animosities to which it has given rise, I have hardly any doubt but that the same spirit of the age, which appears to be so opposed to it, would become so favorable as to admit of its great and sudden advancement. One of the most ordinary weaknesses of the human intellect is to seek to reconcile contrary principles, and to purchase peace at the expense of logic. Thus there have ever been, and will ever be, men who, after having submitted some portion of their religious belief to the principle of authority, will seek to exempt several other parts of their faith from its influence, and to keep their minds floating at random between liberty and obedience. But I am inclined to believe that the number of these thinkers will be less in democratic than in other ages; and that our posterity will tend more and more to a single division into two parts—some relinquishing Christianity entirely, and others returning to the bosom of the Church of Rome.

Source: Alexis de Tocqueville, *Democracy in America*, trans. Henry Reeve (New York: Edward Walker, 1847).

4. *Support for Churches in America (1854)*

On his travels in America the Rev. J. H. Grandpierre noted that despite the number of churches in America, they were always supported by their followers even though donations were voluntary. He also noted the number of churches of each of the denominations in New York and was surprised that there seemed to be no hesitation by the parishioners to support their churches. In fact, it was the voluntarism of American religion that gave it such strength.

We have already confessed that we went to the United States with some prejudices. One of these prejudices related to the sufficiency of the voluntary system, as applied to church support. We doubted very much, whether by this means, and this alone, it was possible to provide adequately for the religious wants of a population of twenty-five millions, scattered over so vast an extent of country. We are compelled in truth to acknowledge, that our opinion on this subject is very much modified; and though we do not mean to affirm that the liberality of American Christians, great as it is, fully meets the wants of so considerable a Protestant community, we own that it has produced the most admirable and astonishing results. In all the States through which we passed, we found churches, not only in the large towns, but in the villages, and even in the smallest and remotest hamlets. Wherever a little group of human habitations is seen, even in the midst of uncultivated fields and forests, one is almost sure to distinguish the steeple of a church, and to recognize the familiar aspect of the school-house.

All these churches are built in a style adapted to the purpose. In the cities, the edifices consecrated to worship, are large, and very splendid. The pulpit, with the red velvet sofa, and arm-chairs, which adorn it, is of massive mahogany or rosewood. The same wood, or oak, is usually employed to decorate the closed pews, which are also comfortably carpeted and cushioned. The churches are mostly lighted with gas, and warmed by means of furnaces. They are repaired every two or three years, both internally and externally, so that they have always the appearance of buildings of a recent date.

Enormous sums are devoted by the Americans to the construction of their churches. That of Dr. Alexander, in New York, cost one hundred and fifty thousand dollars. The cost of Dr. Cheever's, to judge by its appearance, could hardly have been less, and may have been greater. The week I left New York, Dr. Adams laid the corner-stone of a new church, to replace his old one, which had become insufficient for the congregation. As he invited me to be present at this ceremony, I took the liberty of asking him what would be the expense of this new building. "The plans of the architect," he replied, "are for one hundred thousand dollars, but we suppose that this estimate will be exceeded." "And where do you find money?" asked I, "for such costly edifices?" "Among members of my church," replied Dr. A. "A few weeks have sufficed to collect the subscriptions. In America, we think no money so well invested, as that employed in the Lord's service."

There are in New York alone, forty-six Episcopal churches, forty-four Presbyterian, forty-two Methodist, thirty-three Baptist, seventeen Dutch Reformed, nine Congregational, twenty-two Catholic, and two Unitarian—in all, two hundred and seventeen churches, founded and sustained by private zeal—and this number is yearly increasing. It is estimated that the whole number of churches in the United States is thirty-six thousand two hundred and twenty-one, which makes one for every five hundred and thirty-seven free inhabitants. The Christians of America are usually not less liberal in supporting their pastors than in their contributions for their houses of worship. The salaries of the clergymen of Boston and New York vary from two to four and five thousand dollars. I was even told of an Episcopal clergyman in New York, who received seven thousand dollars a year, and whose congregation assure a handsome income to his wife in case of his death. In addition to this, when these well remunerated pastors are fatigued and need repose, it is not unusual to see them go to pass six months or more in travelling in Europe, at the charge of their congregations, who not only pay the expenses of their journey, but provide a substitute for their pulpits during their absence. These cases are by no means of rare occurrence. Perhaps a dozen clergymen may yearly be found travelling on the continent of Europe, in the way I have mentioned.

Source: Rev. J. H. Grandpierre, *A Parisian Pastor's Glance at America* (Boston: Gould and Lincoln, 1854), 57–60.

Forms of Worship

Each religion performed different ceremonies, and each believed that the rituals performed brought the followers closer to God. In the United States it was possible to see the services of any number of religions, and many people, whether foreign travelers or American citizens, took the time to observe and record the services. Their accounts, like that about the Shakers, as they traveled through the country give us a glimpse of the religious fervor of these groups. The religious revival that was taking place in the United States in the early nineteenth century led to camp meetings, which were known for the religious fervor they generated and were commented upon by many who attended them and were left with an impression of the deep religious feeling of their adherents. Some religious practices harkened back to the teachings and actions of Jesus, and the washing of feet on Holy Thursday was a tradition of the Catholic Church that carried on the tradition of Jesus and demonstrated the direct connection that the celebrants felt they had with God.

5. A View of a Shaker Meeting (1790s)

The Shakers, or United Society of Believers in Christ's Second Appearing, emerged during the mid-eighteenth century. Called Shakers because of the ecstatic nature of their services, they were a religious sect thought to have developed from the Quakers. They were unique in that their first leaders were women, and they preached equality between the sexes. They also preached and practiced celibacy, which required them to recruit new members from outside the order. They were able to ride the wave of the First and Second Great Awakenings in the eighteenth and nineteenth centuries in America to gain adherents to their messianic message. Here, William Loughton Smith sits in on one of their services.

Within two or three miles of the Pool is a settlement of shaking Quakers, whose mode of worship we went to see on the Sunday following, viz., the 29th. We arrived there about ten o'clock in the forenoon and found them at work. In a long, low room of a very neat building painted white, were about fifty men and from eighty to one hundred women; the preacher stood in the centre, on his right hand were the men, arranged in rows, on his left the women in similar order; two men with their hands applied to their jaws and two or three women sung, or rather howled sundry strange tunes (one of them was "The Black Joke"), to which the men and women danced in uniform step, occasionally all turning around. The men had taken off their coats and waistcoats and hung them up about the room, and tied up their shirt sleeves; they were most of them in trowsers. The women in close, white caps, short jackets, and stiff petticoats: both sexes had thick shoes which made a horrible clatter and shuffling on the floor: the warmth of the weather and such continuous exercise occasioned a profuse sweating, which appeared all over the shirts and the trowsers of the men, and through the very stays of the women, and produced an horrible smell; some of the men were wringing wet, and the sweat dropped from their faces on the floor. There were occasional intermissions when they all stopped; and the preacher, who is an amazing booby, muttered a few words, something to this effect: "Avoid carnal lusts. Labor to shake off sin; sin is hateful; I hate sin. Power of God. Those who come here must observe our rules and orders; the men come in at the west door, women at the east. Strangers must observe silence at our worship; there must be no talking, whispering, or unnecessary goings in and out. Those who come here and don't observe our rules and orders are the basest of mankind." Then turning to the men (who were all arranged in files and held down their heads with their hands clasped before them): "Labour to shake off sin." Then turning to the women, arranged in the same order: "You also labour to shake off sin. You have had an intermission: those who wish to serve God and to labour, prepare again for labour."

Then the men would pull off their clothes as before, and both sexes resuming their places, the howl would commence and with it the dance. In the intermissions some of the most devout would shake from head to foot, as if seized with shivering fits of the ague. At every cessation of labour, the preacher would make the same address to the spectators, who were very observant of these rules and required no admonition, but he either thought it would recommend him to his congregation or he was at a loss for something to say. However absurd their form of worship, it is not the worst part of their devotions; they reprobate matrimony; if any married persons become members of this church, they must immediately live in a state of separation, and any connection between them is considered criminal and the parties expelled; they continue their sect by making proselytes. Their neighbors give them a good reputation for their scrupulous observance of farming industry and attention to agriculture. Their elders own several farms which have been made over to them by new members and which are cultivated for the good of the society. There were two negroes among the dancers, one of them was the best dancer there; all ages joined in the dance. Their settlement is in a romantic situation, in the midst of a fine country, well-cultivated, and their buildings are very neat.

After dancing for three hours they walked home and exposed themselves without any caution to the open air. Their service lasts from nine to twelve in the forenoon, and two to five in the afternoon.

Source: *Journal of William Loughton Smith, 1790–1791*, ed. Albert Matthews (Cambridge: The University Press, 1917), 48–51.

6. *A Camp Meeting Heats Up (1829)*

Frances Trollope, an English novelist of modest success, wrote a valuable social history of early nineteenth-century America, Domestic Manners of Americans. *The book formed opinions about Americans for many Europeans at the time and is still useful to historians. The following excerpt tells the story of a camp meeting, a religious revival that had gained popularity after the Second Great Awakening in the early 1800s. The camp meetings were not only scenes of religious renewal; they also provided what might be the only social contact for isolated settlers.*

It was in the course of this summer that I found the opportunity I had long wished for, of attending a camp-meeting, and I gladly accepted the invitation of an English lady and gentleman to accompany them in their carriage to the spot where it is held; this was in a wild district on the confines of Indiana.

The prospect of passing a night in the back woods of Indiana was by no means agreeable, but I screwed my courage to the proper pitch, and set forth determined to see with my own eyes, and hear with my own ears, what a camp-meeting really was. I had heard it said that being at a camp-meeting was like standing at the gate of heaven, and seeing it opening before you; I had heard it said, that being at a camp-meeting was like finding yourself within the gates of hell; in either case there must be something to gratify curiosity, and compensate one for the fatigue of a long rumbling ride and a sleepless night.

We reached the ground about an hour before midnight, and the approach to it was highly picturesque. The spot chosen was the verge of an unbroken forest, where a space of about twenty acres appeared to have been partially cleared for the purpose. Tents of different sizes were pitched very near together in a circle round the cleared space; behind them were ranged an exterior circle of carriages of every description, and at the back of each were fastened the horses which had drawn them thither. Through this triple circle of defence we distinguished numerous fires burning brightly within it; and still more numerous lights flickering from the trees that were left in the enclosure. The moon was in meridian splendor above our heads . . . .

When we arrived, the preachers were silent; but we heard issuing from nearly every tent mingled sounds of praying, preaching, singing, and lamentation. . . .

We made the circuit of the tents, pausing where attention was particularly excited by sounds more vehement than ordinary. We contrived to look into many; all were strewed with straw, and the distorted figures that we saw kneeling, sitting, and lying amongst it, joined to the woeful and convulsive cries, gave to each, the air of a cell in Bedlam [Bethlehem Hospital, an insane asylum in London]. . . .

At midnight a horn sounded through the camp, which, we were told, was to call the people from private to public worship; and we presently saw them flocking from all sides to the front of the preachers' stand. Mrs. B. and I contrived to place ourselves with our backs supported against the lower part of this structure, and we were thus enabled to witness the scene which followed without personal danger. There were about two thousand persons assembled.

One of the preachers began in a low nasal tone, and, like all other Methodist preachers, assured us of the enormous depravity of man as he comes from the hands of his Maker, and of his perfect sanctification after he had wrestled sufficiently with the Lord to get hold of him, *et caetera*. The admiration of the crowd was evinced by almost constant cries of "Amen! Amen!" "Jesus! Jesus!" "Glory! Glory!" and the like. But this comparative tranquility did not last long: the preacher told them that "this night was the time fixed upon for anxious sinners to wrestle with the Lord;" that he and his brethren "were at hand to help them," and that such as needed their help were to come forward into "the pen.". . . "The pen" was the space immediately below the preachers' stand; we were therefore placed on the edge of it, and were enabled to see and hear all that took place in the very centre of this extraordinary exhibition.

The crowd fell back at the mention of the *pen*, and for some minutes there was a vacant space before us. The preachers came down from their stand and placed themselves in the midst of it, beginning to sing a hymn, calling upon the penitents to come forth. As they sung they kept turning themselves round to every part of the crowd, and, by degrees, the voices of the whole multitude joined in chorus. This was the only moment at which I perceived any thing like the solemn and beautiful effect, which I had heard ascribed to this woodland worship. It is certain that the combined voices of such a multitude, heard at dead of night, from the depths of their eternal forests, the many fair young faces turned upward, and looking paler and lovelier as they met the moonbeams, the dark figures of the officials in the middle of the circle, the lurid glare thrown by the altar-fires on the woods beyond, did altogether produce a fine and solemn effect, that I shall not easily forget; but ere I had well enjoyed it, the scene changed, and sublimity gave place to horror and disgust. . . .

. . . Above a hundred persons, nearly all females, came forward, uttering howlings and groans, so terrible that I shall never cease to shudder when I recall them. They appeared to drag each other forward, and on the word being given, "let us pray," they all fell on their knees; but this posture was soon changed for others that permitted greater scope for the convulsive movements of their limbs; and they were soon all lying on the ground in an indescribable confusion of heads and legs. They threw about their limbs with such incessant and violent motion, that I was every instant expecting some serious accident to occur. But how am I to describe the sounds that proceeded from this strange mass of human beings? I know no words which can convey an idea of it. Hysterical sobbings, convulsive groans, shrieks and screams the most appalling, burst forth on all sides. I felt sick with horror. As if their hoarse and overstrained voices failed to make noise enough, they soon began to clap their hands violently. . . .

One woman near us continued to "call on the Lord," as it is termed, in the loudest possible tone, and without a moment's interval, for the two hours that we kept our dreadful station. She became frightfully hoarse, and her face so red as to make me expect she would burst a blood-vessel. Among the rest of her rant, she said, "I will hold fast to Jesus, I never will let him go; if they take me to hell, I will still hold him fast, fast, fast!"

Source: Frances Trollope, *Domestic Manners of Americans* (London: Whittaker, Treacher & Co., 1832), 229–41.

7. The Washing of the Feet on Holy Thursday in St. Peter's (1858)

The New Testament tells the story of Jesus washing the feet of his disciples on what Christians would later set aside as Holy Thursday. By washing others' feet, Jesus was humbling himself and teaching his disciples humility. The practice is continued to this day in the Catholic Church when the pope washes the feet of the cardinals, bishops, and priests who attend Holy Thursday service and as cardinals, archbishops, and bishops, as the case may be, do for their priests. It is a practice that is carried out in churches around the world. This poem describes the practice and its significance in the Catholic Church.

ONCE more the temple-gates lie open wide:
Onward, once more,
Advance the Faithful, mounting like a tide
That climbs the shore.

What seek they? Blank the altars stand to-day,
As tombstones hare:
Christ of his raiment was despoiled; and they
His livery wear.

To-day the puissant and the proud have heard
The mandate new:
That which He did, their Master and their Lord,
They also do.

To-day the mitred foreheads, and the crowned,
In meekness bend:
New tasks to-day the sceptred hands have found;
The poor they tend.

To-day those feet which tread in lowliest ways,
Yet follow Christ,
Are by the secular lords of power and praise
Both washed and kissed.

Hail, ordinance sage of hoar antiquity,
Which She retains,
That Church who teaches man how meek should he
The head that reigns!

Source: "The 'Washing of the Feet' on Holy Thursday in St. Peter's," *The Atlantic Monthly* 2, no. 13 (November 1858): 728.

Systems of Belief

The various religious groups in America had different systems of belief that informed daily devotions, morality, and many other aspects of people's lives. Religious authority counted, even if many Americans remained suspicious of clergy. Some religions established moral codes taken from religious texts that were to be followed by their adherents, while others relied on the authority of religious leaders as a guide to salvation and proper behavior. As a predominantly Protestant nation, the systems of belief in the United States were similar. Still, upheavals such as the Revolution led to schisms and even the formation of new church bodies. Thus, for example, some practices that had been part of religious services under the Anglican Church were changed to suit an "American church." Indeed, in an act of independence, the Episcopal Church developed a new book of common prayer to be read at worship.

The variety and diversity of religious practice fascinated Americans. Invariably, as they traveled and visited, they looked into the practices of other faiths and commented on them. Such curiosity bred understanding and also suspicion. What were hard-core Congregationalists to make of the liturgy of a Catholic service conducted in Latin, for example? The Quaker ideas of worship and gaining grace were different from most Christian groups in America, and these beliefs are discussed by a Frenchman visiting the United States, who gives a very detailed account of a Quaker service. Changes that were made in the services of the Protestant churches that marked a change from European practice are discussed by two English visitors. The first comments on how the changes made in the Episcopal Church's services avoided the controversies that surrounded the Anglican Church in England in the early nineteenth century. The other English visitor decries the strict observance of the Sabbath and calls for the allowance of recreation on Sundays in the United States.

8. *Beliefs of the Quakers* (1788)

The Quakers, or the Religious Society of Friends, began their movement in the seventeenth century in England, where despite facing persecution, their membership expanded and reached to the Americas and Africa. To escape persecution in England, William Penn was granted a charter to establish a colony in Pennsylvania where the Quakers could practice their faith. Quakers believed that all could hear the word of Christ, and that there was no need for churchmen or the paying of tithes, which meant more freedom for members. They were a significant part of the movements for the abolition of slavery, promoting equal rights for women, and peace. They also promoted education and the humane treatment of prisoners and the mentally ill, through the founding or reforming of various institutions. Here a visitor to America, Frenchman J. P. Brissot de Warville, describes a Quaker meeting.

The religion of the Quakers is the simplest imaginable. It consists in the voice of conscience, the internal sentiment, the divine instinct, which, in their opinion, God has imparted to every one. This instinct, this light, this grace, which every person brings into the world with him, appears to them the only guide necessary for the conduct of life. But to understand the guide, it is necessary to know it; to be known, it should often be interrogated. Hence, the necessity of frequent meditations; hence the nullity of all formal worship, and the ministration of priests: for they confider [consider] forms as so many obstacles, which turn the attention from the voice within; and priests possessing no more of the Divine Spirit than other men, cannot supply the want of meditation.

I have shown in my Critique on the Travels of Chastellux, how much this meditative worship of the Deity is superior to the mechanical worship of other sects. I have proved that the man who adores his Creator by meditating on his own duties, will necessarily become good, tolerant, just, and beneficent. You have here the key both of the moral character of the Quakers, and of its extraordinary duration. Their virtue is an habit, a second nature.

The Quakers have been much ridiculed for their belief in this interior principle. For their calumniators, some of whom have called themselves philosophers, are ignorant that this belief is not peculiar to the Quakers. We find it in a great number of sages, who have merited the homage of mankind: With Pythagoras, it was the *Eternal Word, the Great Light*,—with Anaxagoras, *the Divine Soul*,—with Socrates, *the Good Spirit, or Demon*,—with Timeus, *the Uncreated Principle*,—with Hieron, *the author of Delight, the God within the Man*,—with Plato, *the eternal, ineffable and perfect Principle of Truth*,—*Truth*,—with Zeno, *the Creator and Father of all]*,—and with Plotinus, *the Root of the Soul*. When these philosophers endeavoured to characterise the influence of this principle within us, they used correspondent expressions. Hieron called it a *domestic God*, an *internal God*,—Socrates Timeus, *the Genius*, or *Angel*,—Plotinus, the *Divine Principle in Man*,—and Plato, *the Rule of the Soul, the Internal Guide, the Foundation of Virtue*.

I do not pretend to explain to you all the religious principles of the Quakers; this would lead me too far; not that their dogmas are very numerous, for their doctrine is more simple and more concise than their morals. But this article, as well their history, ought to be treated at large. I can assure you, that all the French authors who have written on them, without excepting Voltaire, have been ignorant of the true fources [sources] of information. They have contented themselves with seizing the objects to which they could give a cast of ridicule, and have thrown aside every thing that could render that society respectable.

One inviolable practice of theirs, for instance, is, never to dispute about dogmas.

They have cut off an endless chain of disputations, by not admitting the authority either of the Old or New Testament to be superior to that of the internal principles, and by not hiring a class of men for the sole purpose of disputing and tyranizing, under the pretext of instructing. What torrents of blood would have been spared, if the Catholics and Protestants had adopted a rule of conduct so wise; if instead of quarelling about unintelligible words, about writings that may be changed about the authority: of the Church and the Pope, they had believed in the internal Spirit, which for each individual may be the secret guide! This guide has little concern with dogmas, and much with morals.

Among the political principles of the Quakers, the most remarkable are, never to take an oath, and never to take arms. I shall speak of the latter in an article by itself; as to their refusing to take an oath, it may be said, that an oath adds no weight to the declaration of an honest man; and perjury has no terrors for a knave.

Their discipline is as simple as their doctrine. In their marriages, their births, and interments, they use only the forms necessary to verify the existence of the fact.

A Quaker cannot marry a person of another sect; I asked the reason of this; as it appeared to me a sign of intolerance. "The preservation of our society," (replied a Quaker,) "depends on the preservation of the customs which distinguish us from other men. This singularity forces us to be more honest; and if we should unite our families with strangers, who are not of our society, individuals would swerve from our usages, and confound them with others. A Quaker woman who should marry a Presbyterian, submits herself to the authority of a man over whom we have no influence; and the society subsists only by this desire, voluntary, and reciprocal influence."

This influence is directed by their different assemblies. The monthly assemblies are in general composed of several neighbouring congregations. Their functions are to provide for the subsistence of the poor, and the education of their children; to examine the new converts, and prove their morals; to sustain the zeal and the religion of others; to hear and judge their saults by means of superintendents appointed for this purpose; to decide and settle any dispute that may arise either between Quakers, or between a Quaker and a stranger, provided the latter will submit to their arbitrament. This last object is one of the most important; it prevents that cruel scourge so ravaging in other countries, the scourge of lawyers, the source of so much corruption, and the cause of such scandalous divisions. This custom must be of great advantage to strangers who live in the neighbourhood of Quakers. The society excommunicates a member who will not submit to this arbitration.

Appeals are sometimes carried from the monthly to quarterly assemblies; the principal business of the latter, is to superintend the operations of the former.

But the superintendance of the whole society belongs to the annual assemblies. These receive reports from the inferior bodies respecting the state of all parts of the society, give their advice, make regulations, judge definitively on the appeals from the lower assemblies, and write letters to each other, in order to maintain a fraternal correspondence.

There are seven annual assemblies. One at London, to which the Quakers in Ireland send deputies; one in New-England, one at New-York, one for Pennsylvania and New-Jersey, one in Maryland, one in Virginia, one for the two Carolinas and Georgia.

As the Quakers believe that women may be called to the ministry as well as men, and as there are certain articles of discipline which only concern the women, and the observance of which can be superintended only by them, they have likewise their monthly, quarterly, and annual meetings. But they have not the right to make regulations. This method is much more proper to maintain morals among women, than that of our Catholic Confessors: which subjects the feeble sex to the artisice [artifice], the fancies, and the empire of particular men; which opens the door to the most scandalous scenes, and often carries inquisition and dissension into the bosom of families.

The Quakers have no salaried priests; their ministers are such men as are the most remarkable for their zeal; they speak the most frequently in their meetings; but all persons, male and female, have an equal right to speak wherever they feel an inclination.

These ministers, with some approved elders, hold monthly meetings, by themselves, for their own instruction. In these meetings they revise, and order to be printed, such works as they choose to have dist[r]ibuted; and they never fail to take such measures, as that Useful works should fold at a low price.

In all these assemblies, some of which are very numerous, they have no president, and no person who has the least authority. Yet the greatest order and harmony are always at once in any of their most interesting deliberations.

But what will surprise you more is, that in their numerous assemblies, nothing is decided but by unanimity. Each member has a kind of suspensive negative. He has only to say, *I have not clearness;* the question is then adjourned, and not decided till every member is agreed.

This usage appears to me highly honorable to the society; it proves a wonderful union among this band of brothers; it proves that the same spirit animates them, the spirit of reason, of truth, and of the public good. Deliberative assemblies in general, would not be subject to such long and violent discussions, if, like the Quakers, they were disengaged from all personal ambition, and if, to resolve doubts, the members addressed themselves only to the consciences of men.

You will, perhaps, conclude from this, that this society can do but little business. This will be a mistake; no society does more for the public good. It is owing to them, that Philadelphia has hitherto been preserved from the danger of theatres. Their petition this year, to prevent permission being obtained to erect one, has been successful.

A thorough knowledge of the Quakers, my friend, is not to be obtained by going, like Chastellux, for an hour into one of their churches. Enter into their houses; you will find them the abodes of peace, harmony, gentleness, and frugality; tenderness to children, humanity to servants. Go into their hospitals; you will there see the more touching effects of charity, in their unexampled cleanliness, in their aliments, in their beds, and in their scrupulous attentions. Visit the asylums of old age and decrepitude; you will find cloth and linen of the poor, as decent as that of their benefactors. Each one has his chamber, and enjoys not only the necessaries, but many of the agreeables of life.

If you would quit the town, and run over the farms of the Quakers, you will discover a greater degree of neatness, order, and care, among these cultivators, than among any other. If you examine the interior organization of the society, you will find, in every church, a treasury for charity, containing more or less money, according to the wealth of the congregation. This is employed in assisting young tradesmen, in succouring those who have failed in business through misfortune, those who have suffered by fire and other accidents. You will find many rich persons among them, who make it a constant rule to give to this treasury one-tenth of their revenue.

I am persuaded, my friend, that, after having well examined this society under all these details, you would cry out, If tomorrow I were reduced to poverty, and to be destitute of the succour of my friends, GOD grant that I might finish my days in a Quaker hospital: if tomorrow I were to become a farmer, let me have members of this society for my neighbours; they would instruct me by their example and advice, and they would never vex me with law-suits.

Source: J. P. Brissot de Warville, *New Travels in the United States of America. Performed in 1788*, trans. from the French (Dublin: Printed by W. Corbet, for P. Byrne, A. Gueber [etc.], 1792), 401–11.

9. *Sabbatical Observances in England and America* (1838)

The observance of Sunday as a day of prayer and reflection was a practice carried to America by Christians of all faiths. In Puritan New England the strict observance of Sunday was enforced by closing all shops and theaters on this holy day. As America entered the nineteenth century, many cities continued this practice, but as it progressed many also began to ameliorate these laws. Here, British traveler Andrew Bell decries the absence of anything to do on a Sunday in America.

The first Sunday turn-out I saw of the Philadelphian population, confirmed me in my opinion of the peculiar pride the Americans take in dress. There being no positive acknowledged degrees of rank among them, all the world wish to hide their humble stations as much as possible by imposing externals. It might be said of them with more truth than George the Fourth did of the Scotch, on seeing them in holiday attire, "They are a nation of gentlemen." They are certainly, in outward things, a *distingué* people. As I looked, with much interest, at the vast numbers of well-apparelled females, no small proportion of them very beautiful, on their way to the different churches and chapels, I thought of the contrast this country must have presented, at the time of the revolutionary war, when the stock of articles of personal equipment ran so low, from poverty and stoppages of importation, that the ladies were fain to fasten their worn-out clothes with thorns, instead of pins; and when a good sewing-needle was thought worth lending from one distant farm-house to another.

Having ascertained which was the principal Episcopal place of worship, I was directed to Christ church, and had, before entering, the satisfaction of hearing the familiar sounds of a peal of bells, rather imperfect indeed, but the only one I then knew of in, the country. The venerable Bishop White officiated. This patriarch of the, American church was consecrated to his sacred office in England, and had been chaplain to the first American congress: he died some days before I left. The members of the Episcopal community are not so numerous as those of some of the others in Philadelphia—the Presbyterians for instance; but they comprise a large portion of the prime families of the place. As the *élite* of the Americans are Tories in politics, so they are no less churchmen in religion. They seem to participate in the sentiments of old Herbert, as expressed in his "British Church:"

"I joy, dear mother, when I view
Thy perfect lineaments, and hue
Both sweet and bright:
A fine aspect in fit array,
Neither too mean, nor yet too gay,
Shows who is best:
Outlandish looks may not compare;
For all they either painted are,
Or else undrest."

Charles the Second said he thought Presbyterianism was no fit religion for a gentleman; the superior kind of Americans seem to think so too.

Morning and evening service being ended, as I had as yet made few acquaintances, and as my letters of introduction were merely to houses of business, I found the city become miserably dull. Having lived for some years on the continent, and been rather unused to the deadness of all towns where the Protestant religion prevails, I began to call in question, in my private mind—perhaps wrongly—the utility of a total suspension of all amusement, and absence of agreeable relaxation. The Catholics, I thought, had done wisely, in coming to a compromise with poor human nature; and I doubted much whether the conduct of the many were much improved by the rigid observances imposed upon them by the few. I must own I have never been a strict Sabbatarian. I never could find the institution of a Christian Sabbath any where in the New Testament. I have long thought that the Jewish Sabbath, as part of the ceremonial law, and meant to be confined to the Jews, was, by implication, virtually abolished, and no other put in its place. See Matt. Xii. 1–12; Luke xiii. 15–16, and other passages.

The first colonists of this country—the New England settlers particularly—were mostly rigid, not to say fanatical, Puritans; the principal distinction of these schismatics, after their bitter hatred of the Church, was their Judaical way of spending the Sunday; the freedom with which Christ made us free, was foregone by them. Not only so, but spiritual despotism was inconsistently mixed up with free political institutions; and seldom was intolerance carried farther by the most bigoted Catholics, than by these pretended victims of spiritual tyranny at home. They thought fit to take exceptions against the Quaker sect in particular, and passed a law, banishing them from certain of the new settlements under pain of death if they ever returned; I believe some individuals did actually get hanged in consequence. Their laws against infractions of sabbatical observance were rigorous to the last degree; and, as an instance, it is on record, that the head men of Salem punished the captain of a vessel with public flogging, for having saluted his wife in public; this poor man had not seen her for many months, and on his arrival, which unluckily for him happened to be the Sabbath, was naturally overjoyed to meet her. It is even said, that these gloomy bigots would never put malt to ferment near the end of a week, lest it should "work" on the Sabbath; and tied the legs of their dunghill fowls, to prevent them from gallanting the hens. Constables were employed to scour the streets for stragglers, with power to lay hands on violators of gloomy Sabbath sanctities, and force them into the conventicles; or, if refractory, to imprison and set them in the stocks.

Thus rigorously was the observance of the Sabbath established by the early Americans, and the influence of such institutions is felt even now. A punning Frenchman called a London Sunday "un jour de poudins de *plomb*"; an American Sabbath is still more *leaden*. Yet does the sun go on his way rejoicing, the birds sing, the winds blow, the tides rise and fall—of a surety a ritual observance of Sabbath has no sympathy in the visible creation; not to urge that the Sabbath in the synagogue of Pear-street, Philadelphia, has yet four hours to run, when that of the Jews of Duke's Place has finished; while in Palestine, for which, probably, the institution was alone meant, it has even ceased long before. No, the Sabbath has small foundation in external nature; has it any in the general mind of man? If I were captiously asked, Would you shut up the churches, and abolish religion? I would answer such a question by another, What has that to do with it? Do the continental Catholics shut up their churches because the theatres and concert rooms are open?

With respect to ourselves, is there any population in the world more immoral, more besotted, more degraded than ours?—and this, too, in despite of all sabbatical ordinances. If there have been a "reform" in politics since I left the country some ten years ago, there has been none in morals. Look at the condition and habits of a great mass of the London lower classes—mark the crowds of squalid drunken men and wretched women on Saturday and Sunday evenings, with miserable infants in arms, "conceived in gin, and begotten in poverty." What has the Sabbath yet done for them but add to their means of doing themselves harm?

Nothing has spread dissent from the Church all over the country so much as leaving the Sabbath evenings open to schismatical eloquence. Evening lectures, by Church divines, are certainly more common than they were; but it is too late to hope to lessen the amount of dissent by a rivalry in this way.

It would be more effectually done by encouraging public recreations after daily church service. The sects have committed themselves too much to sabbatarianism, to countenance any thing of this kind; and it is only the Church of England which can afford to relax. Once it had puritanical practice forced upon it, but these days are gone by.—Let us refer a little to history. In the year 1618, James the First published his declaration, called the Book of Sports, permitting certain pastimes, and commanded it to be read in all churches. The Puritans held up their hands in holy horror against the indulgence; but of all the principal clergy of the Church, Archbishop Abbot alone opposed himself to it, and would not allow it to be published in his diocese. He was a very mediocre man, and a cunning trimmer all along between his duties to the Church, and his popularity with the undermining Puritans; but unhappily in the end the latter gained the day. Thus we see that the suggestion of a relaxation is not new. If such were needful then, how much more now! When increased habits of confinement and lengthened hours of labour, are, by the progress of society, so much established. Holidays have almost ceased to exist; Sunday is the only instrument put into our hands, whereby to re-civilize a people relapsing into brutality, and make them withal happier and better. The very first step to an improved, a more moral state of things, will be TO OPEN THE THEATRES on Sunday.

Source: Andrew Bell, *Men and Things in America: Being the Experience of a Year's Residence in the United States; in a Series of Letters to a Friend*, by A. Thomason [pseud.] (London: William Smith, 1838), 212–17.

10. The Difference between Church Services in England and America (1857)

The problems that had plagued the Anglican Church both in England and its American colonies had led in many instances to splits within that community. After the Revolution, the American branch of the church renamed itself the Episcopal Church and began to carry out reforms that would avoid the controversies that afflicted the English church. One outside observer, Captain Henry A. Murray, RN, notes how the changes in the services made by the Episcopal Church in America had led to greater unity in the Episcopal Church in America in the nineteenth century.

The Episcopal Church in America is free from the violent factious [factions] that have distracted and thrown obloquy upon the sister church in this country. The puerile struggle about surplices, and candles, and steps up to altars, and Brussels lace offerings, appear to have attracted little attention among those in America, whose theological views assimilate with the extreme high party in England: and I never heard, during my residence in the States, any of that violent and uncharitable language with which discussions on religious topics too frequently abound in this country; nor is the Episcopal community by any means so divided as it is here. The Bishop of New Zealand is far nearer their type than the controversial prelate of Exeter.

The Book of Common Prayer, as arranged by Convention in 1790, is well worthy of notice, and, in many points, of imitation. These pages are not the proper place for a theological discussion, and my only reason for touching upon the subject at all is, that the public voice is constantly calling for some modification of the great length of our present Sunday services, and I therefore conclude that the following observations may be interesting to some of my readers.

The leading points of retrenchment are—removing all repetitions, such as the Lord's Prayer, the Creed, and the Collect for the day; a portion of the close of the Litany is omitted at the discretion of the minister. The Communion Service is not read every Sunday. I suppose the Church authorizes this omission at the discretion of the minister, as I have attended service on more than one occasion when the Communion was not read; when read, Our Lord's commandment, Matthew xxii. 37–40, follows the Commandments of the Old Testament, and a short Collect, followed by the Collect, Epistle, and Gospel for the day, finish that portion of the service. Independent of the regular Psalms, for the day, there are ten separate short collections, any one of which the minister may substitute for the proper Psalms, and the Gloria Patri is only said after the last Psalm.

The leading features of difference from our own "Common Prayer" are as follow:—They appoint proper Second Lessons for the Sunday, instead of leaving them to the chance of the Calendar—they place the Nicene and Apostles' Creed side by side, and leave the minister to select which he prefers, and to use, if he think proper, the word "Hades" instead of Hell. They remove the Athanasian Creed entirely from the Prayer Book, leaving to the minister to explain the mysteries which that creed so summarily disposes of. When it is considered how many Episcopalians are opposed to its damnatory clauses, and how much more nearly the other creeds resemble that model of simplicity, the Lord's Prayer, they appear to have exercised a sound discretion in this excision. Few deep-thinking people, I imagine, can have heard the children of the parish school reading the responses of that creed after the minister, without pain.

Lest the passing opinion of a traveller upon such a subject be deemed hasty or irreverent, I beg to quote Bishop Tom-line's opinion. He says—"Great objections have been made to the clauses which denounce eternal damnation against those who do not believe the faith as here stated; and it certainly is to be lamented that assertions of so peremptory a nature, unexplained and unqualified, should have been used in any human composition. Though I firmly believe that the doctrines of this creed are all founded on Scripture, I cannot but conceive it to be both unnecessary and presumptuous to say that, "except every one do keep them whole and undefiled, without doubt he shall perish everlastingly." Mr. Wheatley also, when writing on the Creed, says, that the third and fourth verses constitute the creed, and that what follows "requires our assent no more than a sermon does, which is made to prove or illustrate a text."—To resume.

They have proper prayers and thanksgivings for individuals who desire their use, instead of, as with us, introducing a few words into the ordinary service. They have provided a liberal collection of psalms and hymns for singing in church, and no others are allowed to be used. Each psalm and hymn has the Gloria Patri suited to it marked at the beginning. The inconvenience of the total want of such a provision in our Church is most palpable.

Not long before I went to America, I was attending a parish church in the country, where a great proportion of the psalms and hymns used were the minister's own composition, and if I recollect right, the book cost half-a-crown. I came up to town, and I found my parish church there had a selection under the sanction of the Bishop of London. Since my return from America, I have gone to the same London church, under the same Bishop, and I have found a totally different book in use.—The foregoing are the principal alterations in the Sunday services.

The alterations in the other services are chiefly the following:—In the full Communion Service, the word "condemnation" is substituted for "damnation," in the notice of intimation. The whole of the damnatory clause in the exhortation, from the word "unworthily" to "sundry kinds of death," is expunged. The first prayer in our Church after the reception, is modified by them into an oblation and invocation, and precedes the reception. The remainder of the service is nearly the same as our own.

They have removed the objectionable opening of the Marriage Service; but, not content with that, they have also removed the whole of the service which follows the minister's blessing after the marriage is pronounced, and thus reduced it to a five minutes' ceremony. While on this subject, I may as well observe that, from inquiries I made, I believe but few of those marriages take place by which husband and wife are prevented from kneeling at the same altar, by which their highest interests can never be a subject of mutual discussion, and by which children are either brought up without any fixed religious ideas at all, or else a compromise is entered into, and the girls are educated in one church and the boys in another. In short, I believe the Romanists in America marry but rarely out of the pale of their own church. I cannot say what the law of divorce is, but it appears to offer far greater facilities than would be approved of in England. A gentleman mentioned two cases to me, in one of which the divorce was obtained by the wife without the husband being aware of it, although living in the same State; in the other, the wife returned to the State from which her husband had taken her, and there obtained a divorce without his knowledge.—To return from this digression. In the Visitation of the Sick they have removed that individual absolution of the minister, the wording of which is so objectionable that, if I am rightly informed, it is rarely used by ministers in England. In the Burial of the Dead, they have changed the two concluding prayers in those sentences which refer to the deceased. The Commination they have entirely expunged. They have added a full service for Visitation of Prisoners, and a Harvest Thanksgiving; and they have provided a form of morning and evening prayer for families.

The foregoing constitute the leading points of difference. Of course there are many minor ones which are merely verbal, such, for instance, as their expunging the scriptural quotation of "King of kings, Lord of lords," from the prayer for the President, probably out of deference to the prejudices of the Republicans, for which omission they have partially atoned by the substitution of the grander expression of "only Ruler of the Universe," in lieu of the more limited term "only Ruler of Princes." To enter into all these verbal changes would be alike tedious and useless. Enough, I trust, has been written to convey a general idea of the most striking and interesting points of difference.

Source: Captain the Hon. Henry A. Murray, R.N., *Lands of the Slave and the Free: or, Cuba, the United States, and Canada* (London: G. Routledge and Co., 1857), 419–23.

Death and Afterlife

The belief in life after death and the existence of heaven was very prevalent in America as a result of the two Great Awakenings of the eighteenth and nineteenth centuries. The belief that those who followed the will of God would be saved and enter into the kingdom of heaven, while those who followed the path of evil would burn in the fires of hell, was a powerful message preached from pulpits, at camp meetings, and in a large religious literature. Many of the preachers of the Second Great Awakening used the images of heaven and hell in their sermons to invoke the fear of hell and to avoid following the path of Satan. The image of a peaceful existence with God in heaven can be seen in the dream of James Finley, and his image is very powerful in creating a sense of a good life leading to a peaceful afterlife. The idea of predestination and of man's innate wickedness was predominant in America in its early colonial period, mainly through Calvinist doctrine, but these beliefs were challenged during the First Awakening of the 1730s and 1740s and led many to question the concept of predestination and eternal damnation. Many denominations in the United States began to emphasize forgiveness and the saving power of God, which can be seen in the observations of those attending services in the United States at the time. In an era when death could come at any age, the death of an infant was one of the most terrible losses any parent could suffer. Solace was offered in the idea that these innocents would be taken into God's loving arms and would experience the love and grace of God in heaven.

11. A Dream of Heaven (1842)

James B. Finley was a Methodist minister known for his revivalist sermons during the Second Great Awakening. Here he gives a view of heaven that he experienced during a dream, which would become part of many of his future sermons.

During my labors on the Dayton district an incident occurred which I must relate, because it is due to the many to whom I promised an account of it that it should be published in my biography.

It was in the summer of 1842. Worn down with fatigue, I was completing my last round of quarterly meetings, and winding up the labors of a very toilsome year. I had scarcely finished my work till I was most violently attacked with bilious fever, and it was with great difficulty I reached home. The disease had taken so violent a hold on my system that I sank rapidly under its power. Every thing that kind attention and medical skill could impart was resorted to, to arrest its ravages, but all was in vain, and my life was despaired of. On the seventh night, in the state of entire insensibility to all around me, when the last ray of hope had departed, and my weeping family and friends were standing around my couch waiting to see me breathe my last, it seemed to me that a heavenly visitant entered my room. It came to my side, and, in the softest and most silvery tones, which fell like rich music on my ear, it said, "I have come to conduct you to another state and place of existence." In an instant I seemed to rise, and, gently borne by my angel guide, I floated out upon the ambient air. Soon the earth was lost in the distance, and around us, on every side were worlds of light and glory. On, on, away, away from the world to luminous worlds afar, we sped with the velocity of thought. At length we reached the gates of paradise; and O, the transporting scenes that fell upon my vision as the emerald portals, wide and high, rolled back upon their golden hinges! Then in its fullest extent, did I realize the invocation of the poet:

"Burst ye emerald gates and bring
To my ruptured vision
All the ecstatic joys that spring
Round the bright Elysian."

Language, however, is inadequate to describe what then, with unveiled eyes, I saw. The vision is indelibly pictured in my heart. Before me, spread out in its beauty, was a sheet of water, clear as crystal, not a single ripple on its surface, and its purity and clearness indescribable. On each side of this lake, or river, rose up the most tall and beautiful trees, covered with all manner of fruits and flowers which were reflected in the bosom of the placid river.

While I stood gazing with joy and rapture at the scene, a convoy of angels was seen floating in the pure ether of that world. They all had long wings, and, although they went with the greatest rapidity, yet their wings were folded close by their side. While I gazed I asked my guide who they were and what their mission. To this he responded, "They are angels, dispatched to the world from whence you came on an errand of mercy." I could hear strains of the most entrancing melody around me, but no one was discoverable but my guide. At length I said, "Will it be possible for me to have a sight of some of the just made perfect in glory?" Just then there came before us three persons; one had the appearance of a male, the other a female, and the third an infant. The appearance of the first two was somewhat similar to the angels I saw, with the exception that they had crowns upon their heads of the purest yellow, and harps in their hands. Their robes, which were full and flowing, were of the purest white. Their countenances were lighted up with a heavenly radiance, and they smiled upon me with ineffable sweetness.

There was nothing with which the blessed babe or child could be compared. It seemed to be about three feet high. Its wings, which were long and most beautiful, were tinged with all the colors of the rainbow. Its dress seemed to be of the whitest silk, covered with the softest white down. The driven snow could not exceed it for whiteness and purity. Its face was all radiant with glory; its very smile now plays around my heart. I gazed and gazed with wonder upon this heavenly child. At length I said, "If I have to return to earth, from whence I came, I should love to take this child with me, and show it to the weeping mothers of earth. Methinks, when they see it, they will never shed another tear over their children when they die." So anxious was I to carry out the desire of my heart, that I made a grasp at the bright and beautiful one, desiring to clasp it in my arms, but it eluded my grasp, and plunged into the river of life. Soon it rose up from the waters, and as the drops fell from its expanding wings, they seemed like diamonds, so brightly did they sparkle. Directing its course to the other shore, it flew up to one of the topmost branches of one of life's fair trees. With a look of most seraphic sweetness it gazed upon me, then commenced singing in heaven's own strains, "To Him that hath loved me, and washed from my sins in his own blood, to him be glory both now and forever. Amen." At that moment the power of the eternal God came upon me, and I began to shout, and, clapping my hands, I sprang from my bed, and was healed as instantly as the lame man in the beautiful porch of the temple, who "went walking, and leaping, and praising God." Overwhelmed by the glory I saw and felt, I could not cease praising God. The next Sabbath I went to camp meeting, filled with the love and power of God. There I told the thousands what I saw and felt, and what God had done for me, and loud were the shouts of glory that reverberated through the forests.

Though years have rolled away since that bright, happy hour, yet the same holy flame is burning in my heart, and I retain the same glorious victory. "Halleluiah! For the Lord God omnipotent reigneth."

Source: James B. Finley, *Autobiography of James B. Finley*, ed. W. P. Strickland (Cincinnati, OH: Methodist Book Concern, 1854), 375–78.

12. Sir Charles Lyell on a More Forgiving God (1840s)

Sir Charles Lyell was a British lawyer, one of the foremost geologists of the nineteenth century, and a friend of Charles Darwin. Lyell made two trips to America in the 1840s and wrote about his experiences. Here he discusses the change made in New England's Protestant churches from a strict Calvinist view of heaven and who can reach it, to the more benign teachings he witnessed in the 1840s.

To account for the toleration prevailing in New England and the states chiefly peopled from thence, we must refer to a combination of many favorable circumstances, some of them of ancient date, and derived from the times of the first Puritan settlers. To these I shall have many opportunities of alluding in the sequel; but I shall mention now a more modern cause, the effect of which was brought vividly before my mind, in conversations with several lawyers of Maine, New Hampshire, and Massachusetts, whom I fell in with on this tour. I mean the reaction against the extreme Calvinism of the church first established in this part of America, a movement which has had a powerful tendency to subdue and mitigate sectarian bitterness. In order to give me some idea of the length to which the old Calvinistic doctrines were instilled into the infant mind, one of my companions presented me with a curious poem, called the "Day of Doom," formerly used as a school book in New England, and which elderly persons known to him had been required, some seventy years ago, to get by rote as children. This task must have occupied no small portion of their time, as this string of doggrel rhymes makes up no less than 224 stanzas of eight lines each. They were written by Michael Wigglesworth, A.M., teacher of the church of Malden, New England, and profess to give a poetical description of the Last Judgment. A great array of Scripture texts, from the Old and New Testament, is cited throughout in the margin as warranty for the orthodoxy of every dogma.

Were such a composition now submitted to any committee of school managers or teachers in New England, they would not only reject it, but the most orthodox among them would shrewdly suspect it to be a "weak invention of the enemy," designed to caricature, or give undue prominence to, precisely those tenets of the dominant Calvinism which the moderate party object to, as outraging human reason and as derogatory to the moral attributes of the Supreme Being. Such, however, were not the feelings of the celebrated Cotton Mather, in the year 1705, when he preached a funeral sermon on the author, which I find prefixed to my copy of the sixth edition, printed in 1715. On this occasion he not only eulogizes Wigglesworth, but affirms that the poem itself contains "plain truths drest up in a plain meter;" and further prophesies, that "as the 'Day of Doom' had been often reprinted in both Englands, it will last till the Day itself shall arrive." Some extracts from this document will aid the reader to estimate the wonderful revolution in popular opinion brought about in one or two generations, by which the harsher and sterner features of the old Calvinistic creed have been nearly eradicated. Its professors, indeed, may still contend as stoutly as ever for the old formularies of their hereditary faith, as they might fight for any other party banner; but their fanatical devotion to its dogmas, and their contempt for all other Christian churches, has happily softened down or disappeared.

The poem opens with the arraignment of all "the quick and dead," who are summoned before the throne of God, and, having each pleaded at the bar, are answered by their Judge. Some of them declare that the Scriptures are "so dark, that they have puzzled the wisest men;" others that, being "heathens," and having never had "the written Word preached to them," they are entitled to pardon; in reply to which, the metaphysical subtleties of the doctrines of election and grace are fully propounded. The next class of offenders might awaken the sympathies of any heart not protected by a breastplate of theological dogmatism:—

"Then to the bar all they drew near
Who died in infancy,
And never had, or good or bad,
Effected personally," &c.

These infants remonstrate against the hardship of having Adam's guilt laid to their charge:—

"Not we, but he, ate of the tree
Whose fruit was interdicted;
Yet on us all, of his sad fall,
The punishment's inflicted."
The Judge replies, that none can suffer "for what they never did:"—

"But what you call old Adam's fall,
And only his trespass,
You call amiss to call it his,
Both his and yours it was.

"He was designed, of all mankind,
To be a public head;
A common root, whence all should shoot,
And stood in all their stead.

"He stood and fell, did ill and well
Not for himself alone,
But for you all, who now his fall
And trespass would disown.

"If he had stood, then all his brood
Had been established," &c.
"Would you have grieved to have received
Though Adam so much good?" &c.

"Since then to share in his welfare
You would have been content,
You may with reason, share in his treason,
And in his punishment."

A great body of Scripture texts are here introduced in confirmation; but the children are told, even including those "who from the womb unto the tomb were straightway carried," that they are to have "the easiest room in hell:"—

"The glorious King, thus answering,
They cease, and plead no longer,
Their consciences must needs confess
His reasons are the stronger."

The pains of hell and the constant renovation of strength to enable the "sinful wight" to bear an eternity of torment, are then dilated upon at such length, and so minutely, and a picture so harrowing to the soul is drawn, as to remind us of the excellent observations on this head of a modern New England divine. "It is not wonderful," he says, "that this means of subjugating the mind should be freely used and dreadfully perverted, when we consider that no talent is required to inspire fear, and that coarse minds and hard hearts are signally gifted for this work of torture." "It is an instrument of tremendous power," he adds, "enabling a Protestant minister, whilst disclaiming papal pretensions, to build up a spiritual despotism, and to beget in those committed to his guidance a passive, servile state of mind, too agitated for deliberate and vigorous thought."

That the pious minister of Malden, however, had no desire to usurp any undue influence over his panic-stricken hearers, is very probable, and that he was only indulging in the usual strain of the preachers of his time, when he told of the "yelling of the damned, as they were burnt eternally in the company of devils," and went on to describe how—

"God's vengeance feeds the flame
With piles of wood and brimstone flood,
That none can quench the same."

We next learn that the peace and calm blessedness of the saints elect, who are received into heaven, is not permitted to be disturbed by compassion for the damned; mothers and fathers feeling no pity for their lost children:—

"The godly wife conceives no grief,
Nor can she shed a tear,

For the sad fate of her dear mate
When she his doom doth hear."

The great distinction between the spirit of the times when these verses were written and the present age, appears to be this, that a paramount importance was then attached to those doctrinal points in which the leading sects differed from each other, whereas now Christianity is more generally considered to consist essentially in believing and obeying those scriptural precepts on which all churches agree.

Source: Sir Charles Lyell, *A Second Visit to the United States of North America*, vol. 1 (New York: Harper & Brothers; London: J. Murray, 1849), 48–52.

13. *On the Death of an Infant to a Mother, by the Authoress of* The Discipline of Life *(1850)*

The death of a child is one of the most wrenching losses that can be experienced by a parent. In this poem published in the Harper's New Monthly Magazine *in 1850, the writer offers comfort to those who have lost their babies, giving hope that they will experience God's love in heaven.*

His languid eyes are closing,
On the pale, placid cheek,
The lashes dark reposing,
So wearily, so weak.
lie gasps with failing breath,
A faint and feeble strife with death;
Fainter and fainter still tis past,
That one soft sigh the last.

Thy watching and thy fearing,
Mother, is over now
The seal of death is bearing
That pale but angel brow,
And now in the deep calm
That follows days of wild alarm,
Thy heart sinks down, and weeps, and weep~
Oer him who silent sleeps.

Oh, Mother, hush thy crying,
The ill of life is oer,
Even now his wings are flying
Unto a happy shore;
Those wings of stainless white
Unfolded neer to earthly sight,
He spreads them now, they bear him hi& ~
Unto the angel company.

From sight of evil shrinking,
From thought of grief like thine
At the first summons sinking
Into the arms divine.
Oh! thou who knowest life,
Temptation, trial, toil and strife,
Wilt thou not still thine aching breast
To bless his early rest?

Source: "The Death of an Infant," *Harper's New Monthly Magazine* 1, no. 2 (July 1850): 183.

SUGGESTED READINGS

Blumenthal, Walter Hart. *Women Camp Followers of the Revolution*. Salem, NH: Ayer, 1992.

Blumin, Stuart M. *The Emergence of the Middle Class: Social Experience in the American City, 1760–1900*. New York: Cambridge University Press, 1989.

Bode, Carl, ed. *American Life in the 1840s*. New York: New York University Press, 1967.

Bowman, Larry. *Captive Americans: Prisoners During the American Revolution*. Athens: Ohio University Press, 1976.

Bradburn, Douglas. *The Citizenship Revolution: Politics and the Creation of the American Union, 1774–1804*. Charlottesville: University of Virginia Press, 2009.

Bruce, Dickson D. *Violence and Culture in the Antebellum South*. Austin: University of Texas Press, 1979.

Callahan, North. *Royal Raiders: The Tories of the American Revolution*. New York: Bobbs-Merrill, 1963.

Clarke, William B. *Ben Franklin's Privateers*. Baton Rouge: Louisiana State University Press, 1956.

Commager, Henry Steele, and Richard B. Morris. *The Spirit of Seventy-six: The Story of the American Revolution as Told by Participants*. New York: Harper & Row, 1975.

Dangerfield, George. *The Reawakening of American Nationalism, 1815–1828*. New York: Harper Torchbooks, 1965.

Davies, K. G. *Documents of the American Revolution 1770–1783, Colonial Office series*. 22 vols. London: Irish University Press, 1976.

Davis, David Brion. *The Problem of Slavery in the Age of Revolution, 1770–1823*. Ithaca, NY: Cornell University Press, 1974.

Demos, John. *Circles and Lines: The Shape of Life in Early America*. Cambridge, MA: Harvard University Press, 2004.

Faragher, John Mack. *Women and Men on the Overland Trail*. New Haven, CT: Yale University Press, 1979.

Fehrenbacher, Don E. *The Era of Expansion, 1800–1848*. New York: John Wiley & Sons, 1969.

Foner, Eric. *Free Soil, Free Labor, Free Men: The Ideology of the Republican Party Before the Civil War*. New York: Oxford University Press, 1970.

Freeman, Joanne B. *Affairs of Honor: National Politics in the New Republic*. New Haven, CT: Yale University Press, 2001.

Glenn, Myra C. *Campaigns against Corporal Punishment: Prison, Sailors, Women, and Children in Antebellum America*. Albany: State University of New York Press, 1984.

Graymont, Barbara. *The Iroquois in the American Revolution*. Syracuse, NY: Syracuse University Press, 1972.

Gumming, William P., and Hugh Rankin, eds. *The Fate of a Nation: The American Revolution Through Contemporary Eyes*. London: Phaidon Press, 1975.

Halttunen, Karen. *Confidence Men and Painted Women: A Study of Middle-Class Culture in America, 1830–1870*. New Haven, CT: Yale University Press, 1982.

Heidler, David S., and Jeanne T. Heidler. *Daily Life in the Early American Republic: Creating a New Nation*. Westport, CT: Greenwood Press, 2004.

Hibbert, Christopher. *Redcoats and Rebels: The American Revolution Through British Eyes*. New York: Avon, 1991.

Higginbotham, Don. *The War of American Independence: Military Attitudes, Policies, and Practice, 1763–1789*. Boston: Northeastern University Press, 1983.

Horn, James P., and Jan Lewis. *The Revolution of 1800: Democracy, Race, and the New Republic*. Charlottesville: University Press of Virginia, 2002.

Howe, Daniel Walker. *What Hath God Wrought: The Transformation of America, 1815–1848*. New York: Oxford University Press, 2007.

Lacour-Gayet, Robert. *Everyday Life in the United States before the Civil War*. New York: Ungar Publishing Company, 1969.

Lancaster, Bruce. *The History of the American Revolution*. New York: American Heritage/Bonanza, 1971.

Larabee, Benjamin W. *The Boston Tea Party*. New York: Oxford University Press, 1964.

Larkin, Jack. *The Reshaping of Everyday Life, 1790–1840*. New York: Harper & Row, 1988.

Levine, Bruce. *Half Slave, Half Free: The Roots of the Civil War*. New York, Hill & Wang, 1992.

Lupiano, Vincent de Paul, and Ken W. Sayers. *It Was a Very Good Year: A Cultural History of the United States from 1776 to the Present*. Hobrook, MA: Bob Adams, 1994.

Marcus, Robert, David Bruner, and Anthony Marcus. *America Firsthand*. Vol. 1, *Readings from Settlement to Reconstruction*.7th ed. Boston, MA: Bedford/St. Martin's, 2007.

Martin, James Kirby, and Mark Edward Lender. *A Respectable Army: The Military Origins of the Republic, 1763–1789*. Arlington Heights, IL: Harlan Davidson, 1982.

Mason, Mathew. *Slavery and Politics in the Early American Republic*. Chapel Hill: University of North Carolina Press, 2006.

Mayfield, John. *The New Nation, 1800–1845*. Rev. ed. New York: Hill & Wang, 1986.

McClelland, Peter D., and Richard J. Zeckenhauser. *Demographic Dimensions of the New Republic: American Interregional Migration, Vital Statistics, and Manumissions, 1800–1860*. New York: Cambridge University Press, 1982.

McCutcheon, Marc. *Everyday Life in the 1800s: A Guide for Writers, Students, and Historians*. Cincinnati, OH: Writer's Digest Books, 1993.

Meltzer, Milton, ed. *The American Revolution: A History in Their Own Words 1750–1800*. New York: Thomas Y. Crowell, 1987.

Miller, John C. *The Federalist Era, 1789–1801*. New York: Harper & Row, 1960.

Moquin, Wayne, ed. *Makers of America—Builders of a New Nation, 1801–1848*. New York: Encyclopedia Britannica Educational Corporation, 1971.

Nash, Gary B. *The Forgotten Fifth: African Americans in the Age of Revolution*. Cambridge, MA: Harvard University Press, 2006.

Nettels, Curtis P. *The Emergence of a National Economy, 1775–1815*. Armonk, NY: M.E. Sharpe, 1977.

Newman, Richard S. *The Transformation of American Abolitionism: Fighting Slavery in the Early Republic*. Chapel Hill: University of North Carolina Press, 2002.

Norton, Mary Beth. *Liberty's Daughters: The Revolutionary Experience of American Women, 1750–1800*. Boston: Little, Brown, 1980.

Nye, Russell Blaine. *The Cultural Life of the New Nation, 1776–1830*. New York: Harper Torchbooks, 1960.

Phillips, Kevin. *The Cousin's War: Religion, Politics & the Triumph of Anglo-America*. New York: Basic Books, 1999.

Purcell, L. Edward, and David F. Burg, eds. *The World Almanac of the American Revolution*. New York: Pharos Books, 1992.

Raphael, Ray. *A People's History of the American Revolution*. New York: New Press, 1991.

Royster, Charles. *A Revolutionary People at War: The Continental Army and American Character, 1775–1783*. Chapel Hill: University of North Carolina Press, 1996.

Saum, Lewis O. *The Popular Mood of Pre–Civil War America*. Westport, CT: Greenwood Press, 1980.

Sewell, Richard H. *A House Divided: Sectionalism and the Civil War, 1848–1865*. Baltimore, MD: Johns Hopkins University Press, 1988.

Simkins, Francis Butler, and Charles Pierce Roland. *A History of the South*. 4th ed. New York: Knopf, 1972.

Smelser, Marshall. *The Democratic Republic, 1801–1815*. New York: Harper & Row, 1968.

Smith, Page. *The Nation Comes of Age: A People's History of the Antebellum Years*. New York: McGraw-Hill, 1981.

Stampp, Kenneth M. *Imperiled Union*. New York: Oxford University Press, 1980.

Tebbel, John. *George Washington's America*. New York: E.P. Dutton, 1954.

Tyler, Alice Felt. *Freedom's Ferment: Phases of American Social History from the Colonial Period to the Outbreak of the Civil War*. New York: Harper & Row, 1962.

Volo, Dorothy Denneen, and James M. Volo. *Daily Life during the American Revolution*. Westport, CT: Greenwood Press, 2003.

Volo, Dorothy Denneen, and James M. Volo. *Daily Life in the Age of Sail*. Westport, CT: Greenwood, 2002.

Volo, James M., and Dorothy Denneen Volo. *The Antebellum Period*. Westport, CT: Greenwood Press, 2004.

Volo, James M., and Dorothy Denneen Volo. *Daily Life on the Old Colonial Frontier*. Westport, CT: Greenwood, 2002.

Waldstreicher, David. *In the Midst of Perpetual Fetes: The Making of American Nationalism, 1776–1820*. Chapel Hill: University of North Carolina Press, 1997.

Watson, Harry L. *Liberty and Power: The Politics of Jacksonian America*. New York: Hill & Wang, 2006.

Wiebe, Robert H. *The Opening of American Society: From the Adoption of the Constitution to the Eve of Disunion*. New York: Vintage Books, 1985.

Wilentz, Sean. *The Rise of American Democracy: Jefferson to Lincoln*. New York: W. W. Norton, 2005.

Wood, Gordon S. *The Creation of the American Republic, 1776–1787*. Chapel Hill: University of North Carolina Press, 1997.

Wright, Gavin. *Slavery and American Economic Development*. Baton Rouge: Louisiana State University Press, 2006.

Wright, Louis B. *Everyday Life in the New Nation, 1787–1860*. New York: Putnam, 1972.

Zeman, Theodore J., ed. *The Greenwood Encyclopedia of Daily Life in America*. Vol. 1, *The War of Independence and Antebellum Expansion and Reform, 1763–1861*. Westport, CT: Greenwood Press, 2009.

INDEX

ABOUT THE EDITOR

THEODORE J. ZEMAN, PhD, earned his doctorate from Temple University, Philadelphia, PA, and is a lecturer in history at Saint Joseph's University and Holy Family University, also in Philadelphia. Dr. Zeman's published works include *Beyond Combat: Essays in Military History in Honor of Russell F. Weigley*, co-edited with Edward G. Longacre and published by the American Philosophical Society, and he served as a volume editor of *The Greenwood Encyclopedia of Daily Life in America, Volume I: The War of American Independence and American Expansion and Reform, 1763–1861*.